GOVERNMENTAL STRUCTURE AND LOCAL PUBLIC FINANCE

Governmental Structure and Local Public Finance

David L. Chicoine

University of Illinois at Urbana–Champaign

Norman Walzer

Western Illinois University

Oelgeschlager, Gunn & Hain,
Publishers, Inc.
Boston, Massachusetts

International Standard Book Number: 0-89946-187-5

Library of Congress Catalog Card Number: 84-11874

Printed in the U.S.A.

Library of Congress Cataloging in Publication Data

Chicoine, David L.
    Governmental structure and local public finance.

    Bibliography: p.
    1. Local finance—Illinois. 2. Local government—Illinois. 3. Special districts—Illinois.
4. Municipal services—Illinois—Finance. I. Chicoine, David L. II. Title.
HJ9227.W3325 1984   352.1'09773   84-11874
ISBN 0-89946-187-5

Contents

List of Tables and Figures

Preface

Since the passage of Proposition 13 and other property tax relief programs in the late 1970s, local public finance has been the subject of intense interest from academics, policymakers, and taxpayers. Local governments have faced restrictions on revenue raising powers at the same time that inflation was seriously eroding their budgets.

There has been a recent proliferation of local government administration and finance studies in which scholars debate the merits of revenue sources and intergovernmental relationships. However, structure of government, numbers of governments involved in providing services, and organizational characteristics have not received the attention they deserve. Arrangements for providing local services – through multipurpose governments or single-function districts – must affect the level of services provided and their cost. This study examines governmental structure relating it to revenues collected, expenditures for services, and public perceptions of the services provided.

Any serious research effort incurs a large debt to colleagues, professional staff, and policymakers willing to discuss the intricacies of local public finance. This study is no exception. Financial support for part of Professor Walzer's time was provided by Professor Samuel K. Gove through the Institute of Government and Public Affairs, University of Illinois in 1978–1979 when the background material was being assembled. Professors Glenn W. Fisher and Terry N. Clark commented on early drafts of the manuscript. Numerous local public officials were willing to spend many hours discussing operating practices and procedures.

D.L.C.
N.W.

Chapter 1

Introduction

During the past century American lives have changed immensely. New methods of transportation that link formerly remote sections of the country permit residents to travel with less time and effort than formerly required. Technological progress has brought great increases in the standard of living and significant changes in lifestyles. A greater awareness of social issues and a need for solutions to more complex problems accompanied this economic progress. America's commitment to aid the less fortunate with food, housing, and other needs has introduced numerous publicly financed programs that are accompanied by administrative governmental complexities.

The growth in public programs and expanded services has not been costless. To implement these changes, citizens have paid higher taxes and public sector payrolls have swelled. The United States went from a philosophy of minimum governmental intervention in economic matters to a posture of relying on governments, at all levels, for protection of the less fortunate, economic development and stabilization, public jobs programs in times of high unemployment, and a host of other initiatives aimed at enhancing living standards.

Increased demands on governments for more and expanded services have affected public agencies at all levels. Municipal services, for instance, initially focused on protecting public health and providing services considered essential for facilitating commerce. Police protection, fire protection, and road and sewerage systems were essential to the prosperity of early urban residents. Cities now provide these services in addition to numerous others such as industrial development assistance, housing mortgage assistance, regulation of conflicting land uses, transportation, and libraries. It is doubtful whether most urban residents could list the vast array of services provided by cities.

The growth in public services and the machinery to provide them have brought a complex maze of governmental units, some of which are unknown to tax-paying citizens. In 1982, for instance, there were 82,637 units of local government in the United States.[1] The governments are arranged in no particular pattern and often are created with little, if any, attention paid to efficient or effective provision of services. Since county and township boundaries were established more than a century ago, shifts in population patterns have created municipalities that extend into more than one county, multiple townships, and many single-purpose districts.

An initial reaction to this governmental fragmentation is a frustrated retreat from this duplication of services, overlapping responsibility, political unresponsiveness, uncoordinated replication, and a less than efficient network for providing even essential services. This view is often supported by reports in research volumes or the news media of communities served by multiple fire protection districts or of residents in the same city paying substantially different tax rates for similar services.

In practice, however, the system persists. When citizens are offered an opportunity to eliminate a governmental unit, the necessary referendum is often unsuccessful. Hearings by state legislative committees regarding attempts to eliminate or consolidate governmental units are met with an outcry from the local officials involved and with little response from the general public, which supposedly is inconvenienced or "over-taxed" by this fragmented governmental structure. The leading proponents for reducing the number of governments are typically researchers and public spirited organizations such as the Advisory Commission on Intergovernmental Relations and the Committee for Economic Development which, based on limited empirical analysis, have determined that the number of governments is too large to be efficient.[2]

Even within the academic and research communities, however, views regarding the appropriate governmental structure or most efficient size of public bodies are not unanimous. A group of economists and political theorists, termed the *public choice school*, argue on efficiency grounds that residents allowed maximum choice in the types of services available and the revenue instruments used to finance them will select the most efficient governmental units and the inefficient ones will fail. This school reasons that residents will select the community in which the tax expenditure package best fits their desires so that localities providing the most desired packages will prosper while those providing too few services, or at too high a tax price, will decline.

This competitiveness between governments will most efficiently allocate government resources, given the restrictive assumptions employed in the reported theoretical models.[3]

PURPOSE OF BOOK

While many research studies discuss the strengths and weaknesses of various governmental arrangements for providing local services, there have been few systematic analyses of the impact of alternative governmental configurations on local public finance. Empirical studies usually focus on a single unit of government or a particular service in order to answer a specific research question.[4]

The analyses in this study examine factors that influence the structure of government used to provide services, the impact of numbers and structure of governments on the revenue composition used to finance services, the importance of fragmentation in determining the costs of the services provided, and the perceptions of residents regarding quality of service. The majority of the discussions in this study are empirically oriented, although a reasonably thorough review of the academic and professional literature is provided.

This book is aimed at three groups of readers. First is the policymaker generally interested in the extent to which forming an additional government, rather than providing the service through an existing general-purpose government, may affect expenditures, revenues, or taxpayer satisfaction. These questions are important to policymakers in state and local governments. When a new government is created, considerable thought must be given to the potential for effectively providing services, collecting revenues, and administering the operations. Most of the time, however, information is not readily available for making comparative decisions about alternative governmental structures. By reviewing previous studies and testing hypotheses put forth in professional literature, some insight into general trends based on the experiences in a large, industrial state has been obtained. Here, the most complex governmental structures and their importance for budgetary outcomes have been analyzed.

A second group of readers includes students of public administration and finance who are interested in alternate governmental structures and their importance in budgetary outcomes. A third group includes lay persons seeking information about local public finance who may be intrigued, if not mystified, by the presence of many overlapping and seemingly uncoordinated governments that provide services. While some of the discussions are technical, the findings are presented at a level that can be understood by the average reader.

Selection of Sample

The research reported in this book examines a set of governments within a single state. In a study of this type it is important to control as many institutional factors as possible. The legal and institutional arrangements for collecting revenues differ among states. For example, states with a local income tax may create incentives for a different configuration of local government than states where intergovernmental aid is provided directly to special districts. States with a restrictive system of local property tax rate limits may have more special-purpose governments than states with few local limits.

By studying a single state, comparable units of government face similar legal constraints, especially those imposed by the state legislature. Demographic and economic characteristics differ, but the external forces delimiting feasible alternatives are most similar when the governments are contained within a single state.

Using a single state, however, has its limitations. In attempting to formulate generalizations from the findings, the political or economic philosophy of policymakers and residents in one region may differ from that in another. This difference is revealed to some degree in a comparison of states with strong township governments with those in which townships do not exist or provide few services. The applicability of the findings in a state without similar governments is limited. This question, however, plagues all social science research, and the best that can be done is to make readers aware of these differences. In this study it is paramount that examples of as many governmental arrangements for providing services as possible be present.

The advantages of studying a single state, thereby standardizing legal requirements and comparability of responsibility for services, led us to select a state with a wide variety of government control. In 1982, Illinois had 6462 units of local government, or one governmental unit for every 1767 residents. The state with the next highest number is Pennsylvania with 5319—an average of one for each 2231 residents.[5]

Illinois also has broad home rule authority for cities with populations of 25,000 and above, cities having held a successful referendum, and counties having an elected administrator. The availability of home rule authority permits insight into an explanation commonly offered for the presence of special districts, namely to avoid restrictive property tax rate limits. Governments in Illinois without home-rule face a system of tax rate limits, not unlike those in most other states.

In addition to having the largest number of governments, Illinois also has a rich variety of governmental types. The Census Bureau classifies governments into five broad classes: counties, townships, municipalities, school districts, and special districts. The latter is further divided into seventeen separate groups of districts. By census count, in 1977 Illinois had 102 counties, 1434 townships, 1280 municipalities, 1050 school districts, and 2597 special districts scattered throughout the state. The special districts in Illinois provide a rich sample of alternate public services. Airports, for example, are financed by no less than five different governmental types.

Illinois also offers a rich diversity in general-purpose governments. The 102 counties range in size from Cook (containing Chicago with a 1980 population of 5,523,190) to Pope County (containing 4404 residents in rural southern Illinois). The structure of general-purpose governments within the counties also differs with eighty-five counties having a township form of government and seventeen without township governments. Municipalities likewise include Chicago at one extreme with 3,005,072 residents in 1980, while small hamlets have 200 residents or less. In fact, only 259 Illinois municipalities contained populations of 5000 or more in 1975.

Municipalities in Illinois also vary in socioeconomic status. For example, Glencoe in the Chicago metro area had a mean per capita income of $23,664 in 1979, while another large city, East St. Louis, had an average 1979 per capita income of $3681. These are just two examples of the diversity among large cities and do not necessarily represent extremes.[6] The point is that the diversity in both socioeconomic conditions and governmental structure makes Illinois a nearly ideal location for studying the impact of governmental structure on the financing of local public services.

Scope of Research

Previous studies of local public finance have usually directed their attention to policy prescriptions. Some researchers have called for consolidation and elimination of small governmental units. Others offer evidence that a large number of governments reduces the monopoly power of a large single government. Studies provide conflicting results about whether greater fragmentation leads to higher or lower expenditures and better or poorer perceptions of service quality.

Suggesting policy changes is not the intent of this research project.

Information about types of services and scales to measure services or compare them across governments has not been perfected to a level at which unambiguous comparisons can be made. The inability to conduct sophisticated cost comparisons, however, does not negate the value of understanding variations in expenditure and revenue patterns that result from arrangement differences for providing services. As far as the authors can determine, there have been few detailed studies of how differences in governmental organization affect revenues, expenditures, and debt within a state containing a wide variety of local governments. Insight into responsibility for services, differences in revenues collected, and variations in resulting services and employment patterns are the major objectives of the present study.

The analyses in this book differ from many previous approaches by aggregating expenditures and revenues to a broader area, counties, rather than focusing on a single governmental type. When examining the effects of differences in government organization on local finance, an aggregation of expenditures or employment across governments within the region is needed. This is especially true in states such as Illinois where services provided by municipalities in one region are financed by special districts or townships elsewhere. A study of the county area permits an examination of the aggregate taxes paid by residents for services received in light of the governmental arrangement involved.[7]

Examining aggregate revenue and expenditure at the county level has a significant limitation, however. Variations in service levels and tax burdens within a county are not considered. Countywide aggregation, nevertheless, is the common approach employed in studies involving governmental structure and represents the most useful alternative given existing data.

Several other considerations should be mentioned before proceeding with this analysis. First, at the time of writing, the most current comprehensive information on local finance is the 1977 Census of Governments. Detailed data on many aspects of local government finance are collected and published on all governments responding to the survey. Information on taxes and expenditures is available on 6619 units of local government in Illinois. Of course, not every government completes the survey form and occasionally data are missing for small governments.

Local public finance researchers also find measuring public services difficult. Expenditure and employment data are readily available as is information on tax rates and revenues collected. However, a consistent set of productivity measures needed to translate input expenditures into services produced is not available. Neither is comprehensive information on pay rates, hours worked, or other characteristics useful for adjusting the expenditure or employment information.

Throughout this research effort, revenues, expenditures, and employment are used as measures of local government activity. Although these indicators provide less information than might have been desired, they shed light on differences in local finance patterns that result from differences in governmental structure.

Need for Study of Local Finance

Recent national events make a comprehensive study of local finance especially timely. The late 1970s brought numerous attempts to impose limits on property taxes, frequently with little or no consideration given to arrangements for providing services and levels of services provided. Limits are imposed by state governments with virtually no consideration for differential impacts on public agencies across the state. For instance, the imposition of an overall property tax limitation on municipalities, townships, and counties provides incentives for policymakers to create additional special districts when the limitations faced by general-purpose governments have been reached. Likewise, little or no forethought is given to the availability of alternate tax revenues or fiscal capacity. Some municipalities, for instance, are highly dependent on property taxes. Others, containing regional shopping centers, rely on sales taxes and have minimal need for a general property tax levy. Limits on property tax rates more seriously affect local governments with few revenue alternatives.

The current interest in possibly reorganizing the structure for delivering local services makes a detailed analysis of local public finance critical.[8] On two occasions the federal government has proposed to transfer programs to state governments and possibly to assume programs formerly provided by states.

It is quite possible that an offshoot of these discussions will involve changes in the local financing and delivery of services. States have formed commissions to examine possible reorganization of local finance. Present systems of local government evolved incrementally over a century. Population and economic shifts have created needs for different services and have created wide disparity in the ability to provide them. The migration of population and economic bases to suburbs from central cities has caused a mismatch between governments with the greatest financial capacity for providing services and those containing the populations with the greatest need. This disparity between governments has brought financial problems for central cities.

The migration of tax base and the lack of conformity between resources and needs are not only limited to large central cities. Outmigration of population and wealth from the center city also has occurred in Illinois' middle-size cities where wealthy residents have moved outside the city but continue to consume services as they work and shop there. Those moving away from the central city have been able to form special districts to obtain selected services without bearing the costs of general administration, police and fire protection, streets, and other services required to maintain the central city as a viable shopping and employment center.

As in many regions of the country, the population turnaround in Illinois has reversed the major rural to urban migration trend of the 1950s and 1960s. Rural counties, particularly in southern Illinois, have experienced dramatic population increases and net inmigration. Many of the new residents are retired and economically independent. Others have sought communities with an advantageous quality of life to rear their families, and because of the diversification of the rural economy are able to return to a rural community. The new population has experienced public services in its former communities that are markedly different from those provided in its new rural town or country home.

The result of these population and resource shifts is that existing methods for providing local services are being challenged. Perhaps certain services could be shifted to county governments to best capture the shifting tax base as it moves beyond city boundaries. Multicounty districts can be formed to provide services to suburban residents if each participant is to pay a fair share. These and similar questions must be answered if current migration patterns continue. Before these policies can be debated meaningfully, however, a comprehensive study of governmental structure is needed.

System of Local Governments

Most surprising, and perhaps disappointing, to public policymakers and scholars is the limited understanding by residents of the governments providing services and the types of services they provide. Residents quickly identify police and fire protection, sewerage treatment, and streets as city services, but few can tell how much is spent on each or what portion of the tax bill is represented by counties, townships, cities, schools, or special districts. Residents are quick to blame the most visible government (cities or counties) for high property taxes, even though their share of the property tax levy is often relatively small.

Before launching into a detailed discussion of governmental structure in Illinois, it is worth examining the responsibility for providing local services, by type of government, nationwide. The most comprehensive information for this comparison is 1977 expenditures.

Expenditures. Table 1.1 shows that school districts, of which there were 15,174 in 1977, were responsible for 36.5 percent of the expenditures by local governments. This is particularly interesting because school districts represented only nineteen percent of the local governments. States differ markedly regarding arrangements for providing education services. For instance, six states reported no school districts indicating that educational services are provided by other governmental units. In Illinois, school districts have primary responsibility for providing elementary and secondary education and function independently from general-purpose governments.

The 25,962 special districts represent 32.5 percent of the local governments in 1977 but account for only five percent of the expenditures. Wide variations among states are found in the number of special districts, with Illinois leading the list at 2745 while Alaska reports no special districts.[9] Responsibility for services provided by special districts varies, and the major service categories in Table 1.1 represent less than half the total expenditures by these districts nationwide. The largest expenditure category was health and hospitals with expenditures for these services representing 23.5 percent of the total.

Municipalities had the second largest expenditures representing 32.2 percent of the total by local governments. Numerically, municipalities represented 23.6 percent of the total, but in 1977, 64.2 percent of the U.S. population resided in areas with a municipal government. Municipalities provide a majority of the most visible services and represent the unit of government with which residents are most familiar. It would surprise many residents to learn that the aggregate expenditure of school districts is larger than that of cities.

The remaining 26.3 percent of the local government expenditures were by counties and townships. The services provided by these governments vary substantially by state with thirty states having no township form of government and Minnesota having 1792 townships. Townships provide the greatest variations in governmental structure of the five major types. Even in states with a relatively large number of townships, this form of government may not exist throughout the state, as in Illinois.

The manner in which the number of governments has changed during the past several decades is of special interest. Table 1.2 provides a comparison of local governments, by type, between 1957 and 1982. Two patterns emerge from this comparison. First is the rather dramatic decline in the total number of governments from 102,328 in 1957 to

Table 1.1. 1977 Direct General Expenditures, by Level of Government (millions of dollars)

Function	All Local Governments	Percent	Counties	Percent	Municipalities	Percent	Townships	Percent	Special Districts	Percent	School Districts	Percent
Direct General Expenditure Total	$169,466.7	100.0%	$38,767.7	22.8%	$54,575.9	32.2%	$5,890.0	3.5%	$8,421.0	5.0%	$61,812.1	36.5%
Education	75,732.5	100.0	5,938.6	7.8	7,440.6	9.8	1,777.1	2.3	172.0	0.2	60,404.2	79.9
Highways	9,239.2	100.0	3,740.4	40.5	4,242.8	45.9	1,038.8	11.2	217.2	2.4	–	–
Public Welfare	11,918.0	100.0	7,288.9	61.2	4,566.9	38.3	62.2	0.5	–	–	–	–
Police & Fire Protection	13,104.2	100.0	2,243.2	17.1	9,895.8	75.5	750.0	5.7	215.2	1.7	–	–
Health & Hospital	11,330.0	100.0	6,050.0	53.4	3,238.2	28.6	68.6	0.6	1,976.2	17.4	–	–
Interest on General Debt	6,257.3	100.0	992.3	15.8	2,644.0	42.3	160.2	2.6	1,052.8	16.8	1,407.9	22.5
All Other	41,882.4	100.0	12,514.2	29.9	22,547.5	53.8	2,033.0	4.9	4,787.6	11.4	–	–

Source: U.S. Bureau of the Census, *Governmental Finances in 1976–77*, (Washington, D.C.: Government Printing Office, 1978).

Table 1.2. Number of Local Governments in the United States

Government Type	1982	1977	1967	1957
Total	82,688	79,862	81,248	102,328
Counties	3,041	3,042	3,049	3,047
Municipalities	19,083	18,862	18,048	17,183
Townships	16,748	16,822	17,105	17,198
School Districts	15,032	15,174	21,782	50,446
Special Districts	28,733	25,962	21,264	14,405
With Property Taxing Power				
Number	65,943	67,780	70,726	n.a.
Percent	80.1	84.9	87.1	n.a.

Source: U.S. Bureau of the Census, *Governmental Organization,* (Washington, D.C.: Government Printing Office, 1983).

82,688 in 1982. This change represents a decrease of 19.2 percent. A more detailed comparison reveals that the major decrease resulted from elimination and consolidation of school districts. In 1982, only 29.8 percent of the school districts reported in 1957 were still in existence.

The second trend reported in Table 1.2 is the growth in number of districts. In 1957 there were an estimated 14,405 special districts but by 1982 the number had increased to 28,733. Many reasons have been offered for growth in special districts and authors differ regarding their strengths and weaknesses. A common explanation is that special districts are created to bypass limitations on property tax rates. When a tax rate limit is reached and residents (or policymakers) demand new or expanded services, the state legislature has often been petitioned for authority to create a new unit of government with its own tax rate limits, thereby increasing the total property taxing capacity.

There are other explanations for growth. The establishment of a single-purpose government permits residents with strong interest in specific services to exert more control over the manner and extent to which the service is provided. Residents fleeing a central city to escape relatively high property taxes may desire city sewer and water services. By creating a single-purpose district, these residents obtain services without bearing the burden of the other costly services associated with a municipality. Central city residents, of course, may benefit if the cost of capital construction is spread over a larger tax base as when the new district overlaps the entire city.

There are other reasons for special districts. Rural residents encounter difficulties obtaining fire protection and library services due to the relatively small number of residents and low density. With the creation of a special district, the high quality fire protection services available

Table 1.3. General Revenue, by Type of Government in 1977 (millions of dollars)

Revenue Source	All Local Governments	Percent	Counties	Percent	Municipalities	Percent	Townships	Percent	Special Districts	Percent	School Districts	Percent
General Revenue, Total	$178,979.0	100.0%	$40,710.1	22.7%	$59,862.2	33.4%	$6,435.3	3.6%	$9,952.2	5.6%	$62,019.7	34.7%
Intergovernmental Revenue	76,948.3	100.0	18,056.4	23.6	23,116.5	30.0	1,829.1	2.3	3,352.6	4.3	30,593.9	39.8
From Federal	16,636.9	100.0	3,741.0	22.5	8,880.4	53.4	493.5	2.9	2,588.4	15.6	933.8	5.6
From State	60,311.4	100.0	14,315.4	23.7	14,236.1	23.6	1,335.6	2.2	764.2	1.3	29,660.1	49.2
General Revenue Own Sources	102,030.7	100.0	22,653.7	22.2	36,745.6	36.0	4,606.1	4.5	6,599.6	6.5	31,425.8	30.8
Tax Revenue	74,794.0	100.0	15,864.8	21.3	26,058.8	34.8	4,060.8	5.4	1,553.1	2.1	27,248.4	36.4
Property Tax	60,275.1	100.0	12,888.4	21.4	15,656.7	26.0	3,722.5	6.1	1,435.8	2.4	26,571.7	44.1
Other Taxes	14,518.9	100.0	2,976.4	20.5	10,402.1	71.6	388.3	2.4	117.3	0.8	676.7	4.7
Charges and Miscellaneous Fees	27,236.6	100.0	6,788.9	24.9	10,678.5	39.2	545.3	2.0	5,046.5	18.5	4,177.5	15.4

Source: U.S. Bureau of the Census, Census of Governments, *Governmental Finances in 1976–77*, (Washington, D.C.: Government Printing Office, 1978).

to urban residents can be extended to those living outside city limits. Alternatively, when limited fire services are desired, a special district can be used to finance a volunteer company. Without the special district option, the service might be provided by the township or county government. The availability of these public services has the effect, however, of discouraging residents on the outskirts from annexing to the city.

As society becomes more urbanized, suburbanization continues, rural areas are revitalized, and population migrates beyond the boundaries of general-purpose governments, a need is created for flexible service arrangements. State governments have responded with broader powers for local governments to cooperate on projects. Illinois, for example, allows special service areas to be created within a city or county. The statutes contain provisions to promote cooperation among local governments.

An important factor reducing the need for special districts in large cities is home rule authority. In Illinois this was granted as part of the 1970 constitution. Home rule units in Illinois face no property tax rate or debt limits which, if researchers are correct, eliminates one important reason for the creation of special districts. More direct evidence on this point will be presented in Chapter 3.

Revenues. An appreciation of the revenues used by local governments nationwide is equally important. Knowledge of the types of revenues employed is especially useful since each revenue source has advantages and limitations. Governments that rely on sales and income taxes experience substantial revenue growth during economic upswings, whereas governments more heavily reliant on property taxes experience greater stability in economic downturns with smaller and delayed growth during upswings. Those governments financing services with user fees may improve resource allocation since consumers are faced with prices for services.

The fact that the burden of the taxes differs by type of tax imposed is also important. A progressive income tax will create a different burden than a property tax. The burden of sales taxes changes when food and drugs are exempted. Thus, knowledge of the types of taxes collected provides broad insight into which groups pay for services and how governments will fare in a recession or growth period.

A comparison of the major revenue sources for local governments in the United States is provided in Table 1.3. To facilitate the comparison, the percentage which each form of local government represents in the aggregate collections is shown. The aggregate revenues are distributed among local governments in a manner similar to expenditures shown in Table 1.1 with municipalities collecting approximately one-third of the revenues, school districts one-third and so on.

The comparison of major revenue sources is more interesting. Municipalities received more than one-half (53.4 percent) of the aid provided to local governments by the federal government. School districts received only 5.6 percent directly from the federal government. However, intergovernmental assistance to school districts from state governments represented 49.2 percent of the total local government support from state governments. A portion of this was obtained by state governments from the federal government. Cities and counties each received slightly less than twenty-five percent of the total intergovernmental aid from the state.

Special districts provide an interesting case since they represent approximately five percent of the expenditures by local governments while simultaneously receiving 15.6 percent of the federal aid. The amount of state aid to special districts nationwide is minimal, representing only 1.3 percent of the total. Likewise, special districts, per se, collect only 2.4 percent of the property taxes nationwide.

The way in which property taxes are distributed might be surprising to many citizens. The major nationwide user of property taxes is school districts which collected 44.1 percent of the total. School districts, however, were shown earlier to represent 36.5 percent of the expenditures. On the other hand, municipalities which represent nearly one-third of the total local expenditures, collect 26.0 percent of the property taxes, based on the national sample.

Municipalities make heavy use of nonproperty tax revenues. This revenue class includes sales taxes, income taxes, and other taxes which grew in popularity following the Second World War. Table 1.3 shows that municipalities were responsible for collecting 71.6 percent of the nonproperty tax revenues. Cities rely on user charges for services with 39.2 percent of charges and miscellaneous fees collected by municipalities. Special districts also seem to have effectively employed this revenue source.

Growth in Government

Another dimension of local government which bears examination is growth in spending and employment. Although detailed local government employment estimates prior to 1951 are not available, it is clear that the size of local government employment since that time has increased substantially. Table 1.4 shows, for example, that in 1951 local governments reported 2.8 million full-time equivalent employees. By 1980, the number was 2.79 times larger, reaching 7.9 million. The largest

Table 1.4. Local Government Full-Time Equivalent Employment (thousands)

Year	All Local Governments	Municipalities	Counties	Townships and Special Districts	School Districts
1951	2,843	1,145	458	179	1,060
1955	3,406	1,252	604	209	1,341
1960	4,217	1,447	728	302	1,729
1965	5,186	1,638	893	368	2,287
1970	6,226	1,922	1,098	420	2,786
1975	7,354	2,142	1,408	561	3,243
1980	7,941	2,166	1,651	655	3,468

Source: U.S. Bureau of the Census, *Historical Statistics of the United States, Colonial Times to 1970* (Washington, D.C.: Government Printing Office, 1975), Series Y272–289, 1100, U.S. Bureau of the Census, *Statistical Abstract of the United States, 1981*, (Washington, D.C.: Government Printing Office, 1981).

relative growth, interestingly, was counties where the employment increase was 3.6 times and township/special districts which expanded employment 3.65 times. Municipalities reported the slowest rate of growth during this thirty year period.

The local government expenditure growth during this interval is even more pronounced. Table 1.5 shows that local nationwide government expenditures increased nearly ten-fold between 1955 and 1980. In 1955, local governments spent $22.5 billion in direct general expenditures. In 1980, the comparable figure was $223.6 billion. An examination of expenditure increases by type of government shows roughly similar increases for counties, municipalities, and school districts but much smaller increases for townships. By far the largest increase occurred in special districts which exhibited expenditures in 1980 of 15.8 times those in 1955.

In making this comparison, recognition must be given to price increases faced by governments. During this period, consumer prices increased significantly. For example, what $100 purchased in 1955 cost $307.73 in 1980. The price increases paid by state and local governments as measured by the Gross National Product Implicit Price Deflator for State and Local Government Purchases increased so that it cost $388.00 in 1980 to purchase what $100 would have bought in 1955.[10] Thus, the impact of inflation was higher on public sector purchases than the private sector. However, there can be no doubt that the local public sector grew during this period.

It must also be realized that not all of the expenditure increases were financed with local revenues. The federal government's support of local services increased dramatically during this period and represents a major stimulus for the expenditure increases reported.

Table 1.5. Direct General Expenditures by Local Governments (millions of dollars)

Year	All Local Governments	Municipalities	Counties	School Districts	Special Districts	Townships
1955	$ 22,534	7,870	4,629	8,168	837	1,029
1960	33,931	11,700	6,600	12,600	1,700	1,300
1965	48,405	15,758	10,000	18,402	2,359	1,886
1970	82,582	27,249	17,036	31,483	3,984	2,830
1975	143,148	47,964	30,903	52,230	7,134	4,918
1980	223,621	70,426	51,383	80,681	13,199	7,931

Source: ACIR, Significant Features of Fiscal Federalism, 1980–81 (Washington, D.C.: Advisory Commission on Intergovernment Relations, 1981).

The national comparison of local governments provides an introduction to the relative importance of each type of local government and its recent growth. However, differences among states in revenue options and responsibilities for services weaken the usefulness of the comparisons. There is thus a need for a more detailed comparison of each type of government within a more tightly controlled setting, such as a single state. That is the purpose of this book.

Organization of Analysis

A description of the structure of local governments in Illinois and an overview of the issues currently surrounding governmental structure in the academic literature facilitates an understanding of the importance of governmental structure on local finance patterns. An understanding of local public finance can be augmented with a review of current thinking in the academic and professional literature. Following the introduction of the public choice literature in the 1950s, numerous articles and books have been written on various aspects of local public finance, and many studies touch on the effects of alternate governmental service arrangements. Rather than attempt to work this research into each analysis and risk being repetitive or miss major contributions, the literature is discussed separately in Chapter 2. Readers not interested in this detailed review can omit the discussion and move directly to the empirical findings.

Chapter 3 describes in detail the types of governments in Illinois and hypothesizes about their occurrence and the institutional factors affecting their future growth. In particular, changes in the number of governments and taxing units are examined both by type of government and location within Illinois. This information helps the reader to better understand the empirical analyses presented in later chapters.

The empirical analysis begins with a study of the impact of number of taxing units on property tax reliance. This follows a detailed discussion of the mechanics of property tax administration. Property taxes are receiving major criticism from those wishing to impose limitations. Relatively little data, however, are available on the relationship between special districts and property tax collections. While national data suggest that special districts are relatively unimportant in property tax collections, a more detailed study suggests that single-purpose districts may be associated with differences in reliance on this revenue source.

Next is an examination of expenditures for services and employment in the local public sector. These analyses are conducted using specific services with an attempt to identify whether expenditures per capita increase, decrease, or are largely not affected when the numbers of governments involved also change. Hypotheses presented in the professional literature are tested when data permit.

The analysis concludes with a discussion of the effects of governmental structure on subjective and objective measures of service quality. Citizens' attitudes are the subjective evaluations analyzed. Recent contributions to the professional literature suggest that more governments are associated with lower perceptions of service quality. The analysis on Illinois data presents similar findings.

SUMMARY

The past half-century has brought a dramatically increased role for local government as demands for public services increased. While not increasing as rapidly as the federal government, expenditures for services provided by local governments have grown markedly.

Considering the present turn back philosophy of the federal and many state governments, and the general climate of tax resistance, it is time to examine the structure under which local public services are provided and determine the impact of differences in organization on the performance of the local governance system. A detailed examination of these effects is presented in subsequent chapters.

NOTES

1. U.S. Bureau of the Census, "Governmental Units in 1982," GC 82 (P)–1, (Washington, D.C.: Government Printing Office, June, 1982) Table A.

2. ACIR, "The Problem of Special Districts in American Government," (Washington, D.C.: Advisory Commission on Intergovernmental Relations, 1964), Henry S. Reuss, *Revenue Sharing: Crutch or Catalyst for State and Local Governments?* (New York: Praeger Publishers, 1970), Committee for Economic Development, *Modernizing Local Government* (New York, NY: Committee for Economic Development, 1966).

3. An extensive public choice literature exists on various aspects of this subject. An early article advancing this position is Charles M. Tiebout, "A Pure Theory of Local Expenditures," *Journal of Political Economy*, Vol. 64, No. 5, October 1952, pp. 416–24. Also, see Dennis C. Mueller, *Public Choice* (Cambridge, UK: Cambridge University Press, 1979); and James M. Buchanan, "Public Finance and Public Choice," *National Tax Journal*, Vol. 28, No. 4, December 1975, pp. 383–394.

4. A notable exception is a major study by John C. Bollens, *Governments in the United States* (Berkeley, CA: University of California Press, 1957).

5. U.S. Bureau of the Census, "Governmental Organization," (Washington, D.C.: Government Printing Office, 1983), Table 2.

6. A detailed description of the differences in large cities in Illinois can be found in Norman Walzer and Glenn W. Fisher, *Cities, Suburbs, and Property Taxes* (Cambridge, MA: Oelgeschlager, Gunn, and Hain, Inc., 1981), especially Chapter 2.

7. An alternative is to trace out the governments providing services to residents in an area and to statistically determine the amount of revenues raised by each government unit from residents in the jurisdiction. This approach is not practical for the number of observations being examined in this study.

8. This position has been advanced on several occasions by the Advisory Commission on Intergovernmental Relations.

9. U.S. Bureau of the Census, "Governmental Organization," Vol. 1, No. 1 (Washington, D.C.: Government Printing Office, 1978), Table 7.

10. "Economic Report of the President," (Washington, D.C.: Government Printing Office, 1981), Table B-3.

Chapter 2

Concepts for Local Government Organization

Local governments provide many goods and services to residents that contribute to the quality of life. Yet the system of governments varies substantially both among and within states. Many of these variations can be linked to historical events, economic growth patterns, demographic shifts, institutional rigidities, and service demands. Growth in expenditures by local governments has attracted the interest of both academics and policymakers trying to understand factors underlying both the growth in numbers and size of local governments. Part of the interest in understanding more about the performance of the local public sector results from the use of local governments as policy vehicles by federal and state governments. An understanding of the local budgetary process that allocates resources and provides public services is necessary for effective use of local governments.

Local governments in the United States can be most easily classified as general-purpose or single-function. General-purpose units provide a wide array of services and commonly include cities, counties, and in some instances, townships. Single function districts usually provide one service within defined boundaries and can be further subdivided into independent and dependent units. Here the distinction rests on the district's autonomy in decisionmaking authority. Dependent districts generally do not have the authority to tax or set service levels independent of a parent government such as a city or county. Independent districts, alternatively, operate autonomously from other local governments following their own work program but still within state constitutional or statutorily defined limits.

Most local units must operate within closely defined state government mandates, but municipalities have the widest range of services and authority. They therefore exercise greater discretion in the provision of services. Counties traditionally function as administrative agents of states in matters such as criminal justice, recording of legal documents, and property assessments. Counties also provide additional services, including health, fire protection, emergency medical services, airports and economic development, depending on whether authority is granted statutorily or constitutionally.

Local governments are commonly found in three general configurations or patterns: (1) a single, general-purpose government centrally providing virtually all local services within an area; (2) a set of fragmented, mutually exclusive, general-purpose governments; (3) a set of overlapping, multilayered governments including both special districts and general-purpose governments. The third configuration is the most common; the degree of overlap depends on the importance of special districts.[1] The use of special districts is one of the major factors contributing to differences in governmental structure.

While the target of some criticism, special districts have been increasing in number nationally and have been hailed as providing great flexibility and possessing inherent advantages in meeting local demands for public services. Over 28,000 special districts were reported in 1982 in the United States. In 1962 the number was 18,323.[2] The interest in single-function districts has partially emanated from the perceived failure of general-purpose governments to cope with modern urban society's changing spatial, economic, social, and political landscapes. Critics, for example, point to the inability of general-purpose governments to solve broad urban problems such as air pollution, public transportation, and crime. To solve these problems, researchers and policymakers have called for geographical and functional reordering of local government responsibilities.[3]

The debate over the structure of local government has attracted scholars from economics, political science, and public administration. While an extensive literature on both the organization of local government and on the fiscal performance of local public economies has developed, there are few empirical studies of the fiscal performance of local governments that focus on the effects of alternative government structures.[4]

PURPOSE OF CHAPTER

This chapter presents a broad framework for analyzing local public sector outcomes emphasizing variations found in the structure of local governments. First is a review of studies involving determinants of local government expenditures with particular attention paid to underlying alternative decision models. Second is a consideration of the possible effects of variations in local government organizational patterns on fiscal behavior. This provides a conceptual framework for identifying testable propositions about the impact of local government structure on local budgetary outcomes. Finally, prior empirical investigations of local government behavior that incorporate analyses of alternate government structures are presented.

Before these topics are presented, local government patterns in the United States are described in general terms to provide a background for exploring the literature discussing their behavior and impact. Of particular interest is the great nationwide diversity in arrangements for providing local services.

LOCAL GOVERNMENT PATTERNS

The local government concept in the United States can largely be traced to Thomas Jefferson's advocacy of "local self government." Local governments or "ward republics" as Jefferson referred to them, were at the heart of his republican government with the three other levels of governance being federal, state, and counties. The ward republics were to care for the poor, provide roads, public safety, education, and elections. The Jeffersonian concept of independent local governments is built on the underlying doctrines of individual sovereignty and individual rationality, understanding, and involvement in governmental affairs. Jefferson's ward republics were closely connected with an agrarian society and functioned under direct, participatory democracy.[5] The traditional Jeffersonian concept of American local government most closely parallels New England towns.

Many regional differences in arrangements for providing local services are found with certain types of governments more dominant in some areas than in others. This is due, in part, to the historical settlement patterns and the experiences of early settlers. Even within a single state many differences exist but, overall, local governments share many basic characteristics.[6]

Municipalities

Many municipalities have broad authority enabling them to provide services at their discretion rather than by a mandate of the state government. The strengthening of home rule powers has greatly expanded the services that can be provided. Not requiring specific state legislative authorization to provide services offers needed flexibility for effective local self governance.[7] However, most municipalities are limited to the powers granted in state statutes or chapters.

Counties

In nearly all states, counties act as administrative agents of state government performing functions such as administration of justice, filing of official documents, construction and maintenance of rural roads and bridges, collection of property taxes, and public health regulation activities. Geographically, the county is the most universal local government in America. With New England towns, its heritage can be traced to British self-government. Counties are historically the dominant local government in unincorporated areas in the South, the mountain states, and the far West. In some states counties provide local school services. In the West, they perform functions similar to those of midwestern townships. The importance of the county in the South and West is a partial reflection of the large plantation and ranch economies that dominate these regions. Small governmental units were less suited to provide essential services in sparsely populated rural areas.

Connecticut, Rhode Island, and Alaska have no county governments. The 3041 counties in the United States average sixty-five per state. Counties are increasingly becoming involved in providing expanded urban functions including public health, hospitals, airports, comprehensive planning with land use controls, and industrial development programs. Since the extension of home rule powers to counties has not been widespread (only about sixty have home rule authority), enabling legislation is required for counties to engage in many of these activities.[8]

Towns and Townships

Unincorporated towns are a dominant local government in New England, performing many functions provided elsewhere by other governments. Typical town functions include education and services provided by counties in other states. Densely settled New England was well served by the unincorporated towns that operated as direct democracies through town meetings. Some towns have now incorporated. Operations, consequently, are carried on through representative assemblies and municipal-type services provided.

Township governments are strongest in New York, New Jersey, Pennsylvania, Michigan, and Wisconsin. These governments provide rural roads and bridges as well as municipal-related services such as water treatment, sewerage, and public safety. Townships also play a significant role in local governance in other midwestern states. The growing importance of townships has come at the expense of counties whose influence is less in the Midwest than in the South and West where townships are generally not found. The township reflects a mixture of the New England town and the southern county.

As a civic unit, the midwestern township should not be confused with the standard thirty-six square mile geographical unit based on the Township and Range Land Survey. It is common for the civic and land unit to coincide. Because of the natural terrain, however, many civic townships are smaller than the standard size. Also, township governments and large municipalities are sometimes coterminous. While many functions performed by townships such as magistrates' courts, tax collection, and in some cases property assessment, have been consolidated or shifted to counties, townships still generally have large responsibilities for transportation services, pauper assistance, and property assessment.

Single-Function Districts

Single-function districts are divisible into school districts and other special district governments. These districts are also legally divisible into independent and dependent units.[9] Dependent districts are agents of cities or counties, created and controlled by these governments to provide additional services. Districts, for example, may be used to finance capital improvements such as water systems, sewerage facilities, or airports. Dependent districts obtain authority from the parent government with the elected officials of the parent body either serving directly as a governing board of the dependent district or directly appointing members to the board.

Independent special districts, on the other hand, employ limited powers authorized by state legislation to undertake public ventures. In contrast to dependent districts, they generally are governed by elected boards, have authority to tax, to set fees on services, to sell bonds and, most importantly, are able to independently determine services ranging from park and recreation services to mosquito abatement. Authorizing statutes generally include requirements of formation, accounting, dissolution, and other operating practices.

Primary growth in the local government system has involved noneducation independent special districts. Nationally, their numbers have continuously increased through the past three decades. Many special districts were formed to provide urban-type services outside municipalities. While special district growth is commonly associated with the process of urbanization, the majority of special districts provide services to nonmetropolitan communities.[10] Special districts, usually created by local referenda, can be appropriate institutions to serve communities with intense preferences for goods and services that general-purpose units cannot or will not provide, and to address problems of boundary, externality, and common resource issues other units are unable to address.

While special districts offer advantages for certain services, special district growth has been frequently criticized for contributing to inefficient and unresponsive local government. The bases for this criticism are: (1) a fragmentation of authority and responsibility, (2) a competition for financial resources, and (3) weakening of general-purpose local governments. Concern over growth in special districts and political fragmentation encouraged five states to control expansion through regulatory agencies or boundary commissions.[11]

School Districts

Historical factors have largely determined the extent to which school and other special districts are employed. Due to the historical dominance of New England towns, for example, independent school districts are relatively unimportant in the Northeast. In the South and the Northeast, education is commonly provided by dependent districts that have boundaries coterminous with towns, cities, or counties. Also, dependent districts associated with county government provide education in the South reflecting the dominance of counties in southern states.

The majority of local education services, however, are provided through independent school districts that have boundaries generally noncoterminous with other jurisdictions and boards determined by separate nonpartisan elections.[12] Using independent school districts to provide education reflects the importance of local schools. With this organization, education is placed under the guidance of specially selected boards and is beyond the control of local politicians. The settlement of the West and related public land policies fostered the early establishment of schools.[13] The establishment of school districts prior to general-purpose local governments partly explains the many independent school districts found in midwestern and western states. Since many of the districts were initially small, school district consolidation has been an almost continuous phenomenon.

Local Government Organization

The wide disparity in local government scenarios complicates the idea of a "typical" local government structure. Organizational patterns, however, can be placed along a continuum with a geographically and functionally fragmented system at one end and a single, general-purpose government providing a full range of local services at the other. Along the continuum are varying degrees of geographical and functional inclusiveness, dependent on the extensiveness of special districts.

The independent cities of Virginia, the New England towns, and the southern rural counties were once the best examples of a single government with a monopoly in the provision of services. However, many of the urban services demanded in the past two decades in New England are provided by special districts. In other areas of the United States, the local government structure is much closer to the fragmented end of the organization continuum. Local services are provided by layers of governments involving counties, school districts, municipalities, and special districts. In the Midwest, townships are also an integral part of the local government structure. A typical metropolitan area has eighty-five units of government including two counties, thirteen townships, twenty-one municipalities, eighteen school districts, and thirty-one special districts.[14]

The optimal structure of local government has been subject to considerable debate in academic and professional literature. There is no concensus on a consistent economic and/or political theory about why additional units of government are created and how they affect local public services. Two schools of thought have developed, both of which are partially based on impressionistic evidence. One group, the reformers, claim that additional governments lead to confusion in responsibility for services, reduced political scrutiny and control, duplication of effort, inefficiencies, and higher per unit costs or expenditures.[15] Local government reorganization attempts that are influenced by the reformers derive much of their foundation from views expressed at the turn of the century.[16] Consolidation or metropolitan governments are prescribed and accompanied by claims that while other sectors of society are becoming increasingly interdependent, political and local governance integration stand still. Political boundaries that coincide with the new expanded community depend on functional and territorial realignment.

The alternative school of thought, public choice, asserts that a greater variety of local governments offers more opportunity for residents to select a desired combination of services at the tax price they are willing to pay. The competition among governments promotes efficiency and greater responsiveness to residents' needs. Public choice proponents see a similarity between the public sector and the private sector where competition weeds out ineffective and inefficient producers. One difficulty, of course, is that free entry and exit in the public sector does not exist. Also, even inefficient governments have taxing powers. Considerable time and effort is required to assemble the information needed to convince the populace to disband a governmental program or body. The time and effort required for such an endeavor quickly outweigh the taxes saved by any individual. This is especially true when capital costs or indebtedness are transferred to an existing governmental agency. Public choice enthusiasts, however, are bolstered by empirical studies that show situations in which a larger number of decentralized governments is associated with lower spending patterns.[17]

While different conceptual views of local government are evident in existing local government structures, little systematic evidence exists that compares the results of alternate organizational forms. There are more normative and conceptual writings on the alleged performance and behavior of alternative local government systems than hard empirical analyses.[18] Many of the investigations of the local public sector have not even considered the institutional variations existing among local governments that provide services. An examination of studies of local government fiscal performance, however, indirectly provides insight into possible implications of alternate organizational structures for local government behavior.

DETERMINANTS OF LOCAL GOVERNMENT EXPENDITURES

Factors that underlie differences in state and local public expenditure have been an interest in public finance since Fabricant reported a public service expenditure function in 1952. Using per capita income, population density and percent urbanization, Fabricant accounted for more than seventy percent of the variation in per capita expenditures among the then forty-eight states.[19] This pioneering effort was followed by numerous studies analyzing interjurisdictional and interarea local government expenditure variations.

Early research on the fiscal behavior of local governments involved empirical tests of plausible cause and effect relationships between factors thought to influence local government expenditure levels in communities and observed expenditures.[20] The interest in these studies was twofold. First was a curiosity about how local public sector resources were allocated and community preferences for public goods and services articulated through the political process, given differences in socioeco-

nomic characteristics. The observed empirical relationships would hope-
fully permit policymakers to predict public expenditures based on demographic and economic factors. Second was an interest in determining
whether large units of government had lower unit service costs as is
found in the private sector.

The major advances in determinant studies during the 1950s and 1960s
involved adding other explanatory variables or "determinants" such as
intergovernmental aid and measures of community tax base. There were
also attempts to either limit the analysis to politically and geographically similar units, such as central cities and school districts, or to study
a set of common services. These studies were all based on a priori expectations about the statistical outcomes, but generally did not include an
underlying decisionmaking process or model of local government
behavior. The lack of an underlying behavioral model complicated an
unambiguous interpretation of how the local budgeting process actually
allocates resources and subsequent policy recommendations. A consistent finding, for example, that higher income is associated with higher
outlays has been interpreted as indicative of a preference by higher
income residents for more services, that public sector compensation is
higher in wealthier communities, and that higher income areas are more
able to support greater spending with less sacrifice. In economic terms,
the factors may be demand- or supply-oriented.[21]

Without a consistent theory, it is difficult to arrive at firm conclusions
or a consensus about the determinants of local fiscal behavior. Thus the
usefulness of these early studies for policy purposes is lessened. Interest
in understanding local government expenditure patterns, however,
increases as federal and state legislators view local governments as vehicles of policy implementation and as local governments provide a larger
share of public services.

Recent refinements in the analysis of local government behavior have
brought better specification of underlying decision models for local
government behavior and have overcome criticisms of earlier studies.[22]
Despite these improvements, however, disagreement about interpretations of the statistical analyses of local government expenditures continues. Determinant studies, however, have reported certain basic patterns. For example, areas with more income, larger tax bases, more
unemployment, a higher proportion of minorities, more extensive urbanization, and higher intergovernmental aid have consistently higher levels
of per capita expenditures.

Empirical studies of local public finance generally focus on expenditures rather than local government output because of measurement and
conceptual difficulties in quantifying public sector output. Even the more
articulate studies have difficulty disentangling variations in quality and

quantity of service, input costs, productivity, and the preferences of voters and taxpayers that cause expenditures to vary among communities. Citizens are both consumers and inputs into the production of local services.[23] This raises the issue of whether expenditures are better viewed as indicators of input rather than proxies for public sector output.[24]

Local government expenditure-demand studies, therefore, have moved from ad hoc statistical analyses of budget outlays toward more rigorous mathematical modeling of fiscal behavior. Basic to this evolution is a finessing of the difficulties inherent in measuring public sector output. By assuming that costs per unit of local government output are constant in a given jurisdiction and production technologies do not vary from jurisdiction to jurisdiction, per capita expenditures have been used as a proxy for output in an expression for the demand for local public services.[25]

The main advantages of a more rigorously specified decisionmaking mechanism over the straightforward statistical approach are the opportunities to test behavioral hypotheses, the inclusion of a price variable, and the more precise specification of federal and state aid variables. Interestingly, in practice, the expenditure-demand equations estimated are generally very similar to the less rigorously formulated, more ad hoc determinant studies. This results mainly from data limitations.[26]

The paradigm most commonly employed to analyze observed patterns in local government expenditures views budgetary outcomes as resulting from well informed choices. These choices are based on underlying preferences and reflect resource constraints. According to this model, the demand for local services is determined by before-tax income, fiscal base, a surrogate for the price or cost of services which accounts for intergovernmental aid, and a set of exogenous taste variables. The more rigorous approach to the underlying expenditure-demand decision process explains how preferences for local services are transformed into decisions about size and scope of local government activities that are reflected in budget outcomes. Changes in preferences, relative prices, and income are considered important determinants of local expenditures.[27]

Decision Models

Deciding whose preferences determine local public sector output or expenditures is fundamental to developing a decisionmaking mechanism for expenditure studies.

Demand-oriented public expenditure studies have usually adopted some form of the median voter approach.[28] This model postulates that voters determine budgetary outcome. Expenditure levels must be consistent with citizens' wishes. Elected officials make tax and expenditure decisions and choose budget outcomes in order to remain in office. The fiscal package that achieves this objective must attract a plurality of votes in elections under majority rule. Tax and expenditure levels representing the preferences of the median voter have been shown to receive the greatest support at elections. Thus the term "median voter" model has evolved.[29] The median voter analyses are usually grouped under the public choice school of thought.[30]

An alternative model of local decisionmaking is the bureaucratic model. Emphasis is on the preferences of government bureaucrats. The motivating force is not the satisfaction of community preferences for local public services but, rather, maximizing budgets.[31] The bureaucratic model has not enjoyed the popularity of the median voter concept of local fiscal behavior in expenditure determinant research.

As opposed to the competitive spirit of the median voter approach, where it is assumed that any government official who spends far from the median will be driven from office by a more accommodating opposition, the logic of the bureaucratic model assumes considerable "monopoly power" held by bureaus and their supporters. Noncompetitive institutions arise because of the costs of organization and differential information. Voters essentially respond as price takers to the bureau's supply of public services as expenditures are maximized. The monopoly power causes expenditures to be generally greater than the expenditure level for the competitive median voter model.

The conceptual approach for explaining expenditure choices in the local public sector that best represents actual decisionmaking is not directly testable. However, the results of empirical investigations that use alternative frameworks give some indication as to which is most applicable. Empirical results that are strong and consistent with the conceptualization of the underlying decisionmaking structure suggest the appropriateness of the assumed public choice process. Most studies of local government expenditure patterns that use some variant of the median voter approach to identify underlying reasons for fiscal differences among local governments and to predict patterns of response to exogenous change have found results generally supportive of this framework.[32]

Empirical Determinant Studies

Local expenditure studies that employ the median voter approach primarily emphasize the price effect. Voters demand more of a public service the lower their share of the local tax bill. The price effect and the impact of income are traditional factors that influence the demand for private goods or services so studies of local public service demands follow accordingly. In addition to price and income factors, other important variables include intergovernmental aid, factor costs, indicators of preferences, and size measures. The statistical results briefly summarized below are intended to provide only a flavor of the seemingly endless studies. The reader is referred to the public finance literature for more detailed discussions.[33]

Most studies agree about the shape of the demand for public services. Demand is price inelastic with a one percent change in price associated with a less than one percent change in service demanded. Expectedly, the price measure is inversely related to per capita expenditures.

Specifying the price variable for an empirical analysis of local public services is no small task. One might argue that the price of a public service to a voter results from the interaction between cost of providing an additional unit of service, degree of local tax exporting, intergovernmental aid, share of the marginal service cost borne by the voter, and amount of the additional unit of service required by the voter. Researchers have measured local public service prices using various combinations of these five variables but generally concentrate on the marginal cost, tax share, and capturability components. Net share of per capita local taxes seems to be the most commonly used price variable.

Except for specific services such as parks and recreation, estimated income elasticities computed from the statistical relationship between expenditures and income are generally positive but less than one. This means that a one percent increase in the median voter's income results in less than one percent increase in per capita expenditures for the local public service. Studies by Borcherding and Deacon, Bergstrom and Goodman, Ohls and Wales, Deacon, Inman, and Johnson are examples of the demand oriented expenditure research.[34] The income elasticities for per capita local government expenditures have generally ranged between .34 and .89.[35]

In the expenditure determinant literature, the importance of the level and type of intergovernmental aid has been of particular interest. Early studies introducing intergovernmental grants as an explanatory variable in regression equations found that grants significantly stimulate local expenditures. A $1 per capita increase in grants was associated with a more than $1 per capita increase in level of outlays. These early efforts failed to consider that in many programs, such as open-ended matching grants, the level of aid and local expenditure are determined simultaneously. Consequently, the estimated statistical relationship between aid and outlays suggested a stronger stimulative effect than might actually be true.[36] A more sophisticated approach to an examination of the effects of intergovernmental grants is to first recognize the differences in grant programs and then to separately study the effects of each type using the underlying decision framework.

Open-ended matching grants, closed-ended unconditional grants, and closed-ended conditional grants are the three general grant types in use.[37] The first group lowers the relative prices of local public services and, with inelastic demands for local public services, will have a substitutive impact. Total expenditures on grant-supported programs increase less than the grant, resulting in a decline in own expenditures which, in turn, results in tax or debt relief. The few studies focusing only on open-ended matching grants substantiate this view.[38]

The unconditional closed-ended lump sum grants increase the income of the community without affecting relative prices. The federal general revenue sharing program and many state aid programs are examples of these grants. With positive income elasticities for public goods, the effect of these programs is generally substitutive and expenditures increase but not necessarily by as much as the grant. The traditional approach to lump sum grant analysis has been to treat changes in lump sum grants as identical to changes in community income. However, because the grant is external money, not locally raised, lump sum transfers may be expected to have a greater impact on local budgets than comparable increases in private income. Gramlich and Galper labeled this possibility the "flypaper theory of incidence."[39] Considerable empirical support exists for the idea that community income and intergovernmental grants have different impacts on local government fiscal behavior.[40]

The third grant, closed-ended and conditional, has been historically by far the dominant form of aid. The expected impact depends on the matching ratio and the funding limits. One review of twenty-four studies found that closed-ended conditional grants are stimulative, with a mean estimated effect being $1.40 per capita for every $1 per capita increase in grants.[41] Another review of studies considering all types of grants suggested that the overall system of intergovernmental aid has a general substitutive effect on local budget outlays with tax relief ranging from $.50 to $.80 per $1 of aid.[42]

The empirical literature identifies both level and structure of intergovernmental aid as important determinants of per capita local government expenditures. This implies that policies characterized by greater local discretion with fewer matching requirements, reflected in the federal domestic aid programs initiated in the 1970s, were less stimulative and more substitutive in impact on local budget outcomes. The 1980s, of course, brought a decrease in federal and state aid as well as greater local discretion. The impact on local expenditures remains to be seen.

The inclusion of taste or need variables in studies of local government expenditures, regardless of the rigor with which the underlying decision model is developed, has been rather ad hoc and subject to a great deal of subjectivity. Taste variables are often selected to study the impact of measures of need on the size of the local public sector and to adjust for preference differences among communities. Common examples of need variables include measures of urbanization such as population or housing densities. Per capita expenditures for certain services, such as fire and police protection, are positively influenced by the degree of urbanization while other service expenditures, such as highways, are inversely associated with these factors. To adjust for preferences, authors have included income levels, demographic change, and socioeconomic factors. Past population changes also have been found to impact fiscal behavior.[43]

While researchers have been successful in identifying statistically strong taste variables, these factors as expenditure determinants must be interpreted with caution. The possible interdependence among taste variables obfuscates the distinction between the importance of these variables. An unambiguous interpretation of the results is often not possible. Obviously, the interpretation of the variables depends on the type of local service studied and the unit of government analyzed.[44]

Many interpretive difficulties can be traced to weaknesses in underlying theoretical models needed for a differentiation between the impacts of demand factors and supply or cost factors. The interpretation of income variables is a case in point. Despite these shortcomings, the inclusion of taste and need variables provides much of the richness found in the determinant literature and contributes to the understanding of observed regularities in local government spending behavior.

Expenditure studies have also been used to investigate the presence of scale economies in the local public sector. Population size is the scale variable commonly used even though there may be little connection between size of district and amount of output produced. While scale economies may exist in certain local government operations, changes in the cost per unit of output are difficult to ascertain from a statistical relationship between per capita expenditures and population size. It is difficult to statistically control for local public service quality differences across jurisdictions that might affect costs. Not unexpectedly, the literature using this approach generally reports mixed results.[45]

While empirical studies are becoming more sophisticated in applying theoretical decision models, many unanswered questions remain. Many of these questions relate, in part, to the shortcomings of the conceptualization of the local budgeting process and the treatment of capital costs as well as the selection of the unit of analysis in expenditure determinant studies.

An important question that needs to be asked is whether the median voter decisionmaking mechanism, the most common framework, captures the complicated bureaucratic decisions involved in setting local government public service levels and whether the restrictions of this model are necessary to understand variations in local government spending. A commonly overlooked restriction of the median voter specification is the need to treat local public outlays as if they were unidimensional and decided on separately as a single-purpose government providing one service. This formulation guarantees that local spending choices are restricted to the question of more versus less spending. The median voter approach is less satisfactory when issues are multidimensional or several issues are decided simultaneously.[46] The median voter approach is thus most appropriate when issues such as the size of a school or park district budget are investigated. However, in support of the median voter approach, limited research on citizen perceptions of public service quality suggests that voters may indeed perceive an underlying unidimensionality in common local public services.[47]

There has been little empirical investigation of capital expenditures using the median voter or any other framework. Major problems with capital expenditures are their lumpiness and potential for postponement. Inclusion of capital outlays causes expenditures in one year to be unrepresentative.[48]

A final shortcoming is the use of a generalized local government structure that views local governments as isolated decisionmaking units. There are abundant studies of either single units such as cities or school districts or the aggregation of jurisdictions within an area, like a county, into a system of local governments. The great diversity in local government structure is ignored in either approach and an important characteristic of the American local public service sector is therefore not recognized. As decisionmaking units, local governments are commonly in juxtaposition to similar units and overlap other jurisdictions. Studying a system of local governments at the county area level is difficult with a framework emphasizing the preferences of the average voter. The median voter model loses much of its meaning in this context.

In addition, all general-purpose local governments and special districts within a county may not respond similarly to changes in various economic or demographic factors. Without an understanding of how political processes and structures vary in response to institutional diversity, no a priori method of adjusting the median voter approach or other underlying decisionmaking mechanism for local differences exists.[49]

Alternative Approaches

In addition to the determinant studies, two other approaches to the study of the demand for local public services warrant mentioning. One is to analyze voting patterns directly in order to gain insight into preferences for public sector output. This approach is limited because it requires

direct referenda on public service provision. Demands for local education as exhibited through school tax referenda are the most common
application of voting data analysis.[50]

The second alternative approach to the study of local service demand
builds on the early work by Tiebout.[51] Taxpayers reveal their preferences for local public services by locating in communities that provide
the preferred bundle of public services and tax burdens. Perceived net
benefits from local public services are claimed to be reflected in real property values. By studying the relationships between value of property,
particularly single family homes in local markets, and public service
levels, researchers have attempted to gain insight into the value of local
public output. Combining public service valuations and levels of services
results in a local demand. As opposed to the other approaches, this paradigm assumes local public service and tax levels are constant and the
location of voters is variable. Empirical work following the property market approach extends the seminal study of Oates who showed that
median property value is positively influenced by a community's level
of public spending.[52]

An analysis of local budget outcomes needs to consider the structural
differences characteristic of local government systems. Rigorous decisionmaking frameworks are not easily formulated for multiservice, multilayered local government systems. Thus, a better understanding of the
interaction between institutional diversity and taxing or spending policies
is possible only by empirically studying existing patterns of behavior
amidst structural variation. For an underlying decisionmaking paradigm,
it may be sufficient that local governments respond consistently to price
or budget changes and that output levels reflect local preferences and
available resources in a general framework. Using this approach, an empirical analysis of the impact of structural variation on local government
fiscal behavior will provide an improved understanding of local government operations prior to the more systematic testing of hypotheses derived
from a yet incomplete general theory of local government.

To proceed in this direction, the literature regarding local government
structure in a federal system is reviewed in the following section. Based
on this review, we can formulate broad expectations about the relationship between local government structure and fiscal behavior.

LOCAL GOVERNMENT ORGANIZATION
AND PERFORMANCE

Two aspects of the organization of local political apparatus are
of interest: size of local government units (geographic inclusiveness) and

multiplicity of decisionmaking structures (functional inclusiveness). Despite the pleas for reform and change in the institutional structure of local governments in the United States beginning in the late 1880s, the definitive answer to the basic question, "What difference does it make?", has yet to be found. While local governance performance may respond to structural change, little positive evidence has been presented for the benefits of reorganization along either the size or fragmentation dimension.[53]

Reform literature focuses primarily on the degree to which local governments effectively provide for the agreed upon mix and level of services. It does not weigh heavily the effect of government structure on the process of registering citizen preferences for local public services. The fragmented authority that results from small, multilayered, overlapping single-purpose districts is the fundamental source of institutional failure in the governance of many areas. The commitment of small jurisdictions to parochial interests obstructs an achievement of the overall public interest of the larger community. Greater efficiency through scale economies and strengthened political control through centralization are captured by consolidating local government authority, functionally and territorially, in a single jurisdiction.

Such restructuring will professionalize local service provision and reduce constituency confusion, frustration, and transaction costs. Regional problems such as air pollution are handled more effectively when a single government is responsibile for a large area. Because special district governments represent the greatest degree of fragmentation and jurisdictional overlap, they would be eliminated by the reform tradition.[54]

The public choice school, on the other hand, sees local governments as aggregators of individual preferences on issues requiring public action. Within this context, jurisdictional boundaries of local government are an important element through which citizens express their preferences. Accordingly, a system of small multiple governments, each with a unique level and mix of services, is preferable to a monopolistic government's one level of services. In this context, special districts are useful for communities with strong preferences for certain services or boundary problems such as air pollution. Public choice, with its competitive market model of local government, offers two principles of government organization: intrajurisdictional homogeneity and smallness.[55]

In addressing the effectiveness of government in providing services, public choice scholars distinguish the provision of services and preference revelation through the collective choice process from service production.[56] Focus is on the characteristics of services with a recognition that production efficiencies and scale economies are service specific. Alternate organizational arrangements may thus be better suited to provide different local services with no single size or government structure appropriate for all services.

In addition, intergovernmental agreements, such as contracting, allow governments to capture production efficiencies independent of their size. The importance of simultaneously considering the nature of public services and structural organization is emphasized. There is no a priori determination of whether small or large or fragmented or consolidated systems are "better." With the diverse characteristics of problems and services for which collective provision is desirable, the public choice approach would imply a diversity of local governments including small general and special purpose units with large scale governmental units to resolve regional problems. The selection of any particular structure is left to available empirical evidence rather than the prima facie acceptance of any particular set of propositions.

Imbedded in the constructs of the reform and public choice approaches are implications for the impact of local government structure on the supply and demand for local public sector output. By examining these implications, expectations about the relationship between governmental organization in terms of both geographic and functional inclusiveness, and local fiscal behavior can be identified. In the following section, the importance of governmental structure is examined within the framework of its effect on the demand and supply of local services.[57]

Demand Factors

Structural aspects of local government organization may impact the demand for local services in several ways. First is the effect on the preference aggregating functions of local governments. Second is the impact on the ability to match benefits and costs of public services due to differences in boundaries. Third is the effect on the amount of services provided.

It is generally accepted that economic efficiency in the provision of public services is enhanced by providing services that correspond to the tastes of individuals through a system of local governments. Being responsive to citizen demands is an endeared quality of local governance. Furthermore, smaller homogeneous governmental units that provide services in accord with local preferences are advantageous. The advantage emanates first from the greater likelihood that preferences of consumers will be similar and second from the greater influence any one individual may expect to exert on the level and mix of collectively provided services with smaller governments. Where the number of jurisdictions in an area is large and the average size of jurisdictions small, preferences within the government units may be more uniform so voters are confident local tax levies and associated expenditures are for services thought to be beneficial and highly valued. From this, one might expect higher demand for services, increased local public output, and greater per capita expenditures in areas with highly fragmented local government systems.[58]

This effect should be particularly strong when earmarked levies are used and when there is wide variation in service preferences among communities. Education is an example. Conversely, for services such as fire protection, where preference variation is minimal and there is general fund support, governmental fragmentation may not affect local fiscal behavior.

There is a possibility that a fragmented decisionmaking system, characterized by extensive special district government with no two districts having identical constituencies, may frustrate the rational collective choice process. This would occur if the same individuals are prevented from considering complementary and substitutive relations among the services provided by special districts. Compromises across different services through log-rolling, for example, would not be available due to the separation of the choice processes. Individuals with strong preferences would benefit from this structure. The fragmented local government system would also be a disadvantage to all individuals by raising the costs of gathering information and participating in the collective choice. Thus, residents with strong preferences could strongly influence the level of services. Because of the fractured political authority in an area served by many overlapping but not juxtapositioned special districts, there may be higher levels of services and thus expenditures and taxes.[59]

Conceptually, a government should be large enough to include all affected individuals. Matching those who receive benefits and those who pay for them is called "fiscal equivalence."[60] However, when individuals who benefit from services provided by a local government reside outside the jurisdiction, externalities or spillovers occur.[61] Most local services produce some externalities or spillovers. Where spillovers occur, citizens of the providing government do not demand the optimal level of output. Furthermore, when many small general-purpose governments are clustered in one area, boundary problems cause more spillovers to occur. One effect of spillovers on local fiscal behavior associated with alternate organizational arrangements is lower spending in fragmented structures.

However, the judicious use of special district governments to establish jurisdictional boundaries that coincide with services burdened with extensive spillovers, such as air pollution control, may have the opposite budgetary impact. This circumstance, however, is not expected to dominate the measure of government fragmentation in any area and would hardly compromise the more general case where benefit spillovers encourage lower outlays in fragmented local government structures.

The third demand factor is the contention that local governments do not automatically function as competitive suppliers of public services and that they tend to be monopolistic. This behavior, allegedly, is linked to an emergence of bureaucratic systems within local governments that evolve as governments grow.[62] Monopolistic behavior can prevail only in the absence of competitive forces. These forces, using the market analogy, emanate in part from a structure composed of territorially and functionally fragmented special and general-purpose governments. If monopolistic behavior exists, fragmented government structures that are driven by the forces of competition would more efficiently meet local service demands and have lower expenditure levels.[63]

This brief review of the impact of local government structure on fiscal performance through public service demand factors argues that the interaction between the preference aggregating function of local government and the structure of political authority may result in higher expenditures when the organization of local government is fragmented. On the other hand, both benefit spillovers and potential monopolistic behavior suggest that fragmented decentralized systems have relatively lower expenditure levels in comparison to more centralized and consolidated structures. While suggesting some plausible expectations, a framework for the unambiguous interpretation of empirical results focused on demand factors certainly does not emerge. However, what we present here provides a base for further study.

Supply Considerations

The most discussed supply factor in studies of local government organization and fiscal performance is the influence of the size of government on the unit cost of public services. In addition to size, however, group size and fiscal illusion may also influence expenditures and taxes through the supply side of local public service budgets.

If local governments produce their own services and there are substantial scale economies, a system of numerous small governments will cause higher expenditures for the same level of output than a geographically more inclusive system. Scale economies are technology specific. The most efficient level of production therefore depends on the type of service. No single size of government is likely to be appropriate for all collectively produced services. Labor intensive, user oriented services may have few economies of scale while major economies are possible when capital intensive services are produced in large scale, like sewage disposal, public transportation, water supply and hospitals.[64]

The support for a large centralized government structure to take advantage of lower costs through scale economies loses some prescriptive quality when service production is separated from service provision. Purchasing services from other governments or from private producers allows smaller governments to take advantage of scale economies. However, purchase arrangements are potentially greater for some services than others. Difficulties may be greater: (1) when large, durable, specialized capital facilities are required, (2) when the services are difficult to quantify and price, (3) when the services are politically sensitive and (4) when the function is a coordinating, planning and administering activity.[65]

The potential and possibility for service contracting would argue against scale economies causing generally higher outlays in a community served by a fragmented governance system. But savings may also be available to centralized government organizations because public services are often complementary in their provision. Such savings arise from the sharing or joint utilization of inputs in the production of separate services. For example, one dispatcher may be able to handle both police and fire services, thereby reducing the cost of these services when provided by a multiservice government compared with provision by special districts.

The structural variation among communities will affect local fiscal performance through the cost of services depending on the extent that scale economies and complementary service provision are accommodated by local governance systems. Fragmented structures dominated by small special districts where service contracting and intergovernmental cooperation are not practiced may have higher costs and consequently higher expenditures.

With full information, no institutional or historical rigidities, and with structural flexibility, the organization of governments in communities should adjust as technologies and service demands change. No considerable cost advantages need thus be expected due to structural variation. However, information problems and other political and historical constraints may limit these adjustments and cause budget outcomes among communities to vary because of cost aspects linked to structural differences.

The second supply consideration is the size or the population of the community. The contention is that expenditures on services, in total, may be observed to vary among governments because of population size differences. For many services, up to a point, an increase in community population reduces per capita costs or the price of services faced by residents. The lower price would cause higher service levels to be demanded.

Because, as reported earlier, the demand for local government services is price inelastic, expenditures would be less in governments with more population.

However, most local services are subject to crowding, such as highway congestion. The effect of crowding on per capita costs or service prices is positive, increasing prices above those in places with fewer people and less crowding. In the more populous communities, the higher prices from crowding will reduce the services demanded. This combination of higher per capita costs or prices and reduced service levels due to demand inelasticities will cause higher expenditures to be observed in more populous governments. This suggests that in areas with a simpler government organization, more people per government may indeed have higher expenditures driven by the shift in costs linked to the size and density of the jurisdiction's population.[66]

The opposite relationship between expenditures and population per government in an area arises from the notion that smaller communities can capture lower per capita public service costs, and thus more services, by increasing their population through inmigration. Inmigration is encouraged by strategically oversupplying selected services identified as important in location choices.[67] If communities engage in such strategic behavior, governance organizations characterized by many low population governments should have relatively higher expenditure levels than organizations with more people per government.

The third supply factor is structural illusion. If local government taxing and spending depends on residents' knowledge about local service costs and associated tax prices, it is possible the local government structure will affect the outcome. The more complex, geographically decentralized and functionally diverse the structure of local government, the greater the amount of diverse information citizens need to form a perception on the price of local public output.[68]

If residents underestimate costs or tax prices, more services will be demanded than if their perceptions were accurate. An increase in the complexity of the structure raises the cost of gathering required information for intelligent voting decisions. The higher costs involved are expected to cause reduced effort to gather information and a reduction in accuracy of perceptions of local service costs. A lower perceived tax price with higher levels of services caused by "structural illusion" would increase per capita expenditures in areas characterized by structurally complex local governance systems when compared with more inclusive organizations.

To summarize, no unambiguous expectations about the effect of local government organization and fiscal performance associated with supply factors can be stated. Scale economies and complementarities suggest that small fragmented government systems may possibly have higher budget outlays because of production inefficiencies. Agglomeration economies suggest that both small fragmented and large inclusive structures may have higher expenditures while structural illusion in complex fragmented systems may bring about larger outlays through taxpayers' inaccurate perceptions of local government costs.

EMPIRICAL EVIDENCE

The number of studies analyzing local government structure in general, and interrelationships between structure and fiscal performance in particular is not large. Some empirical research has focused on isolating the relationships between organizational structure and budgetary behavior using statistical techniques. Other studies have considered the implications of governmental structure for different measures of fiscal performance, such as taxes and service quality, presenting descriptive as well as statistical evidence. These studies are summarized in Table 2.1. A separate but relevant line of inquiry is directed at assessing voter response to proposed local government reorganization through consolidation.

Expenditures and Structure

Researchers who are interested in analyzing the relationship between expenditures as a measure of local government budgetary performance and the distribution of collective choice authority among political jurisdictions in a community, generally have adopted the expenditure determinant approach. Per capita expenditures are regressed on selected explanatory variables one of which is a measure of local government structure. In general, data are aggregated to counties so that a structural variable can be incorporated.

Adams focused on the impact of benefit spillovers on local public sector outlays in a study of expenditures on seven local public services.[69] The number of jurisdictions in county areas was included as a structural variable in a study of police, fire, sewage disposal, sanitation, recreation, street maintenance, and general control expenditures in 478 nonrural U.S. counties. In all expenditure functions, except street maintenance and general control, a larger number of jurisdictions was associated with lower per capita expenditures. The negative relationship was attributed to an underprovision of public services caused by benefit spillovers. If there are added costs from duplication and overlap, they are offset by the spillover phenomena. As additional evidence of possible complemen-

Table 2.1. Empirical Evidence on Local Government Structure and Fiscal Performance

Study	Unit of Analysis	Structural Variable	Major Hypothesis	Findings
I. Expenditures and Structure				
Adams (1965)	478 nonrural U.S. county areas	number of governments	benefit spillover complementarity	lower expenditures with more governments except for general control expenditures
Isserman (1976)	New Jersey county areas	number of governments	benefit spillover	lower expenditures with more governments
Baird & Landon (1972)	central county areas from 125 largest U.S. metro areas	number of governments, residents/government	political responsiveness	higher expenditures with more governments
Campbell & Sacks (1967)	U.S. central cities and metro areas	residents/government, area/government	inefficiencies in fragmentation	no relationship
Wagner & Weber (1975)	148 U.S. metro county areas	0–1 variable for school organization, number of cities	monopoly behavior of centralized structure	small counties: lower expenditures with centralization, larger counties: higher expenditures with centralization, higher expenditures with more cities
Dilorenzo (1983)	65 largest U.S. metro county areas	expenditure and revenue concentration ratios	monopoly behavior of centralized structure	lower expenditures with decentralized governments
Sjoquist (1982)	48 southern U.S. central cities	number of governments in metro area	competitive behavior of decentralized structure	lower expenditures with decentralized governments
Minge (1976)	special districts and cities	cemetery expenditures	inefficiencies in fragmentation	higher expenditures with fragmented governments

Study	Sample	Variable	Concept	Findings
Dilorenzo (1981)	county areas in 5 states	0–1 variable for special district use	monopoly behavior in centralized structure efficiencies	lower expenditures with decentralized governments
Martin & Wagner (1978)	county areas in 4 states	0–1 variable for structure variation	monopoly behavior of centralized structures	lower expenditures with decentralized governments
Hawkins & Dye (1971)	U.S. metro areas	number of governments	inefficiencies in centralization	no relationship between expenditures and centralization
Cook (1973)	cities in Ontario, Canada	0–1 variable for consolidated and unconsolidated	efficiencies in consolidation	higher expenditures with consolidation
Gustely (1977)	cities in Florida	0–1 variable for consolidated and unconsolidated	efficiencies in consolidation	higher expenditures with consolidation
II. Taxes and Structure				
Baird & Landon (1972)	central county areas from 125 largest U.S. metro areas	number of governments	political responsiveness	higher property taxes with more governments
Chicoine & Walzer (1982)	Illinois county areas	number of governments per 10,000 population	structural illusion	higher property taxes with more governments
III. Service Quality and Structure				
Christenson & Sachs (1980)	North Carolina county areas	number of employees, number of employees per capita, number of employees per government, number of governments, number of governments per capita	size increases perceived quality, centralization increases perceived quality	higher service quality with larger government, lower service quality with decentralization
Ostrom (1976)	urban neighborhoods	police department size	size increases service quality	lower service quality with large police department and service quality unrelated to size

tarity in production, Adams reports a positive relationship between number of jurisdictions and general control expenditures. Other variables included in addition to number of jurisdictions were population density, a measure of urbanization, income, and percent inmigration.

Isserman challenged Adams' interpretation that a reduction in number of jurisdictions leads to higher per capita expenditures and to a more optimal allocation of resources in the public sector. Isserman noted that while political fragmentation and interjurisdictional spillovers may lead to lower spending on local government services, no optimal benchmark is available to suggest whether this level is too low.[70]

Based on New Jersey counties, Isserman also found an inverse relationship between number of jurisdictions and per capita expenditures for all services, and selected services. He noted that using observations from a single state eliminates the need to adjust for differences in functional responsibilities existing among levels of government across states. In contrast to Adams, Isserman found a negative coefficient for expenditures on general control. He also notes: (1) that while statistically significant, number of jurisdictions as a measure of the organizational structure of the local public sector had little explanatory power and (2) number of jusridictions is an indirect measure of the extent of benefit spillovers and requires cautious interpretation of empirical results.

Baird and Landon used data from the central counties of the 125 largest U.S. metropolitan areas to test the hypothesis that a larger number of small governments serving an area results in relatively higher outlays. Small governments were hypothesized to be more politically responsive, resulting in the provision of more highly valued services.[71] Expenditure determinant functions were estimated for four services, including education. Expenditures by cities were aggregated by county for sewerage, police, and fire services. School district outlays were summed. Structural variables included the natural logarithm of the number of jurisdictions in each county and residents per district. The latter was also included as a scale variable.

The results were generally consistent. Per capita expenditures for all services studied except fire protection were positively related to the number of the respective jurisdictions. The impact of fragmentation was greatest for education, a service where individual preferences vary substantially, and less for sewerage, a capital intensive service where individual preferences vary little. A ten percent increase in number of school districts was associated with a $7.17 per pupil increase in educational expenditures. An increase of ten percent in the number of cities caused a $.82 increase in per capita police outlays.

Campbell and Sacks include a chapter on the determinants of fiscal behavior in *Metropolitan America: Fiscal Patterns and Governmental Systems*.[72] Central cities, areas outside central cities, and entire metropolitan areas are the units of analysis. In estimating expenditure functions across thirty-six metropolitan areas, populations per government and area per government were not significantly related to expenditures. Campbell and Sacks concluded that their findings may be affected by measurement problems in the government structure variables.

The proposition that monopoly behavior is characteristic of a functionally inclusive government structure was tested by Wagner and Weber. They studied local public expenditures in 164 metropolitan county areas in sixteen southern states.[73] The empirical investigation compared total expenditures for counties in Maryland, North Carolina, Tennessee, and Virginia with total expenditures for county areas in the remaining twelve southern states. These four states have government systems characterized by dependent school systems while education is the responsibility of independent school districts in the remaining states. Intercept and slope binary variables distinguished counties with dependent school systems from those with independent districts. The number of municipalities in each county was also included as a determinant to adjust for the budgetary consequences of different degrees of geographical fragmentation.

From their analyses, Wagner and Weber conclude that the two structural forms of government differ significantly with respect to determinants of fiscal behavior. Among smaller counties studied, government systems with dependent school districts were generally associated with lower expenditures. This is attributed to complementary service provision, particularly administrative efficiencies, that cause lower outlays in the functionally inclusive structure. For the larger counties (those with a population over 150,000), however, government structures characterized by dependent school systems experienced relatively higher per capita outlays. Here, Wagner and Weber suggest a dominance of monopoly behavior in functionally inclusive government systems forcing expenditures up. The number of municipalities was negatively related to outlays, suggesting that geographical fragmentation was associated with lower expenditures. This is consistent with the benefit spillover hypothesis studied by Adams and Isserman.

Dilorenzo also studied the monopolistic behavior of governments by estimating expenditure equations for five common services plus general expenditures with data from sixty-five selected urban county areas.[74] He interprets the positive correlation between government concentration measures and expenditures as evidence that consolidated governance structures produce public goods less efficiently than if there were greater interjurisdictional competition. Dilorenzo introduced the percentage of total government spending and total own tax revenues collected in a county area by the four largest jurisdictions as structural variables.

Exploring the notion that local governments within a metropolitan area engage in competitive strategic behavior, Sjoquist applied the median voter framework in a study of forty-eight southern SMSA central cities.[75] The expenditure demand equation for each central city median voter includes the number of jurisdictions in the metropolitan area. The results show an inverse relationship between the number of jurisdictions and per capita total expenditures with a ten percent increase in governments associated with an estimated 3.18 percent reduction in per capita outlays. Sjoquist interprets this relationship as an indication that in metropolitan areas local governments decrease their expenditures in response to competitive pressures and the possible migration of their tax base. This strategic behavior became more pronounced as the number of jurisdictions increased and the governance structure became more decentralized.

Minge and Dilorenzo approached the local government organization issue somewhat differently in their respective studies by focusing on special districts.[76] In a purely descriptive approach, Minge contrasted cemetery expenditures in Wyoming communities where services were provided by the municipal government with expenditures by cemetery districts. Advancing economic, administrative and political reasons for cemetery districts spending more than municipalities for similar services, Minge compared average per capita outlays for cemeteries. He observed: (1) cemetery districts spent, on average, $8.62 per capita while municipal cemetery outlays were $3.35, (2) of these amounts, $3.67 and $1.56 were tax revenues from the districts and the municipalities respectively, and (3) cemetery district officials tended to favor tax revenues as opposed to fee revenues to support cemetery services. Minge concluded that creating a special district to provide a particular service, rather than leaving the financial responsibility with a general purpose government, results in a higher outlay. Generalizing, Minge's analysis suggests functionally fragmented systems of government that are dominated by special districts are associated with higher per capita expenditures.

Taking a similar approach, Dilorenzo examined the expenditure effects of legislation in several states aimed at restricting the use of single purpose governments to provide local services. Based on economies of scale arguments, expectations about bureaucratic behavior, information flow, and potential monopoly behavior, Dilorenzo hypothesized that restricting the use of special districts tends to increase the cost for local services if public service demands are price inelastic. This hypothesis was tested by estimating an expenditure function for total outlays, water supply, fire protection, sewage disposal, and housing and urban renewal expenditures in 1967 and 1977 using observations from California, Oregon, Texas, Kentucky, and West Virginia county areas. California and Oregon are the two states that most severely restricted the growth of special districts in the early 1970s. A binary variable distinguished California and Oregon county areas from those in the three control states.

The sign and significant change in the magnitude of the coefficients on the binary variables in the 1967 and 1977 expenditure functions caused Dilorenzo to conclude that per capita expenditures, in general and for all the selected services except housing and urban renewal, were strikingly increased in the two states that imposed effective restrictions on single-purpose district growth. To generalize, systems of local government, functionally fragmented and characterized by special districts, should have lower per capita budget outlays. This stands in direct conflict with Minge's findings.

A conclusion that political competition reduces expenditures was reached by Martin and Wagner from their analysis of the California local agency formation commissions.[77] Again, binary variables were used to measure structural variation. The focus here is on the restrictions of new municipal incorporation in California and the effect on the change in total expenditures in county areas. There is evidence that restricting public competition by limiting the incorporation of new municipalities caused expenditures to increase faster than usual between 1962 and 1967.

Based on descriptive and correlation analyses, Hawkins and Dye conclude that neither fragmentation nor centralization affects local government per capita spending levels in metropolitan areas.[78] They emphasize that in relative terms metropolitan areas are less fragmented than nonmetropolitan areas. That is, the number of residents per government is higher in metropolitan areas. Other correlations noted were that: (1) the older and more affluent a metropolitan area, the more complex its governmental structure, and (2) a major explanation of governmental fragmentation is the growth in special districts. A new observation is that while governmental fragmentation measured by number of governments is related to special district governments, reliance on these types of governments measured in terms of revenues and expenditures is not strongly associated with an increase in their number.

Some empirical research has been undertaken to investigate the effects of government reorganization in those metropolitan areas where consolidation proposals were approved by voters. Questions relating to the overall impacts of large scale multiservice consolidations are the topics of Cook's study of the Toronto area consolidation and Gustely's study of the Dade County, Florida consolidation. At issue in both studies is the effect of consolidation on expenditure levels.[79]

Cook examined the effects of the federation of thirteen autonomous Toronto area municipalities on educational expenditures. Cook estimated an expenditure determinant function using observations for the Toronto area cities and other Ontario cities for a year prior and a year after the consolidation. She then concluded that the federation significantly raised operating expenditures for education. A binary variable was used to distinguish between the two samples of cities and analyze the impact of consolidation. The higher expenditures, Cook explains, were caused by service equalization and enhancement (quantity and quality) which swamped any expenditure reductions associated with scale economies.

Gustely used a similar method to estimate the effects of government reorganization through consolidation in the Dade County, Florida metropolitan area. Contrary to hypothesized expectations, but consistent with Cook's findings, expenditures increased after consolidation. For analytical purposes, Gustely grouped common local public services into (1) those that were provided locally, such as parks and sewers, (2) those in which some consolidation occurred with the county involved in delivery, such as police, fire, and highways, (3) all remaining services, and (4) all services.

Gustely presumed that the increased outlays accompanying reorganization resulted from both the elimination of few public employees because of preexisting labor agreements and the equalization of public sector wage scales at the higher center city level. Both factors increased per unit labor costs after consolidation.

The empirical studies using the expenditure approach do not agree on the effects of local government structure on fiscal behavior. Calling on a number of the alternative conceptual arguments, researchers examined different aspects of the structure question and studied alternate organizational characteristics. Some concentrated on geographical fragmentation while others looked at functional fragmentation. Of the thirteen studies reviewed, seven found more decentralized local governments, as measured by number of governments or use of special districts associated with lower per capita expenditures. Two studies observed higher expenditure levels with a decentralized local political apparatus, and two studies concluded no relationship existed or both conditions can be found depending on the size of community under investigation. The lack of consensus is not surprising given the general absence of a rigorous decisionmaking framework specifying a theory of local government, and differences in responsibility for services among the governments studied.

Other Aspects of Fiscal Behavior and Structure

Measures of fiscal behavior other than expenditures have also been studied in terms of the relationship between local public sector performance and organization. While not as numerous as the expenditure studies, each provides additional evidence on the fragmentation issue.

In addition to studying expenditures, Baird and Landon tried to explain differences in per capita taxes among 125 central metropolitan counties using number of governments as a structural measure. They reported a positive relationship between number of governments and level of taxation which is consistent with their expenditure analysis.[80] A similar result was reported by Chicoine and Walzer. Studying per capita property tax collections and the ratio of property taxes to income in Illinois county areas, more governments per 10,000 people were associated with higher tax levels.

An interest in factors influencing citizens' perceptions of service quality led Christenson and Sachs to consider local public sector size and structure.[81] Citizens' perceptions of the quality of common public services in 100 counties in North Carolina were used as the criteria for measuring organizational performance. They report that size of government, measured by employment, was positively related to the perceived quality of local services. More importantly, the number of jurisdictions per capita was negatively related to the perceived quality of services. These findings suggest the public's perception of quality of local public services, at least in North Carolina, was lower in communities served by decentralized local governments.

In studies of police services and the size of police departments, Ostrom generally found that service quality and size were inversely related.[82] This is in contrast to the aggregate statistical findings reported by Christenson and Sachs. Ostrom surveyed residents in selected comparable urban neighborhoods served by small and large police departments to investigate the effect of size on service quality.

Voter Support for Reorganization

The proposal most commonly offered for reorganizing local governments is metropolitan consolidation.[83] The only exception identified is the comprehensive voter review process required by the 1972 Montana constitution and implemented through elected citizen study commissions in every Montana county in the mid 1970s. While analyses of the metropolitan reorganization efforts generally focus on pre- and post-referenda events rather than pre- and post-government performance, these investigations provide added insight into the acceptance of local government organizational changes by voters. Studies by Gustely and Cook are exceptions since they analyze budgetary outcomes resulting from consolidation in Dade County, Florida and Toronto, respectively.

The Advisory Commission on Intergovernmental Relations analyzed eighteen metropolitan reorganization efforts in the early 1960s to isolate factors that seem to affect voter reaction towards reorganization plans.[84] Of the eighteen referenda included in the study, eight plans were passed. The proposals, the study concluded, faced a largely apathetic public with only one in four eligible voters participating. Successful proposals generally did not have difficulty obtaining concurrent majorities inside and outside central cities. Arguments against concurrent majority requirements are common.

Marando summarized the outcome of forty-seven reorganization efforts from 1945 to 1974.[85] He characterized metropolitan consolidation as unique to smaller (less than one million people) single-county metropolitan areas likely located in the southern part of the United States. Only twelve of the forty-seven reorganization efforts analyzed were successful and five of these were in Virginia. Thus, there have been three rejections for every voter acceptance. Generally, the issues identified by Marando as stimulating most reorganization efforts were not critical. Unique local conditions appeared to be the most important factors influencing the acceptance of reorganization proposals by voters. For example, the criminal indictments of local officials and the disaccreditation of schools are pointed out as critical preconditions for the passage of the Jacksonville-Duval County, Florida consolidation.

Marando terms the study of reorganization proposals by civic and government leaders a ritualistic component of a process that appears to have little weight with the public or carryover to the ballot box. Voters outside the center city turned out in higher percentages than did city residents and generally opposed reorganization to a greater extent than did city residents. The findings of the fiscal effects of structural reorganization through consolidation on local expenditures that are summarized in Table 2.1 provide some support for the general voter rejection of the majority of reorganization proposals.

In contrast to the reorganization of metropolitan areas, voters in every county in Montana were asked to cast ballots on extensive reorganizational proposals developed by elected citizen commissioners. As reported by McKinsey and Koehn and Lopach and McKinsey, no community was required to change its form or structure of governance but each was provided a multitude of organizational options including the existing system from which to select an alternative.[86] This review was required in the 1972 Montana constitution which stipulates subsequent local government reviews at ten-year intervals. Of the structural changes proposed by the 122 commissions, sixty-five percent were classed by McKinsey and Koehn as major while ten percent involved major jurisdictional adjustments. The outcome of the voter reviews was the approval of one-in-six proposals suggesting general voter satisfaction with the current governmental organization in Montana.

SUMMARY

The basic principles of local government in the United States are linked to philosophies established during this country's colonial period. Based strongly on the ideas of individualistic rights and the importance of citizen preferences in the local governance of communities, the structure of local government systems that has evolved reflects both the rich heritage and the environmental qualities characterizing various regions of the country. While the organizational structure of the political apparatus through which demands for local collectively provided services are met varies substantially among communities, the impact of the structural variation on local public sector performance is not well-understood.

In contrast, other factors, such as income, wealth, demographics and service costs have often been considered determinants of the performance of local governments. The underlying decision models of local collective choice providing the conceptual logic for a study of local government behavior through expenditure studies are now more rigorously specified. This has improved the quality and policy relevance of this type of research. The most common conceptual construct to the local public decisionmaking process is the median voter approach. While encouraging the more accurate specification of expenditure determinant studies, the median voter paradigm appears better characterized as a framework for studying observed public expenditure outcomes than a vehicle for estimating individual public service demand functions per se.

Missing, however, is a general theory of local government that incorporates and is cognizant of the structural variation in the distribution of collective decisionmaking that characterizes most local government systems. Most studies have applied a generalized structural model even though government structure varies dramatically among communities. However, since there is little usable empirical evidence on local government organizational structure, there is no a priori way to adjust conceptual local choice models for structural differences. This should not, however, deter the use of available conceptual abstractions as a framework to provide some systematic guidelines in the analysis of complex empirical phenomena such as the interaction of the structure of the local public sector and budgetary outcomes.

The warrantability of the reform tradition's general prescriptions for local government reorganization and the public choice approach to the organization of local political structures need additional empirical analysis. Imbedded in these paradigms are causal expectations that, when organized according to the economic logic of supply and demand, provide plausible impacts of overall local government structural variation on fiscal performance. However, the demand and supply factors certainly cannot be summarized in a cadre of unambiguous expectations about the relationship between measures of local government fragmentation and budgetary outcome. The relative dominance and importance of the individual factors is an empirical question.

The majority of the empirical research providing evidence on the interaction between local government organization and fiscal behavior has: (1) applied some variant of the expenditure determinant approach, (2) emphasized the importance of either geographical fragmentation or functional inclusiveness, (3) developed arguments based on one, or possibly two of the supply-demand factors, and (4) focused on metropolitan areas. The majority of the studies find per capita expenditures, the measure of fiscal behavior, inversely related with the number of local governments. This suggests a more territorially and functionally fragmented decentralized system of government in an area has been generally associated with lower outlays. The conclusions of the statistical studies are consistent with the general failure of voter referenda on metropolitan area government reorganization proposals that called for consolidation. A fragmented local political apparatus, however, has also been shown to be associated with a lower public perception of service quality.

This inverse relationship is certainly not a consensus. Four studies reported opposite results or found that local government structure was unimportant in accounting for variations in local budget outcomes. As with all empirical investigations of complex phenomena, shortcomings in theoretical construct, scope, data, measurements, and statistical precision plague this research.

One obvious limitation of the empirical research on this topic is the focus on the expenditure side of local budgets with relatively little attention paid to the impact on taxes, revenue levels, dependence, or revenue structure of variations in government organization. Also, measures of government organization have tended to be unidimensional reflecting only the number of jurisdictions and usually unadjusted for population. The use of a structural measure incorporating additional attributes would be an improvement.

Previous research has often focused only on metropolitan areas and included units of observations from several states. Nonmetropolitan communities commonly have local government systems that are more fragmented than urban areas. This fact has not received attention nor have adjustments generally been made for differences in public sector responsibilities across states when multistate observations were used. Furthermore, the relationship between public perceptions of services, as a measure of local public sector output, and the governance structure deserves additional attention.

The remainder of this study addresses the issues reviewed in this chapter and builds on past research to empirically examine the economics of the local government sector. Emphasis will be on organizational structure. Illinois, an economically and geographically diversified state, provides an excellent setting for the empirical analysis. This state is a unique laboratory in which to further investigate the issues surrounding the structure and organization of local government and associated fiscal behavior because of the rich diversity in types of local governments and arrangements for providing services. The next chapter examines the government structure in Illinois.

NOTES

1. William Cape, Leon B. Groves and Burton M. Michaels, *Government by Special Districts* (Lawrence, KA: Kansas University, 1969).
2. U.S. Bureau of the Census, "Governmental Units in 1982," GC 82(P)-1 (Washington, D.C.: Government Printing Office, June 1982): Table A.
3. See Committee for Economic Development, *Modernizing Local Government* (New York, NY: Committee for Economic Development, 1966).
4. A recent overview of the local government finance literature is available in Robert P. Inman, "The Fiscal Performance of Local Governments: An Interpretative Review," in Peter Mieszkowski and Mahlon Straszheim, eds. *Current Issues in Urban Economics* (Baltimore, MD: Johns Hopkins University Press, 1979), pp. 270–321.
5. The underlying theory and basic concepts of local self government are discussed in Anwar Syed, *The Political Theory of American Local Government* (New York, NY: Random House, Inc., 1966), pp. 38–52.
6. Committee for Economic Development, 1966, pp. 24–32 provides an overview of types of local governments and regional variations. Also see Daniel R. Grant and H. C. Nixon, *State and Local Government in America* (Boston, MA: Allyn and Bacon, 1982).
7. For an extensive discussion of home rule see Luther Gulick, *The Metropolitan Problem and American Ideas* (New York, NY: Alfred A. Knopf, 1962).
8. An exhaustive study of county governments is provided in Herbert Sydney Duncombe, *Modern County Government* (Washington, D.C.: National Association of Counties, 1977).
9. See Robert B. Hawkins, Jr., *Self Government by District: Myth and Reality* (Palo Alto, CA: Hoover Institution Press and Stanford University, 1976), pp. 2–27; John C. Bollens, *Special District Governments in the United States* (Berkeley, CA: University of California Press, 1957) and Cape, Graves and Michaels, 1969.

10. Robert B. Hawkins, Jr., "Special Districts in Nonmetropolitan Areas: Some Policy and Research Issues," *National Conference on Nonmetropolitan Community Services Research* (Washington, D.C.: U.S. Senate Committee on Agriculture, Nutrition and Forestry Print, 1977), pp. 157–166.

11. Hawkins, 1976, pp. 14–21. Evidence presented in Paul B. Downing and Thomas J. Dilorenzo, "User Charges and Special Districts," in R. Arnson and E. Schwartz, eds. *Management Policies in Local Government Finance* (Washington, D.C.: International City Management Association, 1981), pp. 184–210, suggests between 1972 and 1977 the "boundary commission states" of California, Nevada, New Mexico, Oregon and Washington appear to have successfully curtailed special district growth. However, this trend did not hold for the 1977–1982 period.

12. Nationwide, in 1977 there were 16548 school systems of which 15174 were independent and 1374 were dependent. See U.S. Bureau of the Census, *Governmental Organization*, Vol. 1, No. 1, GC77(1)–1 (Washington, D.C.: U.S. Government Printing Office, 1978), Table 9.

13. Frederick Eby and Charles Flinn Arrowood, *The Development of Modern Education in Theory, Organization and Practice* (New York, NY: Prentice-Hall, Inc., 1937), pp. 547–553.

14. Grant and Nixon, 1982, p. 386.

15. See ACIR, "Alternative Approaches to Governmental Reorganization in Metropolitan Areas," (Washington, D.C.: Advisory Commission on Intergovernmental Relations, 1962), and Grant and Nixon, 1982, pp. 378–410.

16. See, for example, H. G. Wells, *Mankind in the Making* (Leipzig: Bernard Tauchnitz, 1903). Also see Syed, 1966, pp. 101–121, and H. Paul Friesema, "The Metropolis and the Maze of Local Government." *Urban Affairs Quarterly*, Vol. 2, No. 2, December 1966, pp. 68–90.

17. See Robert L. Bish, *The Public Economy of Metropolitan Areas* (Chicago, IL: Markham/Rand McNally, 1971), and Clifford S. Russell, ed. *Collective Decision Making: Applications from Public Choice Theory* (Baltimore, MD: The Johns Hopkins University Press, 1979). Empirical evidence is presented in Thomas J. Dilorenzo, "Economic Competition and Political Competition: An Empirical Note," *Public Choice*, Vol. 40, No. 2, 1981, pp. 203–209.

18. Discussions on this point by Vincent Ostrom, Charles M. Tiebout and Robert Warren, "The Organization of Government in Metropolitan Areas: A Theoretical Inquiry," *American Political Science Review*, Vol. 55, No. 4, December 1961, pp. 831–843 are offered as examples.

19. S. Fabricant, *The Trend in Government Activity Since 1900* (New York, NY: National Bureau of Economic Research, 1952).

20. Reviews of this literature are numerous. See, for example, J. E. Fredland, *Determinants of State and Local Government Expenditures: An Annotated Bibliography* (Washington, D.C.: The Urban Institute, 1974).

21. Inman, 1979, pp. 272–274.

22. See Roy Bahl, Marvin Johnson and Michael Wasylenko, "State and Local Government Expenditure Determinants: The Traditional View and a New Approach" in Roy Bahl, Jesse Burkhead and Bernard Jump, Jr., eds. *Public Employment and State and Local Government Finance* (Cambridge, MA: Ballinger Publishing Co., 1980), pp. 65–119.

23. Wallace E. Oates, "On Local Finance and the Tiebout Model," *American Economic Review*, Vol. 71, No. 2, May 1981, pp. 93–98.

24. Elinor Ostrom, "Metropolitan Reform: Propositions Derived from Two Traditions," *Social Science Quarterly*, Vol. 53, No. 3, December 1972, p. 488.

25. See Bahl, Johnson and Wasylenko, 1980, pp. 83–85.

26. Dennis C. Mueller, *Public Choice* (New York, NY: Cambridge University Press, 1979), pp. 106–111.

27. Robert T. Deacon, "Review of the Literature on the Demand for Public Services," *National Conference on Nonmetropolitan Community Services Research* (Washington, D.C.: U.S. Senate on Agriculture, Nutrition and Forestry Print, 1977), pp. 207–230.

28. See Bahl, Johnson and Wasylenko, 1980, pp. 73–83, Inman, 1979, pp. 278–283 and Dennis C. Mueller, "Public Choice: A Survey," *Journal of Economic Literature*, Vol. 14, No. 2, June 1976, pp. 408–410 for a more complete discussion of the assumptions and specification of the median voter model. Also see Werner W. Pommerehne, "Institutional Approaches to Public Expenditure: Empirical Evidence from Swiss Municipalities," *Journal of Public Economics*, Vol. 9, No. 2, April 1978, pp. 255–280.

29. D. Black, *The Theory of Committees and Elections* (Cambridge: Cambridge University Press, 1958).

30. See Mueller, 1979.

31. William A. Niskanen, Jr., *Bureaucracy and Representative Government* (Chicago, IL: Aldine-Atherton, 1971). For theoretical extensions see William Orzechowski, "Economic Models of Bureaucracy: Survey, Extensions and Evidence," in Thomas E. Borcherding, ed., *Budgets and Bureaucrats: The Sources of Governmental Growth* (Durham, NC: Duke University Press, 1977), pp. 229–259. See Dolores T. Martin and Richard B. McKenzie, "Bureaucratic Profits, Migration Costs and the Consolidation of Local Government," *Public Choice*, Vol. 23, Fall 1975, pp. 95–100 for an empirical test of this concept. Romer and Rosenthal claim this model performs better than the median voter approach in explaining local government behavior. See Thomas Romer and Howard Rosenthal, "Bureaucrats Versus Voters: On the Political Economy of Resource Allocation by Direct Democracy," *Quarterly Journal of Economics*, Vol. 53, No. 4, November 1979, pp. 536–588.

32. Deacon, 1977, pp. 211–214. See Thomas Romer and Howard Rosenthal, "The Elusive Median Voter," *Journal of Public Economics*, Vol. 12, No. 2, October 1979, pp. 143–170 for a review of empirical studies using the median voter model and a critique of this approach. The claim is that empirical evidence does not verify the decisiveness of the median voter.

33. This review draws from Deacon, 1977, Inman, 1979, and Bahl, Johnson and Wasylenko, 1980.

34. Thomas E. Borcherding and Robert T. Deacon, "The Demand for the Services of Non-Federal Governments," *American Economic Review*, Vol. 62, No. 5, December 1972, pp. 891–901; Theodore C. Bergstrom and Robert P. Goodman, "Private Demands for Public Goods," *American Economic Review*, Vol. 63, No. 2, July 1973, pp. 280–296; Robert T. Deacon, "A Demand Model for the Local Public Sector," *Review of Economics and Statistics*, Vol. 50, No. 2, May 1978, pp. 184–192; James C. Ohls and Terence J. Wales, "Supply and Demand for State and Local Services," *Review of Economics and Statistics*, Vol. 54, No. 4, November 1972, pp. 424–430; Robert P. Inman, "Testing Political Economy's 'as if' Proposition: Is the Median Income Voter Really Decisive?" *Public Choice*, Vol. 33, No. 4, 1978, pp. 45–65; and Marvin B. Johnson, "Community Income, Intergovernmental Grants and Local School District Fiscal Behavior," in Peter Mieszkowski and William H. Oakland, eds. *Fiscal Federalism and Grants-in-Aid* (Washington, D.C.: The Urban Institute, 1979), pp. 51–77.

35. For a good summary of the price and income elasticities of local public service demands determined through expenditure analyses see Inman, 1979, pp. 285–289.

36. Elliot Morss, "Some Thoughts on the Determinants of State and Local Government Expenditures," *National Tax Journal*, Vol. 19, No. 1, March 1966, pp. 95–103.

37. A good summary of the basic propositions on the impact of intergovernmental aid on state and local budget outcomes is found in James A. Wilde, "Grants-in-Aid: The Analytics of Design and Response," *National Tax Journal*, Vol. 24, No. 2, June 1971, pp. 573–584.

38. Edward M. Gramlich, "Intergovernmental Grants: A Review of the Empirical Literature" in Wallace E. Oates, ed., *The Political Economy of Fiscal Federalism* (Lexington, MA: Lexington Books, 1977), pp. 219–239.

39. Edward M. Gramlich and Harvey Galper, "State and Local Fiscal Behavior and Federal Grant Policy," *Brookings Papers on Economic Activity* No. 1 (Washington, D.C.: Brookings Institution, 1973), pp. 15–58.

40. See Paul N. Courant, Edward M. Gramlich and Daniel L. Rubinfeld, "The Stimulative Effects of Intergovernmental Grants: or Why Money Sticks Where It Hits" in Peter Mieszkowski and William H. Oakland, eds. *Fiscal Federalism and Grants-in-Aid* (Washington, D.C.: The Urban Institute, 1979), pp. 1–21 for additional discussion on this point. Also see Martin C. McGuire, "The Analysis of Federal Grants Into Price and Income Components," pp. 31–50 and Johnson, 1979, in this same volume for empirical evidence on the flypaper theory.

41. Gramlich, 1977, pp. 231–234.

42. Inman, 1979, pp. 289–292.

43. See Robert P. Inman, "The Fiscal Performance of Local Governments: An Interpretive Review," unpublished manuscript, 1976 for a most comprehensive presentation of these studies.

44. See Bahl, Johnson and Wasylenko, 1980, pp. 94–96 for additional discussion of these points.

45. Inman, 1976, p. 48.

46. Mueller, 1979, p. 107. Also see Pommerehne, 1978.

47. James A. Christenson, "Quality of Community Services: A Macrounidimensional Approach with Experiential Data," *Rural Sociology*, Vol. 41, No. 4, Winter 1976, pp. 509–525.

48. See Inman, 1979, pp. 276–278 for a discussion of extending the expenditure demand framework to include borrowing and public capital expenditures.

49. V. Lane Rawlins and Richard P. Nathan, "The Field Network Evaluation Studies of Intergovernmental Grants: A Contrast with the Orthodox Economic Approach," *American Economic Review*, Vol. 72, No. 2, May 1982, pp. 98–102. Pommerehne, 1978, shows that institutional factors do impact expenditures and thus should be included in politico-economic models.

50. See Deacon, 1977, pp. 215–220 for an overview of the direct analysis of voting data. For a specific application see George M. Peterson, "The Demand for Public Schooling: A Study in Voting and Expenditure Theory," (Washington, D.C.: The Urban Institute, 1973).

51. Charles M. Tiebout, "A Pure Theory of Local Expenditures," *Journal of Political Economy*, Vol. 64, No. 5, October 1956, pp. 416–424.

52. See Deacon, 1977, pp. 220–223 for an elaboration on this approach to the study of public service demands; Wallace Oates, "The Effects of Property Taxes and Local Public Spending on Property Values: An Empirical Study of Tax Capitalization and the Tiebout Hypothesis," *Journal of Political Economy*, Vol. 77, No. 6, November/December 1969, pp. 947–971. The Tiebout hypothesis that competition among numerous jurisdictions is sufficient to guarantee public sector efficiency has been shown to not hold. See Joseph E. Stiglitz, "The Theory of Local Public Goods," in M. S. Feldstein and R. P. Inman, eds. *The Economics of Public Services* (London: McMillan Press, 1977), pp. 274–333 and Dennis Epple and Allan Zelenitz, "The Implications of Competition

Among Jurisdictions: Does Tiebout Need Politics?" *Journal of Political Economy*, Vol. 89, No. 6, December 1981, pp. 1197–1217. Ellickson in Bryan Ellickson, "Jurisdictional Fragmentation and Residential Choice," *American Economic Review*, Vol. 51, No. 2, May 1971, pp. 334–339, combines the expenditure determinant approach and locational approach and presents a conceptual framework that simultaneously treats residential location decisions and the determination of local public sector output. Also see Dennis Epple and Allan Zelenitz, "The Roles of Jurisdictional Competition and of Collective Choice Institutions in the Market of Local Public Goods," *American Economic Review*, Vol. 71, No. 2, May 1981, pp. 87–92 and David L. Sjoquist, "The Effect of the Number of Local Governments on Central City Expenditures," *National Tax Journal*, Vol. 35, No. 1, March 1982, pp. 79–87.

53. For a review of the evolution of the reformists see Alan K. Campbell and Guthrie S. Birkhead, "Municipal Reform Revisited: The 1970s Compared with the 1920s," in Alan K. Campbell and Roy W. Bahl, eds. *State and Local Government: The Political Economy of Reform* (New York, NY: The Free Press, 1976), pp. 1–17. Grant and Nixon, 1982, pp. 383–388 present the reform arguments.

54. See Robert L. Bish, "Public Choice Theory: Research Issues for Nonmetropolitan Areas," *National Conference on Nonmetropolitan Community Services Research* (Washington, D.C.: U.S. Senate on Agriculture, Nutrition and Forestry Print, 1977), pp. 125–140, George R. McDowell, "An Analytical Framework for Extension Community Development Programming in Local Government," *American Journal of Agricultural Economics*, Vol. 60, No. 3, August 1978, pp. 416–424 and Ostrom, 1972 for other comparisons of the reform tradition and public choice. See Friesema, 1966, for a structural critique of the "conventional wisdom" on local government reorganization.

55. Lyle C. Fitch, "Fiscal and Productive Efficiency in Urban Government Systems," in Amos H. Hawley and Vincent P. Rock, eds. *Metropolitan America in Contemporary Perspective* (New York, NY: Sage Publications, 1975), pp. 405–407.

56. See Phillip M. Gregg, "Units and Levels of Analysis: A Problem Policy Analysis in Federal Systems," *Publius*, Vol. 4, No. 4, Fall 1974, pp. 59–86.

57. The issue of the optimal organization of government in a federal system is theoretically addressed by Gordon Tullock, "Federalism: Problems of Scale," *Public Choice*, Vol. 6, Spring 1969, pp. 19–29, Mancur Olson, Jr., "The Principle of 'Fiscal Equivalence': The Division of Responsibilities Among Different Levels of Government," *American Economic Review*, Vol. 59, No. 2, May 1969, pp. 479–487, Jerome Rothenberg, "Local Decentralization and the Theory of Optimal Government" in Julius Margolis, ed., *The Analysis of Public Output* (New York, NY: National Bureau of Economic Research, 1970), pp. 31–64, and Wallace E. Oates, *Fiscal Federalism* (New York, NY: Harcourt, Brace, Jovanovich, Inc., 1972) especially Chapter 1.

58. Robert N. Baird and John H. Landon, "Political Fragmentation, Income Distribution and the Demand for Government Services," *Nebraska Journal of Economics and Business*, Vol. 11, No. 4, Autumn 1972, pp. 171–184.

59. Tullock, 1969, pp. 28–29, argues that if voters' wishes are to be served by government then communication through the voting process is essential. However, voters cannot be overburdened by information costs. While he suggests a good deal of empirical work is required, his speculation is that each voter be in the jurisdiction of between five and eight overlapping separate government units, including national and state, for an optimum. Terry N. Clark, "Community Structure, Decision-Making, Budget Expenditures, and Urban Renewal in 51 American Communities," *American Sociological Review*, Vol. 33, No. 4, August 1968, pp. 576–593 found that decentralization increased expenditures in the communities he studied.

60. For an example of the conceptual research on this issue see Herbert Mohring, "The

Optimal Provision of Public Goods: Yet Another Comment," *Journal of Political Economy*, Vol. 81, No. 3, May/June 1973, pp. 778–785 and the references contained therein.

61. Olson, 1969. The argument made here is in terms of benefit spillovers leading to fewer services and lower outlays. Of course, costs can also spill over. In the case of costs the opposite would be expected with fragmented structures exhibiting, comparatively, higher levels of outlays. However, net spillovers from local government services are expected to be dominated by benefits.

62. See, for example, William A. Niskanen, Jr., "Bureaucrats and Politicians," *Journal of Law and Economics*, Vol. 18, No. 3, December 1975, pp. 617–644 and Romer and Rosenthal, 1979.

63. See Richard E. Wagner and Warren E. Weber, "Competition, Monopoly, and the Organization of Government in Metropolitan Areas," *Journal of Law and Economics*, Vol. 18, No. 3, December 1975, pp. 661–684. The authors' empirical results indicate that communities, particularly larger ones, with functionally inclusive government systems do have higher expenditures. Also see Dilorenzo, 1983.

64. Ostrom, 1972, p. 482. For example, see Norman Walzer, "Economies of Scale and Municipal Police Services: The Illinois Experience," *Review of Economics and Statistics*, Vol. 54, No. 4, November 1972, pp. 431–438. Also see William F. Fox, Jerome M. Stam, W. Maureen Godsey and Susan D. Brown, "Economies of Size in Local Government: An Annotated Bibliography," RDRR NO. 9. United States Department of Agriculture (Washington, D.C.: Government Printing Office, 1979).

65. See Jerome Rothenberg, "Comment: Competition, Monopoly, and the Organization of Government in Metropolitan Areas," *Journal of Law and Economics*, Vol. 18, No. 3, December 1975, p. 688.

66. James M. Litrack and Wallace E. Oates, "Group Size and the Output of Public Goods: Theory and an Application to State-Local Finance in the United States," *Public Finance*, Vol. 25, No. 1, 1970, pp. 42–58.

67. Henry J. Aaron, "Local Public Expenditures and the 'Migration Effect'," *Western Economic Journal*, Vol. 7, No. 4, December 1969, pp. 385–390.

68. See Richard E. Wagner, "Revenue Structure, Fiscal Illusion, and Budgetary Choice," *Public Choice*, Vol. 25, Spring 1976, pp. 45–61, for an application of this concept to the revenue structure of government. These ideas are also discussed in Charles J. Goetz, "Fiscal Illusion in State and Local Finance" in Thomas E. Borcherding, ed. *Budgets and Bureaucrats: The Sources of Government Growth* (Durham, NC: Duke University Press, 1977), pp. 176–187. Pommerehne and Schneider in Werner W. Pommerehne and Friedrich Schneider, "Fiscal Illusion, Political Institutions and Local Public Spending," *Kyklos*, Vol. 31, No. 3, 1978, pp. 381–408 demonstrate the impact of institutional variation on the implications of fiscal illusion for spending behavior.

69. Robert F. Adams, "On the Variation in the Consumption of Public Services," *Review of Economics and Statistics*, Vol. 47, No. 4, November 1965, pp. 400–405.

70. Andrew M. Isserman, "Interjurisdictional Spillovers, Political Fragmentation and the Level of Public Services: A Re-Examination," *Urban Studies*, Vol. 13, No. 1, February 1976, pp. 1–12.

71. Baird and Landon, 1972.

72. Alan K. Campbell and Seymour Sacks, *Metropolitan America: Fiscal Patterns and Governmental Systems* (New York, NY: The Free Press, 1967).

73. Wagner and Weber, 1975. For a comment on Sjoquist see George Palumbo, "City Government Expenditures and City Government Reality: A Comment on Sjoquist," *National Tax Journal*, Vol. 36, No. 2, June 1983, pp. 249–252.

74. Dilorenzo, 1983.

75. Sjoquist, 1982.

76. David Minge, "Special Districts and the Level of Public Expenditures," *Journal of Urban Law*, Vol. 53, 1976, pp. 701–718, and Thomas J. Dilorenzo, "The Expenditure Effects of Restricting Competition in Local Public Service Industries: The Case of Special Districts," *Public Choice*, Vol. 37, No. 3, 1981, pp. 569–578.

77. Dolores Tremewan Martin and Richard E. Wagner, "The Institutional Framework for Municipal Incorporation: An Economic Analysis of Local Agency Formation Commissions in California," *Journal of Law and Economics*, Vol. 21, No. 2, October 1978, pp. 409–426.

78. Brett W. Hawkins and Thomas R. Dye, "Metropolitan 'Fragmentation': A Research Note," in Thomas R. Dye and Brett W. Hawkins, eds. *Politics in the Metropolis: A Reader in Conflict and Cooperation*, 2nd edition (Columbus, OH: Charles E. Merrill Publishing Company, 1971), pp. 493–499.

79. Gail C. A. Cook, "Effect of Metropolitan Government on Resource Allocation: The Case of Education in Toronto," *National Tax Journal*, Vol. 26, No. 4, December 1973, pp. 585–590, and Richard D. Gustely, "The Allocational and Distributional Impacts of Governmental Consolidation: The Dade County Experience," *Urban Affairs Quarterly*, Vol. 12, No. 3, March 1977, pp. 349–364.

80. Baird and Landon, 1972; David L. Chicoine and Norman Walzer, "Number of Taxing Units and Property Tax Collections," *Regional Science Perspectives*, Vol. 12, No. 2, 1982, pp. 3–12. See Thomas G. Cowing and A. G. Holtmann, *The Economics of Local Public Service Consolidation* (Lexington, MA: Lexington Books, D. C. Heath and Co., 1976) for service industry case studies useful in developing restructuring policies for the organization of service provision. The case studies demonstrate the application of demand and supply factors in developing individual service industry recommendations.

81. James A. Christenson and Carolyn E. Sachs, "The Impact of Government Size and Number of Administrative Units on the Quality of Public Services," *Administrative Science Quarterly*, Vol. 25, No. 2, March 1980, pp. 89–101.

82. Elinor Ostrom, "Size and Performance in a Federal System," *Publius*, Vol. 6, No. 2, Spring 1976, pp. 33–73. The literature on perceptual evaluations is discussed in more depth in a later chapter.

83. See Steven P. Erie, John J. Kirlin, and Francine F. Rabinovitz, "Can Something Be Done?: Propositions on the Performance of Metropolitan Institutions," in Lowden Wingo, ed. *Reform of Metropolitan Governments* (Baltimore, MD: The Johns Hopkins Press, 1972), pp. 7–41 for a classification of consolidation and reform approaches as well as a general analysis of successful reorganizations.

84. ACIR, "Factors Affecting Voter Reactions to Governmental Reorganization in Metropolitan Areas" (Washington, D.C.: Advisory Commission on Intergovernmental Relations, 1962), M-15.

85. Vincent L. Marando, "The Politics of Metropolitan Reform," in Alan K. Campbell and Roy W. Bahl, eds. *State and Local Government: The Political Economy of Reform* (New York, NY: The Free Press, 1976), pp. 24–49. Also see Walter A. Rosenbaum and Gladys M. Kammerer, *Against Long Odds: The Theory and Practice of Successful Governmental Consolidation* (Beverly Hills, CA: Sage Publications, 1974). Consolidation issues are continuously being placed before voters. In November 1982 voters in the Battle Creek, Michigan area agreed to consolidate the city of Battle Creek and the surrounding township. However, voters in Louisville-Jefferson County, Kentucky turned back a city-county consolidation proposal.

86. Lauren S. McKinsey and Peter H. Koehn, "Montana Voter Review of Local Government: Implications for Policy and Research," in *National Conference on Nonmetropolitan Community Services Research* (Washington, D.C.: U.S. Senate Committe on

Agriculture, Nutrition, and Forestry Print, 1977), pp. 149–156; James J. Lopach and Lauren S. McKinsey, "Local Government Reform by Referendum: Lessons from Montana's Voter Review Experience," *State and Local Government Review*, Vol. 11, No. 1, January 1979, pp. 35–39.

Chapter 3

Structure of Local Governments

Arrangements for providing local public services vary not only by state but differ within states. Patterns of development and the institutional arrangements for providing services within regions evolved historically. Perhaps the most common characteristic of governmental structure has been the creation of governments based on perceived needs of residents. Shifting populations demand additional services and taxing units are created to meet specific requests. The creation of an additional government may be a response to a small group of vocal residents with little or no consideration for the overall impact on other units of government nor for whether existing governments might provide the service at lower cost.

The pattern of local governments which developed over many years is a maze of overlapping and seemingly uncoordinated governments, most having access to the property tax as a revenue source. The conditions under which these governments were originally created did not remain static as the tax base shifted. Needs for services changed but the governments were rarely reorganized or reevaluated. Rather, services were requested and additional governments were created.

This chapter examines the governmental structure for providing local services in Illinois, a state with the greatest variety of governmental units. The number of units, their growth experiences, the decisionmaking framework involved, and personnel who provide the services are examined. In addition, a detailed examination of socioeconomic characteristics in areas with more or fewer taxing units is conducted to obtain insight into factors underlying governmental structure. Particular attention is paid to testing the hypothesis that new governments are created to bypass local taxing limits.

Throughout this chapter, the focus is on numbers of taxing units and numbers of governments. As far as taxpayers are concerned, the authority of a unit of government to levy property taxes may be more important than the number of governments. However, some public agencies do not collect property taxes; rather they depend on user charges and/or finance services with assistance from the federal or state government.

STRUCTURE OF GOVERNMENT

The power to create local governments usually resides within the state legislature. A procedure is available for residents to petition the state legislature to create a new government for the purpose of providing stated services with access to specified revenue sources.[1] In those states with property tax and debt limits, a newly created government has its own set of taxing and borrowing powers. Increasing the number of governments, therefore, directly increases regional taxing and borrowing authority.

Local Governments in the United States

In 1977, there were 79,862 units of local government in the United States of which 67,780 had authority to collect taxes.[2] On the average, there was one unit of local government for each 2668 residents. These governments are not spread evenly throughout the United States, and individual states differ markedly with respect to the amount of governmental fragmentation.[3] Table 3.1 compares the number of local governments by state, and is adjusted for population size.

Table 3.1. Number of Local Governments by State

State	Number of Local Governments	Percent Change 1967–1977	Population Per Local Government
Alabama	949	19.2%	3,809
Alaska	150	143.5	2,433
Arizona	420	6.6	5,267
Arkansas	1,346	7.5	1,568
California	3,806	−1.5	5,570
Colorado	1,459	16.5	1,742

Table 3.1. *continued*

State	Number of Local Governments	Percent Change 1967–1977	Population Per Local Government
Connecticut	434	5.1	7,143
Delaware	210	23.4	2,757
Dist. of Columbia	2	–	356,000
Florida	911	10.1	9,086
Georgia	1,263	5.0	3,904
Hawaii	19	–	45,684
Idaho	972	11.6	836
Illinois	6,620	2.6	1,691
Indiana	2,854	6.9	1,862
Iowa	1,852	2.8	1,545
Kansas	3,725	1.6	612
Kentucky	1,183	24.2	2,863
Lousiana	458	– 37.5	8,310
Maine	779	11.6	1,358
Maryland	426	18.0	9,676
Massachusetts	766	17.1	7,590
Michigan	2,633	– 9.3	3,460
Minnesota	3,437	– 17.8	1,141
Mississippi	835	6.6	2,804
Missouri	2,937	0.7	1,623
Montana	958	– 13.1	779
Nebraska	3,485	– 20.6	443
Nevada	182	24.5	3,242
New Hampshire	506	– 1.7	1,605
New Jersey	1,517	6.8	4,834
New Mexico	313	1.9	3,655
New York	3,309	– 5.0	5,463
North Carolina	874	16.2	6,222
North Dakota	2,707	– 1.8	235
Ohio	3,285	0.1	3,268
Oklahoma	1,675	– 5.5	1,621
Oregon	1,447	– 0.6	1,578
Pennsylvania	5,246	5.0	2,261
Rhode Island	120	10.0	7,758
South Carolina	585	4.3	4,814
South Dakota	1,727	– 50.8	394
Tennessee	905	14.4	4,611
Texas	3,883	12.7	3,151
Utah	492	10.5	2,445
Vermont	647	– 1.4	730
Virginia	389	4.3	12,805
Washington	1,666	0.8	2,136
West Virginia	5 95	30.7	3,024
Wisconsin	2,518	1.1	1,822
Wyoming	385	– 18.4	977

Source: U.S. Bureau of the Census, *Governmental Organization* (Washington, D.C.: Government Printing Office, 1978).

The comparisons in Table 3.1 have several points of interest. First is the great diversity among states in arrangements for providing local services. Illinois leads with 6620 units of local government and a population of 11,197,000 in 1977 – one unit of local government for each 1691 residents.[4] Not all of these governments collect property taxes, however. In 1977, 5522 units (83.4 percent) of local governments had property taxing authority.

The state with the fewest local governments, excluding the District of Columbia, was Hawaii with only nineteen, of which fifteen can collect property taxes. Hawaii is an unusual example because it contains only one municipal government and one school district for 868,000 residents. The majority of its local governments are special districts.

Besides Hawaii, Rhode Island has the smallest number of local governments with 120, followed by Alaska with 150, and Nevada with 182. A simple comparison of the 6620 in Illinois with the 120 in Rhode Island can be misleading, since Rhode Island contains 931,000 residents compared with more than eleven million in Illinois. Since there is reason to expect larger states to have more units of government, an adjustment must be made for population.

The ratio of population to number of local governments is shown in Table 3.1. We find that Illinois is *much more* representative of other states when number of governments is adjusted for population size. Illinois has one local government for each 1691 residents, thereby ranking above the average of one government per 2668 residents nationwide. The greatest density of governments, however, is found in smaller states such as North Dakota with one local government for each 235 residents or South Dakota with one for each 394 residents. By this comparison Illinois ranks seventeenth from the highest.

Although number of governments rather than taxing units is used in this comparison, the rank held by Illinois does not change materially when only units with property taxing authority are included. A few states differ substantially between two measures, however. In Pennsylvania, 62.6 percent of local governments have the authority to levy property taxes compared with the 83.4 percent in Illinois.

Trends. Differences in the growth of governments among states between 1967 and 1977 also provide insight into governmental fragmentation. The percentage changes range from a −50.8 percent in South Dakota to a 143.5 percent increase in Alaska. A 1.7 percent nationwide decline occurred during this period. With a range as wide as in Table 3.1, averages need to be examined in more detail. Fourteen states reported declines in total numbers and four states reported no change or an increase smaller than one percent. The largest numerical decline was in South Dakota with a decrease of 1783 units of government in this period. Minnesota reported a decrease of 747 units of government and Nevada reported a decrease of 906. On the other hand, the major numerical growth occurred in Texas (437), Kentucky (321), and Pennsylvania (248). Illinois was representative with an increase of 2.6 percent. There are many possible reasons for these changes and several explanations will be presented later.

A comparison of growth by type of government between 1967 and 1977 is reported in Table 3.2. The major growth in this period has come from special districts. One might hypothesize that the creation of these governments is related to desires for services outside of incorporated municipal areas. Outmigration from central cities causes residents who desire specialized services to petition the state legislature to create a new government providing only these select services. Often there are economies of scale in water treatment and distribution facilities or sewage waste disposal. By extending the services beyond city limits, local officials can provide additional services with relatively little increase in cost. If the services are financed through property taxes, the additional tax base can offset part of the operating costs of services provided in the city limits.

Types of Taxing Units. While an understanding of the trends in number of governments is needed, an appreciation of the differences in the types of local governments providing services is also important. It is difficult to analyze government structure when the governing board of one governmental unit with taxing power and independent operating authority is appointed directly by officials in another agency.

In other instances the budget of one government must be approved by the governing board of another. A typical case in Illinois involved road districts. A road district is usually coterminous with a township and the road district commissioner is elected independently. The township board, at one time had to approve the budget of the commissioner and levy the required property taxes. Interlinkages among officials make it difficult to classify the governmental units that are independent in status. Since there are more than 1400 road districts in Illinois, classifying them separately from townships greatly increases the number of governments. The Bureau of Census does not consider road districts distinct from townships, except in the seventeen counties without townships.

Local governments are commonly divided into two broad types—general-purpose and single-purpose districts. General-purpose governments coordinate functions and provide a wider diversity of services than single-purpose units. Services are provided to residents within the legally prescribed boundaries of the general-purpose government, although in

Table 3.2. Percent Change of Local Governments and School Districts, 1967–1977

State	Counties	Municipalities	Townships	School Districts	Special Districts
Alabama	–	16.7%	–	6.7%	33.9%
Alaska	– 11.1%	178.4	–	–	–
Arizona	–	12.9	–	– 5.0	39.5
Arkansas	–	10.4	–	– 5.5	20.5
California	–	3.3	–	– 10.5	2.7
Colorado	–	4.4	–	– 3.1	27.0
Connecticut	–	– 2.9	–	77.8	6.8
Delaware	–	5.8	–	– 50.0	95.4
Dist. of Columbia	–	–	–	–	–
Florida	– 1.5	1.6	–	41.8	16.5
Georgia	–	3.5	–	– 3.1	14.5
Hawaii	–	–	–	–	–
Idaho	–	2.6	–	– 2.5	19.3
Illinois	–	1.4	0.3%	– 21.3	18.7
Indiana	– 1.1	2.4	– 0.1	– 23.1	43.0
Iowa	–	1.1	–	– 2.9	19.3
Kansas	–	0.3	– 6.1	– 9.2	17.6
Kentucky	– 0.8	12.8	–	– 9.5	75.1
Louisiana	–	11.1	–	– 1.5	– 91.0
Maine	–	14.3	1.3	32.3	40.2
Maryland	–	–	–	–	34.8
Massachusetts	–	–	–	70.5	32.8
Michigan	–	1.7	– 0.6	– 35.2	52.7
Minnesota	–	0.6	– 1.4	– 65.7	77.7
Mississippi	–	5.6	–	3.1	11.8
Missouri	–	7.0	– 5.0	– 34.0	37.2
Montana	–	0.8	–	– 34.8	48.8
Nebraska	–	– 0.7	– 3.1	– 48.5	25.2
Nevada	– 5.9	–	–	–	38.9
New Hampshire	–	–	– 0.5	– 12.2	15.7
New Jersey	–	–	–	5.2	22.2
New Mexico	–	5.7	–	– 2.2	3.1
New York	–	0.3	– 0.1	– 19.2	– 0.1
North Carolina	–	8.0	–	–	40.5
North Dakota	–	1.1	– 1.3	– 35.7	36.2
Ohio	–	0.2	– 0.4	– 11.1	36.8
Oklahoma	–	8.6	–	– 34.9	89.7
Oregon	–	7.7	–	– 5.8	– 0.4
Pennsylvania	–	1.0	– 0.3	– 22.4	25.3
Rhode Island	–	–	–	–	16.4
South Carolina	–	1.9	–	– 13.9	23.0
South Dakota	–	1.6	– 3.8	– 90.2	39.6
Tennessee	–	9.8	–	–	22.0
Texas	–	20.7	–	– 13.0	42.4
Utah	–	1.4	–	–	27.0

Table 3.2. *continued*

State	Counties	Municipalities	Townships	School Districts	Special Districts
Vermont	–	– 12.3	– 0.4	1.9	– 6.9
Virginia	– 1.0	–	–	–	35.4
Washington	–	– 0.7	– 100.0	– 12.8	13.1
West Virginia	–	0.9	–	–	115.0
Wisconsin	–	1.4	0.9	– 21.0	206.5
Wyoming	–	3.4	–	– 68.9	17.3

Source: U.S. Bureau of the Census, *Governmental Organization* (Washington, D.C.: Government Printing Office, 1978).

some instances services are sold to nonresidents through a system of user charges. In Illinois, general-purpose governments include counties, municipalities, and townships.

A second governmental unit is the special district providing a single public service. The enabling statutes which contain fairly tight regulations regarding available revenue sources list allowable services. The most common single-purpose governments, nationwide, are school districts which in 1977 represented 32.5 percent of the local governments. In addition to school districts, there is a multitude of special districts providing fire protection, parks and recreation, mosquito abatement, water and sewerage, libraries, and other services.

To better understand the structure of local governments, a comparison of the major local governments by type is presented in Table 3.3. States differ widely in number of townships with only twenty states reporting this form of government. Minnesota, for instance, contains 1792 townships while Rhode Island has only thirty-one. Presence of a specific governmental form in a state, of course, says little about its relative importance in providing local services. The Census Bureau groups states into those with strong township governments and those without. This classification is based on powers available.[5] Illinois is included among midwestern states with strong townships. States containing townships also differ in the extent of population covered. In Indiana, for instance, 99.9 percent of the residents are included in townships while in Missouri, only 6.8 percent of the residents receive services from townships and 69.4 percent of the Illinois population are in townships. In fact, among states containing townships, Illinois ranked third in population covered, following Indiana and Vermont.[6]

Some of the services provided by townships in Illinois are provided by special districts in other states. For instance, Table 3.3 shows that California contains no townships but ranks relatively high in special districts.

Table 3.3. Local Government Structure in 1977

State	Counties	Municipalities	Townships	School Districts	Special Districts
Alabama	67	419	–	127	336
Alaska	8	142	–	–	
Arizona	14	70	–	230	106
Arkansas	75	467	–	380	424
California	57	413	–	1,109	2,227
Colorado	62	262	–	185	950
Connecticut	–	33	149	16	236
Delaware	3	55	–	25	127
Dist. of Columbia	–	1	–	–	1
Florida	66	389	–	95	361
Georgia	158	530	–	188	387
Hawaii	3	1	–	–	15
Idaho	44	199	–	117	612
Illinois	102	1,274	1,436	1,063	2,745
Indiana	91	563	1,008	307	885
Iowa	99	955	–	464	334
Kansas	105	625	1,449	327	1,219
Kentucky	119	405	–	181	478
Louisiana	62	300	–	66	30
Maine	16	24	475	86	178
Maryland	23	151	–	–	252
Massachusetts	12	39	312	75	32
Michigan	83	531	1,245	606	168
Minnesota	87	855	1,792	440	263
Mississippi	82	283	–	166	304
Missouri	114	916	326	574	1,007
Montana	56	126	–	465	311
Nebraska	93	534	471	195	1,192
Nevada	16	17	–	17	132
New Hampshire	10	13	221	159	103
New Jersey	21	335	232	549	380
New Mexico	32	93	–	88	100
New York	57	618	930	740	964
North Carolina	100	472	–	–	302
North Dakota	53	361	1,360	346	587
Ohio	88	935	1,319	631	312
Oklahoma	77	567	–	625	406
Oregon	36	239	–	375	797
Pennsylvania	66	1,015	1,549	581	2,035
Rhode Island	–	8	31	3	78
South Carolina	46	264	–	93	182
South Dakota	64	311	1,010	194	148
Tennessee	94	326	–	14	471
Texas	254	1,066	–	1,138	1,425
Utah	29	216	–	40	207
Vermont	14	57	237	272	67

Table 3.3. *continued*

State	Counties	Municipalities	Townships	School Districts	Special Districts
Virginia	95	229	–	–	65
Washington	39	265	–	302	1,060
West Virginia	55	227	–	55	258
Wisconsin	72	576	1,270	410	190
Wyoming	23	90	–	55	217

Source: U.S. Bureau of the Census, *Governmental Organization* (Washington, D.C.: Government Printing Office, 1978).

Other states, including Kansas and Pennsylvania, have relatively large numbers of both townships and special districts. Illinois has the largest number of special districts and ranked fourth in townships.

Government in Illinois

The fact that Illinois has the most complex system of local governments is clear from previous discussions. More important is an understanding of the structure of local governments and the relative importance of each type in order to identify the effects on local public finance.

General-purpose governments, such as counties, provide broad services to both urban and rural residents. Elections, judicial systems, rural highways, finance, and tax collection activities quickly come to mind. In the past, counties were logical extensions of services that state governments provided. Many state programs are now administered in cooperation with counties.

Municipalities usually provide services that are immediately consumed by residents and those for which there is reason to have large variations by communities. These services include police and fire protection, streets, sanitation facilities, and libraries. The spatial arrangement of cities, size distribution, and level of services provided result partly from historical development patterns and fortuitous circumstances. Historically, cities that attracted railroads prospered at least until the railroads discontinued operations. The present-day counterpart of the railroad expansion is modern highway facilities. Municipal officials continually seek to upgrade highway access essential to attracting industry, providing jobs, and thereby increasing the population.

Townships are especially interesting in Illinois. Whether a county contains townships (seventeen do not) depends on the philosophy of early settlers. The southern part of Illinois was settled by pioneers from the southern states who were accustomed to plantations a philosophy of central control and strong county government. Other parts of Illinois were settled by pioneers with a tradition of local governance emanating from the New England town. Counties first settled predominantly by southerners do not contain township governments while remaining counties do. Services provided by townships in the latter are provided by other government units in the former.

With minor exceptions the numbers of counties, townships, and municipalities do not change regularly. Only a few cities have been created or incorporated since World War II. Sometimes the boundaries of townships change, usually when city and township boundaries are coterminous and the city boundaries have changed with annexation.

The number of school districts has declined with consolidations both in Illinois and nationwide as small school systems with limited course offerings were folded into larger systems. In Illinois, there was a decrease of 287 school districts, a reduction of 21.3 percent between 1967 and 1977. The Illinois decrease is smaller than the 30.3 percent decline nationwide.

An increase in number of special districts offsets the decline in number of school districts. Between 1967 and 1977 the number of special districts grew from 2313 to 2745, an increase of 18.7 percent. Numerically, the increase in special districts outweighed the decline in school districts, slightly increasing the total number of governments in Illinois (2.6 percent), although the number of governments declined 1.7 percent nationally.

The increase of 18.7 percent in Illinois special districts masks wide diversity in growth patterns by type of government. In particular, a rather marked increase is found both numerically and percentage-wise in certain types of districts. Sixty-four new fire protection districts and 103 park and recreation districts were created during this period. There were seventy-nine more drainage districts in 1977 than in 1967 and thirty-six new sewerage districts were established. Library districts increased by fifty-one.

The effects of these districts on taxing and spending patterns are not obvious from the information in Table 3.4. Drainage districts are financed largely by benefit levies on those gaining from the services. A portion of the financing of the fire protection districts comes from user charges. The same is true of the park districts. While the financing patterns will be more fully considered in later chapters, it is clear that the proportion of taxing units with access to property taxes has declined slightly. In 1967, 85.3 percent of the units could levy property taxes but a decade later this percentage had decreased to 83.4 percent although the number of governments had increased and the proportion using property taxes decreased.

A discussion of the number and shifts in the distribution of govern-

Table 3.4. Local Governments in Illinois

Type of Government	Illinois			U.S.		
	1967	1977	%	1967	1977	%
Counties	102	102	0.0%	3,049	3,042	−0.2%
Townships	1,432	1,436	1.4	17,105	16,822	−1.7
Municipalities	1,256	1,274	0.3	18,048	18,862	4.5
School Districts	1,350	1,063	−21.3	21,782	15,174	−30.3
Special Districts	2,313	2,745	18.7	21,264	25,962	22.1
Fire Protection	704	770	9.4	3,665	4,187	14.2
Highways	22	23	4.5	774	652	−15.8
Health	19	22	15.8	234	350	49.6
Hospitals	35	33	−5.7	537	715	33.1
Housing & Urban Renewal	110	97	−11.8	1,565	2,408	53.9
Libraries	40	91	127.5	410	586	42.9
Drainage	798	877	9.9	2,193	2,255	2.8
Flood Control	24	33	37.5	662	681	2.9
Irrigation & Water Consumption	5	4	−20.0	904	934	3.3
Soil Conservation	98	90	−8.2	2,571	2,431	−5.4
Parks & Recreation	218	321	47.2	613	829	35.2
Sewerage	115	151	31.3	1,233	1,610	30.6
Water Supply	49	68	38.8	2,140	2,480	15.9
Other Utilities	1	10	1,000.0	126	224	77.8
Cemeteries	38	88	131.6	1,397	1,615	15.6
Sewerage & Water Supply	3	15	400.0	298	1,065	257.4
Other	34	52	52.9	1,942	2,940	51.4
Total	6,453	6,620	2.6	81,248	79,862	−1.7
Units with Property Tax Authority	5,507	5,522	0.3	70,726	67,780	−4.2
Percentage	85.3%	83.4%		87.0%	84.9%	

Source: U.S. Bureau of the Census, *Governmental Organization* (Washington, D.C.: Government Printing Office, 1978).

ments naturally leads to an inquiry into possible explanations for the existence of such complex governmental structures as are found in a state like Illinois. Scholars have long debated not only the reasons for the creation of governments but also the benefits or disadvantages of alternative governmental arrangements. There are at least four explanations commonly offered for the creation of governments and their ability to survive.[7]

Tax Rate and Debt Limit Avoidance. One common explanation for the creation of special purpose governments is avoidance of restrictive tax rates and debt limits imposed by state legislatures.[8] The claim is that general purpose governments reach taxing or borrowing limits, either actual or politically imposed, and are unable to finance allegedly desired new services. To finance these services, additional districts are established by petitioning the state legislature. The new governments bring additional taxing powers and debt authorization.

In the past, the establishment of an additional taxing district was relatively simple since taxpayers offered little resistance at required public hearings. In recent years, with the growing concern about size of government and property taxes in particular, taxpayers are more vocal when they suspect an increase in property taxes. Since the property tax collection system is a two-year procedure and not well-understood by taxpayers, an additional taxing unit may pass unnoticed. However, since California's Proposition 13, taxpayer groups have become much more sophisticated in their understanding of the property tax collection process and are more watchful of the public purse. A blatant attempt to bypass tax or debt limits could now face considerable resistance in many areas.[9]

If the avoidance of tax rate and debt limits was a significant reason for the establishment of new taxing units, then the adoption of the Illinois constitution in 1970 removed some of the incentives. The constitution provides broad home rule authority for municipalities larger than 25,000 in population and those passing a referendum. Counties with an elected chief executive officer also possess home rule powers. Governments with home rule powers are generally not subject to state property tax and debt limits. A minor exception concerns length of time for which debt can be incurred. Thus, at least in those areas with home rule authority, one reason for creating taxing districts may have been eliminated.

Avoid Legal Boundaries. While bypassing state tax and debt limitations may be one explanation for additional taxing districts, there are other explanations. When desired services cannot be effectively provided by existing governments, or only with significant legal difficulties, additional districts may be the best alternative. State constitutions do not provide local governments with a great deal of flexibility in working out intergovernmental cooperative arrangements. Special legislation at the state level may be required before two local governments can work out a system of cooperation in providing a service.

In some instances it is simpler to create a new unit of government to provide a service than to work out administrative obstacles between two or more local governments. The major obstacles may involve difficulties in coordinating schedules or in determining which government is responsible for how much of the service. Creating a new government bypasses these issues and starts operations anew.

A decided advantage of a new district is that it need not include all residents in existing governments. By using a special district, portions of the surrounding county can be served along with residents of a municipality, for example. This may be particularly important when distance is a major factor in providing the service, such as with fire protection. Farmers may want fire protection districts organized by proximity to the fire station. Providing effective and efficient fire protection to rural residents may require special districts. Subdivisions on the outskirts of a city offer another example. Residents in large subdivisions that do not wish to contract with the neighboring city for full fire protection service may find special districts a desirable vehicle to obtain fire protection without purchasing other municipal services.

Avoid Bureaucratic Obstacles. Attempts to circumvent existing governmental policies may also be reasons for creating special districts. Residents interested in special services may find it advantageous to bypass the bureaucratic requirements of general-purpose governments and avoid competing with other services for funds.[10] In a tight budget year, for example, library spending might be replaced by expenditures on police or fire protection. However, if library services are financed with a special district, there is no competition for the funds and local officials are constrained only by the tax limits or the public's willingness to support the services.

The complexity of the local government system also reinforces special districts by masking responsibility for property tax increases. Only after a considerable expenditure of effort and an understanding of local finance are taxpayers able to determine which local governments are responsible for property tax increases. This condition has been changing recently as more sophisticated computerized billing procedures provide detailed information to taxpayers regarding the sources of property tax levies.

Part-Time Citizen Involvement. Special districts also evolve because some residents like to participate in government on a part-time basis. Small single-purpose governments offer opportunities to serve on boards that require relatively little time but provide visibility. The contacts which develop and the exposure obtained can assist participants in promoting careers in other fields. Long advanced a model to explain local decisionmaking in the context of an ecology of games in which participants interact in the public sector in an effort to win other games in which the stakes are higher. Public sector decisions are viewed as a result of strategies developed by the participants.[11]

There are probably many other reasons for providing local public services with single-purpose governments. The property tax system in most states affords an excellent setting for these governments to remain viable. Once the unit of government has been established, the property taxes to support it are collected annually up to a maximum rate with limited inspection of the way in which the funds are spent. Minimal legal requirements, such as passing a tax levy and perhaps an appropriation ordinance, are required. The county clerk automatically extends the taxes against the property tax base in the jurisdiction. Since the portion collected by any single special district in the entire property tax bill is relatively small and since most residents do not understand the tax system, residents do not take the trouble to eliminate or consolidate taxing units unless and until there is a concerted effort on a statewide or regional basis.[12]

Within Illinois, there are considerable differences among counties in the numbers of local governments even when adjusted for population. A comparison of counties based on numbers and types of governments is provided in Table 3.5. The counties range from one government for each 9692 residents in Cook, a densely populated county containing the City of Chicago, to one unit of local government for each 191 residents in rural Iroquois County. While this comparison makes no adjustment for size of district or importance in spending and taxing authority, it does illustrate the diversity contained within one state.

One generalization appropriate from the comparison by county is that larger, more densely populated counties have lower government to population ratios. There may be several reasons for this finding. First is the fact that in small, rural counties the governments represent part-time agencies with little taxing and spending. A cemetery district is a good example. A second reason is that after a special district has been established, the population served can increase considerably without need for another district. In fact, as noted earlier, a potential advantage of a single-purpose district is to achieve economies of scale in services with high fixed costs such as sewerage treatment or water purification. Thus, larger areas have fewer governments per 10,000 residents than smaller, less densely populated counties.[13] A third possible reason is special needs for governments in rural counties. Fire protection facilities are typically provided to rural residents through a special district because of sparse populations. Thus, one would expect to find more fire protection districts in rural counties.

Table 3.5 also shows percentage change in number of governments between 1967 and 1977. The counties ranged from a 91.7 percent increase in Moultrie County (population 13,569) to a 18.6 percent decline in Lawrence (population 17,697). Only five of the 102 counties experienced a decrease in number of governments and twelve counties reported increases of fifty percent or more. A casual examination of the data in Table 3.5 suggests that the recent growth in governments occurred in the rural counties.

Table 3.5. Number of Taxing Units by County, 1977

County	1975 Population	Municipality	Townships	School District	Special District	Population Per Government	Percent Change 1967–1977
Adams	70,184	14	23	7	30	936	19.0%
Alexander	11,788	4	–	7	11	513	64.3
Bond	14,660	10	9	9	13	349	75.0
Boone	26,592	3	9	7	9	917	3.6
Brown	5,476	4	9	3	8	219	38.9
Bureau	37,262	23	25	37	43	289	15.2
Calhoun	5,553	5	–	5	10	264	50.0
Carroll	19,191	7	14	10	22	355	17.4
Cass	14,025	5	11	5	17	360	8.3
Champaign	162,304	24	30	27	98	902	13.9
Christian	36,745	14	17	18	81	280	23.6
Clark	16,342	4	15	9	13	389	20.0
Clay	14,999	6	12	11	9	385	– 2.5
Clinton	29,557	14	15	17	34	365	28.6
Coles	50,134	6	12	12	56	576	74.0
Cook	5,369,328	5,131	29	160	233	9,691	18.9
Crawford	19,760	6	10	9	24	395	28.2
Cumberland	10,320	4	8	8	9	344	30.4
DeKalb	70,886	13	19	25	40	723	25.6
DeWitt	16,918	7	13	14	25	282	30.4
Douglas	19,091	9	9	11	55	225	23.2
DuPage	553,670	38	9	53	105	2,687	19.8
Edgar	21,511	8	15	14	42	269	12.7
Edwards	7,439	5	–	3	16	298	78.6
Effingham	27,404	10	15	10	21	481	39.0
Fayette	20,666	7	20	14	22	323	23.1
Ford	15,079	9	12	14	37	207	40.4
Franklin	41,001	17	12	18	10	707	13.7
Fulton	42,944	20	26	18	57	352	35.6
Gallatin	7,274	7	10	7	12	197	32.1
Greene	16,897	9	13	6	14	393	19.4
Grundy	28,025	15	17	25	18	369	43.4
Hamilton	8,509	5	12	11	11	213	14.3
Hancock	21,996	15	25	12	18	320	– 1.4
Hardin	5,149	3	–	3	6	396	62.5
Henderson	8,480	9	11	8	8	229	15.6
Henry	55,802	15	24	16	50	526	23.3
Iroquois	33,446	21	26	27	100	191	15.9
Jackson	53,950	11	16	14	21	856	12.5
Jasper	11,198	7	11	6	11	311	– 10.0
Jefferson	34,052	9	16	28	11	524	30.0
Jersey	19,414	7	11	4	10	588	37.5
JoDaviess	22,389	10	23	11	15	373	15.4
Johnson	8,742	7	–	10	9	324	12.5
Kane	262,675	22	16	19	43	2,600	31.2
Kankakee	96,228	18	17	21	54	867	16.8
Kendall	30,734	8	9	14	17	627	25.6
Knox	61,298	15	21	15	26	786	18.2
Lake	407,373	48	18	58	79	1,997	22.9

Table 3.5. *continued*

County	1975 Population	Municipality	Townships	School District	Special District	Population Per Government	Percent Change 1967–1977
LaSalle	109,771	25	37	50	44	699	24.6%
Lawrence	17,697	6	9	4	28	369	–18.6
Lee	36,013	12	22	24	34	387	36.8
Livingston	41,026	16	30	30	37	360	32.6
Logan	31,066	11	17	18	28	414	10.3
McDonough	39,609	10	19	9	19	683	18.4
McHenry	125,981	27	17	29	40	1,105	18.8
McLean	114,284	21	31	18	53	922	8.8
Macon	126,439	11	17	16	57	1,240	15.9
Macoupin	46,084	26	26	14	14	569	15.7
Madison	249,685	27	24	23	67	1,758	22.4
Marion	40,168	14	17	18	19	582	13.1
Marshall	13,301	8	12	18	15	246	42.1
Mason	18,159	9	13	8	31	293	26.5
Massac	13,943	3	–	13	7	581	14.3
Menard	10,761	5	–	7	12	430	66.7
Mercer	17,668	12	15	9	17	327	25.6
Monroe	18,977	6	–	7	19	575	32.0
Montgomery	30,682	20	19	20	50	281	32.5
Morgan	35,792	10	–	12	13	994	38.5
Moultrie	13,569	7	8	11	42	197	91.7
Ogle	43,228	11	25	20	26	521	15.3
Peoria	119,023	15	20	21	38	1,253	–10.4
Perry	20,454	6	–	15	10	639	33.3
Piatt	16,077	9	8	8	44	230	12.9
Pike	19,301	18	24	7	18	284	9.7
Pope	4,226	3	–	2	9	282	66.7
Pulaski	8,756	7	–	4	8	438	33.3
Putnam	5,467	6	4	5	12	195	33.3
Randolph	32,747	14	–	10	14	840	21.9
Richland	17,316	5	9	6	11	541	52.4
RockIsland	165,313	15	18	15	39	1,879	22.2
St.Clair	280,946	30	22	35	51	2,021	10.3
Saline	26,643	7	13	5	22	555	33.3
Sangamon	169,753	25	27	19	38	1,543	7.8
Schuyler	8,097	4	13	8	12	213	46.2
Scott	6,180	7	–	3	8	325	18.8
Shelby	23,116	11	24	17	28	285	14.1
Stark	7,329	4	8	8	9	244	–6.3
Stephenson	48,075	11	18	13	28	677	34.0
Tazewell	125,189	17	19	27	56	1,043	25.0
Union	16,088	6	–	13	11	519	40.9
Vermillion	97,466	20	19	25	66	744	–2.2
Wabash	13,385	4	–	5	28	352	65.2
Warren	21,353	5	15	11	9	521	28.1
Washington	14,845	12	16	17	18	232	14.3
Wayne	17,260	9	20	19	27	227	7.0
White	16,534	10	10	12	20	312	1.9

Table 3.5. *continued*

County	1975 Population	Municipality	Townships	School District	Special District	Population Per Government	Percent Change 1967–1977
Whiteside	64,024	11	22	17	58	587	10.1%
Will	296,224	27	24	41	87	1,646	32.4
Williamson	52,075	16	–	14	14	1,157	55.2
Winnebago	245,040	10	14	15	32	3,402	– 18.2
Woodford	29,727	17	17	12	32	376	33.9

Source: U.S. Bureau of the Census, *Governmental Organization*, (Washington, D.C.: Government Printing Office, 1978).

CORRELATES OF GOVERNMENTAL STRUCTURE

With background on patterns of governmental structure and changes during the past decade, an examination of factors associated with alternative governmental structures within Illinois is possible. To undertake this analysis, the number of taxing units per 10,000 residents was computed for each of the Illinois counties, excluding Cook. Cook County was not included because of its size and the fact that it is not similar to other counties in Illinois. Also, Cook is the only Illinois county government with home rule authority. Multiple regression analysis is used to identify socioeconomic and/or political variables associated with differences among counties in governmental structure.

Determinants of Structure

A review of the available academic and professional literature did not disclose empirical analyses of determinants of governmental structure. Much of the literature involves discussions of historical settlement patterns and postulates reasons for the creation of new units of government. It becomes difficult to formulate a conceptual model that considers all of the many possible influences determining governmental structure. In the following analysis, independent variables are included that might logically be related to structure of government based on economic or political rationales. However, no attempt has been made to develop a theory of government formation. This analysis merely tests possible hypotheses about governmental fragmentation.

The *percentage change in population* from 1970 to 1975 is included to differentiate growing from declining areas. Population changes in Illinois counties reveal several trends. Metropolitan counties exhibit greater growth, although certain nonmetropolitan counties grew and some metropolitan counties declined. In total, sixty-five Illinois counties experienced an increase in population between 1970 and 1975. Growing areas may have more governments if special districts are used to meet residents' demands for services in areas not served by existing governments. Operating against this trend, however, is the fact that metropolitan areas are larger and the number of governments per 10,000 residents is known to be smaller in more densely settled areas. Also, metro areas may have more home rule units not constrained by tax and debt limits. The percentage of population residing in home rule units, however, is included as a separate variable. A negative relationship is expected between population change and number of governments per 10,000.

Assessed valuation per capita is included to capture the effects of differences in county wealth. Assessed valuation includes agricultural, commercial, and residential properties. Wealthy counties are expected to have a greater number of governments per population if it is true that wealthy families migrate from central cities to suburban areas and preferences for specialized services can be provided through special districts. This idea rests on the assumption that wealthy residents can translate their desires for certain services, such as libraries or parks into taxing units that encompass the wealth of the entire city. Goldberg and Scott have categorized local services into inferior and normal goods and have empirically tested use patterns and income.[14]

The *rural/urban status of the county* is included to adjust for differences in the service needs and the conditions under which they must be provided. In rural areas, the need for cooperation in the provision of fire protection, sewerage treatment, and similar services is greater, and more opportunities for effective use of single-function districts may exist. A positive significant relationship between percent of residents in rural areas and number of governments is expected.

The *per capita income change* is included to adjust for the change in prosperity. Income growth is likely to be associated with increases in the demands for specialized services. These demands can be met through additional taxing districts. Therefore, counties experiencing income increases can be expected to have more taxing units per 10,000 residents.

Restrictive taxing and spending limits have been offered as one explanation for the presence of single-purpose governments. If this explanation is correct, then counties in which a larger percentage of the population is included in governments containing home rule powers could be expected to have fewer governments. A variable showing the percentage of population residing in governments having home rule authority was included. Those counties with a greater percentage of residents in home rule governments should have fewer government units per population of 10,000 if taxing and debt limits are a valid reason for the creation of special districts.

Political attitudes toward public services and government growth should be a major determinant of governmental structure. Detailed information on political philosophy is not readily available, however. One measure, albeit crude, is the percentage of votes cast for each major party in the previous presidential election. The usual interpretation is that Republicans hold conservative views while Democrats favor more governmental programs. To introduce this information into the analysis, the percentage of votes cast for the major Republican candidate has been assigned a negative sign (indicating less government) and the democrats have been given a positive sign (indicating more government). This is a generalization and may involve considerable error, but represents the best information available. A positive relationship between number of governments and political attitude is hypothesized.

A significant negative correlation exists between percentage rural and change in income between 1970 and 1975. Rural areas tend to have lower income increases. This finding is not unexpected in light of recent experiences. Correlations between percent rural and income change and between percentage rural and home rule population could bring multicollinearity problems in subsequent regressions. Consequently, two models were estimated to determine the stability of the models.

Empirical Findings

The multiple regression results using number of taxing units per 10,000 residents as a dependent variable are shown in Table 3.6. The signs are as hypothesized and all of the variables, with the exception of political attitude, are significant at the five percent level. This analysis presents several key findings. First is the importance of home rule. Counties in which a larger percentage of the population resides in units of government (municipalities) containing home rule and with no tax rate or debt limits had a smaller number of governments per 10,000 residents. This association is an interesting finding since it supports the idea that special districts may provide a way to avoid tax and debt limits. In model A, this variable was the fourth most significant in explaining variation in the dependent variable. However, the correlation coefficient between percent rural and percent home rule was $-.65$ which makes it difficult to separate the effects of each variable. To better determine the importance of the home rule variable, the regression equation was estimated without percent rural and the coefficient of the home rule variable went

Table 3.6. Determinants of Governmental Structure[a]

Variable	Model A		Model B	
	Regression Coefficient	Beta Coefficient	Regression Coefficient	Beta Coefficent
Percent Population Change 1970–1975	−.46* (3.16)	−.17	−.40* (2.43)	−.15
Per Capita Assessed Valuation	.001* (3.54)	.22	.008* (2.57)	.18
Percent Rural, 1970	.22* (5.33)	.41	−	−
Percent Income Change 1970–1974	.30* (3.55)	.26	.50* (5.85)	.44
Percent Home Rule	−12.23* (2.87)	−.20	−24.11* (5.86)	−.39
Political Attitude, 1976	−.03 (.87)	−.05	−.03 (.77)	−.05
Constant	−10.92		−8.47	
R^2 Adjusted	.72		.64	
F–Ratio	43.83		36.39	
S.E.E.	6.80		7.72	

[a] Dependent variable is taxing units per 10,000 residents. Absolute values of t statistics are in parenthesis.
* Significant at five percent level.

from −12.23 to −24.11. The t-value also increased. The beta coefficient shows that the home rule variable increased from twenty percent to thirty-nine percent. This finding indicates that additional work is needed to separate the effects of tax rate limits from population size and urbanization.

A second finding is the negative association between number of governments per 10,000 residents and the percent population change from 1970 to 1975. Counties that grew faster in the first half of the 1970s had a significantly lower number of taxing units per 10,000. There are several explanations for this finding. First, the causality may run from number of taxing units to population change rather than the reverse. There is substantial empirical literature in which researchers have tested the Tiebout hypothesis described earlier to determine whether number of governments or types of services attract more or fewer residents.[15] This line of reasoning claims that more fragmented governmental systems are better able to meet citizens' wishes for services and therefore will attract more residents. However, later analyses in Chapter 6 indicate that, in Illinois, more fragmentation is associated with lower perceptions of service.

It is equally plausible, however, that population growth is a reason for the creation of new taxing units to provide services in formerly rural areas. A subdivision outside city limits or countryside acreage development may provide the stimulus for a sewerage district, water district, or fire protection district.

The significant negative relationship between population growth in the first half of the 1970s and the smaller number of governments per 10,000 residents probably reflects the fact that population increases faster than number of governments. In faster growing areas the number of governments has not increased proportionally. This is not unexpected since larger areas traditionally have fewer governments per resident.

The significant association between governmental structure and income change between 1970 and 1974 provides an interesting comment on previous research.[16] Areas in which residents have had greater income increases also had more governments per population in 1977. This is compatible with the idea that services provided by special districts may be income elastic. Higher incomes translate into higher demands for services and new districts are created to provide them when residents migrate outside city limits. A more complete test of this hypothesis requires income data for rural residents but this information is not now readily available for the sample. However, both wealth as measured by per capita assessed valuation and change in income had strong and positive associations with the number of taxing units in 1977.

Overall, these variables accounted for approximately seventy-two percent of the variation in the dependent variables when model A, including percent rural, was estimated and sixty-four percent of the variation when model B, without percent rural was used. The coefficients in the models were reasonably stable and strong with signs that can be easily explained. The political attitude measure was disappointing but represents only a first attempt to incorporate an indicator of political attitude.

DECISIONMAKING ENVIRONMENT

Examining number of governments in a county provides insight into the structural framework through which decisions about local services are made. Background for understanding the impact of this structure on local public finance is provided by a brief examination of the functions of each type of government, the size distribution of jurisdictions, and the responsibilities of public officials. While the information presented below is Illinois specific, it is generally transferable to other states.

Counties

County governments in Illinois provide a broad range of services. Some services are an extension of the state government when counties are a fiscal agent and administrative unit exercising political, executive, and judicial powers. The county is used by many state and federal agencies to organize and administer programs. There are numerous ways to classify counties, including size, urban or rural, and form of government, depending on the intent of the analysis.[17]

County governments provide different types of services, depending on the region in which they are located. A recent nationwide study of county government grouped the services provided into seventeen broad categories ranging from police protection and corrections to parks and recreation. Land-use planning, public health, transportation programs, and a diverse variety of other services are often provided by urban counties.[18] In small rural counties the range of county activities is much narrower. Virtually all counties enforce and administer state laws, collect property taxes, conduct elections, coordinate welfare activities, record legal documents, maintain rural roads, coordinate the road districts or local transportation units, and administer a judicial system. Beyond these basic functions, county governments differ markedly depending on size and location within Illinois.

There are 102 counties in Illinois, and no areas in the state lie outside the jurisdiction of a county government. The governing body in the eighty-four counties that are organized by township and have a population of less than 3,000,000 consists of a board of from five to twenty-nine members elected at large or by district. In the seventeen non-township counties, the governing body is composed of at least three commissioners elected at large. In Cook County special provisions require that ten members of a fifteen commissioner board be elected from the city of Chicago with the remainder from the county area surrounding the city. Counties that have an elected chief executive officer qualify for home rule powers. At present, only Cook County has home rule although several other counties have unsuccessfully attempted to obtain home rule through a referendum.

The composition and representation of the county board is periodically subject to change. By July 1, 1981, the county board was required to redistrict in order to comply with the decision of the United States Supreme Court for "one-person one-vote." The county board is empowered to alter the number of members as well as the method of selection and is responsible for legislative and administrative functions. To carry out its responsibilities, the board works with independently elected and appointed officials. Each county has a clerk, sheriff, and treasurer. Other offices differ by counties.

The elected *county clerk* maintains an accurate listing of county property owners which is used in administering the property tax. The clerk keeps minutes at meetings of the county board, administers elections, and is responsible for maintaining birth, death, marriage, and property transfer records in the county.

The elected *sheriff* serves as the law enforcement officer for the county government. Duties of this office include maintenance of the county jail and courthouse, provision of law enforcement services to unincorporated areas, and serving legal papers for the court.

The *county treasurer* mails property tax bills and serves as treasurer for the county or any unit of government requesting assistance (except library districts). The major function of this office is to administer state and local funds received by the county government, including collecting property taxes and distributing the revenues to local governments within the county.

Other officials, elected or appointed, assist in carrying out county services. These officials include: a recorder, separate from the county clerk, elected in counties with population in excess of 60,000; an auditor with responsibility for auditing bills and payments of the county; a coroner to hold inquests into violent, unattended, or unexplained deaths; a state's attorney responsible for representing the county in legal matters; an elected superintendent of the educational service region in charge of monitoring the conditions of public schools in the county; a county highway superintendent, and a county supervisor of assessments.

Counties differ regarding the number of officials and the amount of time spent by each. In smaller counties, positions may be adequately filled on a part-time basis. In some instances, personnel serve more than one county. A brief synopsis of county offices in Illinois is provided in Table 3.7.

County governments have changed during the past twenty years, largely increasing the scope of their services. They once served primarily rural portions of the counties, but now their services include urban areas as well. In some cases, the county officials coordinate activities conducted by townships. The county highway superintendent, for instance, coordinates the work and payment schedules of the township highway commissioner, and the county supervisor of assessments works with township property tax assessors.[19]

The State of Illinois coordinates public assistance programs at the

Table 3.7. County Government Officials in Illinois

Office	Terms (years)	Comments
County Board:		
In Commission Counties (3)	3	Elected at large
In Cook County (15)	4	Ten from city of Chicago; 5 from Cook County outside of Chicago
In Township Counties	4	Number of members may vary from 5 to 29; election at large or by district
Other Boards:		
Regional Board of School Trustees (7)	6	Not more than 1 shall be a resident of any one congressional township, unless fewer than seven townships, when not more than 2 shall reside in same township
Board of Appeals (2)	4	Elected at large; Cook County only
Board of Assessors (5)	6	Counties 150,000 to 1,000,000 population; assessing officer may be appointed in lieu of elected board
Board of Review (3)	6	Counties 150,000 to 1,000,000 population; may be elected at large or appointed
Other Offices:		
Supervisor of Assessments	4	Counties 150,000 and over; Elected at large in counties 150,000 and over and those passing authorizing referenda; appointed in other counties
Auditor	4	Counties 75,000 to 500,000 population; elected at large; in smaller counties may also exist as appointive office
Clerk of the Circuit Court	4	Elected at large
Coroner	4	Position is optional; may be elective or appointive
County Clerk	4	Position is mandatory; method of selection and term may be changed by referendum
Recorder of Deeds	4	Counties 60,000 or more population; may be elected or appointed
Regional Superintendent of Schools	4	Elected at large; commonly serving multicounty region
Sheriff	4	Position is mandatory; method of selection and term may be changed by referendum
State's Attorney	4	Elected at large
Treasurer	4	Position is mandatory; method of selection and term may be changed by referendum

Source: U.S. Bureau of the Census, *Popularly Elected Officials* (Washington, D.C.: Government Printing Office, 1979).

Table 3.8. Size Distribution of Illinois Counties, 1980

Size	Number of Counties	Population in Class (000)	Cumulative % of Population
250,000 or more	7	7,474	65.4%
100,000 to 249,999	11	1,705	80.3
50,000 to 99,999	9	597	85.6
25,000 to 49,999	24	895	93.4
10,000 to 24,999	37	655	99.1
5,000 to 9,999	13	97	99.9
Less than 5,000	1	4	100.0
	102	1,427	

Source: U.S. Bureau of the Census, *1980 Census of Population*, (Washington, D.C.: Government Printing Office, 1981).

county level. Likewise, the federal government has county offices to coordinate its agricultural and soil conservation programs. Residents often are confused about which offices are financed by local property taxes and which are part of the state and federal system.

Counties in Illinois in 1980 ranged in population from 5.25 million in Cook to 4404 residents in Pope. In 1980, Cook County contained forty-six percent of the state population. When the five remaining counties larger than 250,000 are added, the group represented nearly two-thirds of the Illinois population. In numbers of residents, ninety-six counties contain only twenty percent of the state population and exactly half of the counties (fifty-one) have fewer than 25,000 residents as shown by the comparison in Table 3.8.

Townships

Townships, during Illinois' territorial period, were administrative subdivisions of the county. Not until after 1848 did townships become distinct taxing units in the state.[20] As noted earlier, eighty-five of the 102 Illinois counties contain township governments with the remaining seventeen having a commission form of government. Township jurisdictional authority overlaps incorporated areas located within their boundaries. Some larger cities have a coterminous township unit with authority for township services inside the city.

The 1970 Illinois constitution defines townships as units of local government that "exercise limited governmental power or powers in respect to limited governmental subjects" that "shall have only powers granted by law."[21] Although the statutes allow townships to provide as many as thirty-nine services, townships are usually associated with property assessment for tax purposes, construction and maintenance of rural roads and bridges, and provision of short-term welfare assistance.[22]

Property assessment involves determining the value of property for taxation purposes. Assessment is the initial, and most important, step in the property tax administration cycle, and is performed by a township assessor elected at large. Recent legislation has created assessment districts so that the minimum size is 1000 residents. A further discussion of the township role in the property tax system is provided in Chapter 4.

The township supervisor coordinates short-term general assistance and aid to the medically indigent in times of emergency, and to individuals unqualified for programs funded by the state or federal government. Assistance for longer periods can also be obtained by those in long-term care facilities. The funds may be granted in the form of payments to landlords for housing, payment of utility bills and vouchers for food or clothing, depending on the supervisor's perception of the most effective method of providing the service. Assistance is also provided through referrals to public or private organizations.

These assistance programs are supported by a township levy of up to 10¢ per $100 of assessed valuation.[23] After the resources generated by the required levy have been exhausted, the State of Illinois assumes the additional costs. However, townships receiving state funds must abide by administrative procedures of the Illinois Department of Public Aid. In those townships not receiving state funds, the pauper assistance program is largely at the discretion of the township supervisor.

Townships and road districts are equally responsible for constructing and maintaining roads and bridges outside municipalities.[24] This includes residential streets in developed, unincorporated areas, and low volume roads in rural areas. The activities performed range from daily grading and pothole filling to major bridge construction.

The road district function is the largest activity performed by townships when measured by tax levies or expenditures. Local support for the road and bridge activities is supplemented by state motor fuel tax rebates, administered through the office of the county superintendent of highways. Townships qualify for these funds either by levying a direct tax of 8¢ per $100 of assessed valuation, or by transferring an equivalent amount of money to the road and bridge fund.

Townships provide unincorporated areas with other services such as weed control and fire protection. Cemeteries, libraries, parks and hospital facilities, and similar activities can be provided, but require a referendum. Few townships provide many of these specialized services because the population and tax base needed for support are seldom available.

Recent population shifts and economic trends are changing the township role in providing services. While population increases and urban expansions have decreased the rural road mileage, many rural roads are experiencing increased use from commuter traffic. Suburbanization and rural population growth have increased the urban-type road services. Also, as growing urban areas attract more disadvantaged residents, an increased burden is placed on township pauper assistance programs.

Township Officials. Each township elects a supervisor, a board of trustees, an assessor, a town clerk and, in most cases, a highway commissioner.[25] Some also elect a township collector. When coterminous with municipal boundaries, township offices can be consolidated with city offices through a referendum. The township supervisor is the chief administrative official managing the general assistance programs and serving as treasurer for the road and bridge fund.

The township board of trustees includes four elected members plus the township supervisor. The board manages township finances, including setting salaries for officials, adopting budgets, and passing levies. At least two meetings of the board are held per year at which payments for bills are approved. Additional meetings are scheduled as needed.

The township assessor is responsible for the assessment of property in counties other than Cook.[26] Township assessors in Cook County serve as assistants to the elected county assessor. In St. Clair County, the township assessor serves as a deputy of the county board of assessors. All property must be reviewed and reassessed every four years. Between quadrennial reassessment years, the township assessor revalues property whose condition has significantly changed or was inaccurately assessed and makes additions or deletions to the tax rolls as needed. Farm property is assessed annually.

A township collector, separate from the clerk, is elected in only five counties—Cook, Madison, Peoria, Sangamon, and Will. The duties of this office are similar to those of the county collector—to collect and distribute property taxes to local governments. This office can be abolished by referendum, except in Cook County.

A highway commissioner (road commissioner) is elected in townships with at least five miles of road. This commissioner is responsible for roads and bridges in the district and prepares a budget which must be submitted to the town board.

Size Distribution. In recent years, the need for and viability of township governments, especially in urban areas, have been challenged.[27] While a government small enough to hold a town meeting is conceptually attractive, small governments can have significant limitations. Critics charge that because of changes in transportation modes, township services could be provided more effectively by cities or counties. Property assessment and general assistance could perhaps be provided at

Table 3.9. Size Distribution of Illinois Townships

Population Size	1980			1970		
	Number of Townships	Population (000)	Cumulative Percent of Population	Number of Townships	Population (000)	Cumulative Percent of Population
100,000 and over	13	1,733	21.3%	11	1,527	20.4%
50,000 to 99,999	22	1,698	42.2	23	1,686	43.0
25,000 to 49,999	40	1,433	59.9	34	1,195	59.0
10,000 to 24,999	76	1,209	74.8	73	1,129	74.1
5,000 to 9,999	81	563	81.7	73	518	81.0
2,500 to 4,999	154	535	88.3	133	454	87.1
1,000 to 2,499	375	584	95.5	370	566	94.7
Less than 1,000	674	368	100.0	717	399	100.0
Total	1,435	8,124		1,434	7,476	

Compiled from U.S. Bureau of the Census, *Final Population and Housing Unit Counts: Advance Reports*, (Washington, D.C.: Government Printing Office, 1980).

the county level with greater uniformity. Economies of scale might be realized with county road districts or consolidation at least of the very smallest townships.

Proponents of township governments claim that larger districts or provision of services to rural residents by county governments will cause the rural residents to be overlooked in favor of more populous areas. The priorities for expenditures on public services will be established by urban residents while rural residents suffer.

A common criticism of townships in Illinois is that they are too small to provide a wide variety of services. The size distribution of Illinois townships is shown in Table 3.9. Nearly one-half (674) of Illinois townships contain populations of fewer than 1000. Some rural townships contain as few as 100 or 200 residents. Townships range in size from Southwest Township in Crawford County with eighty residents to Thorton Township in Cook County with a population of 196,611 in 1975. A few townships coterminous with municipalities have a large population but directly provide few functions.

In 1980, approximately seventy percent of the Illinois population resided in townships, but only sixty percent of the township population lived in townships with 25,000 or more residents. While one view is that small townships provide services at a higher cost per unit, one might note that the 1970 constitution made provisions for dissolution or consolidation and residents have yet to make use of this option.

Municipalities

Municipalities in Illinois have authority to provide many services, even though the vast majority are constrained by Dillon's Rule, a restrictive interpretation of municipal authority. Cities range in size from Chicago, with slightly more than three million residents to more than 600 cities and villages with populations fewer than 1000. In 1977 the majority (83.9 percent) of the Illinois population resided within municipal boundaries making Illinois a leader among states in urbanized population. The comparable figure nationwide was 64.3 percent.

Size of city is important in an analysis of local public finance in Illinois because cities of 25,000 people and larger automatically received home rule powers that allow much greater latitude in decisionmaking powers than in non-home rule cities.[28] Home rule cities do not face tax rate and deficit limits and possess greater freedom in restructuring municipal government to serve constituents. At present approximately ninety cities in Illinois possess home rule authority.

Illinois is unusual in its size distribution of cities as shown in Table 3.10. Chicago contained 26.3 percent of the state's population, 3,005,072

Table 3.10. Size Distribution of Illinois Municipalities

Population Size	1980			1970		
	Number of Cities	Population (000)	Cumulative Percent of Population	Number of Cities	Population (000)	Cumulative Percent of Population
200,000 and over	1	3,005	31.5%	1	3,369	36.2%
100,000 to 199,999	2	264	34.3	2	274	39.2
50,000 to 99,999	17	1,133	46.1	17	1,146	51.5
25,000 to 49,999	44	1,541	62.3	38	1,282	65.3
10,000 to 24,999	112	1,766	80.8	93	1,451	80.9
5,000 to 9,999	97	689	88.0	92	659	88.0
2,500 to 4,999	128	461	92.9	128	456	92.9
1,000 to 2,499	252	393	97.0	238	367	96.9
Less than 1,000	624	288	100.0	654	291	100.0
Total	1,277	9,540		1,263	9,296	

Compiled from U.S. Bureau of the Census, *Final Population and Housing Unit Counts: Advance Reports,* (Washington, D.C.: Government Printing Office, 1980)

residents in 1980, a decrease of 10.8 percent from 3,369,357 in 1970.[29] The city of Chicago, in 1970, contained 61.3 percent of the population in Cook County. By 1980, the proportion in Chicago had decreased to 57.2 percent. A relative loss of population by central cities is commonplace among major metropolitan areas, at least those with more than one million residents. Accompanying the population loss has been a relative decline in employment, except possibly in services and finance, insurance or real estate.

In 1980, there were 624 Illinois cities with a population of less than 1,000. A limited range of public services is provided in these communities. A part-time police officer with minimal training or a part-time volunteer fire company is common. The volunteer fire department is sometimes augmented by mutual aid pacts with neighboring cities.

Municipalities in Illinois are either cities or villages.[30] Most residents are probably unaware that the structure of the governing body varies. Most municipalities have a mayor-council form of government, composed of an elected mayor, city clerk, and treasurer. Two council members are elected from each ward unless the council structure has been changed in home rule cities. The size of the council differs with city size. The mayor appoints department heads and other officials with approval from the council.

An alternate governmental structure is the village-trustee form in which six trustees are elected at large. In cities of 25,000 or larger, trustees may be elected by district to four year terms. A village president and clerk are also elected. The treasurer and other nonelected officials are appointed by the president with consent of the trustees.

A third type of government is the commission form. An elected mayor and four commissioners constitute the governing body. Candidates may campaign for leadership of a particular department or the assignment of responsibilities can be decided after the election. Each commissioner administers a major program and the commissioners collectively appoint a city clerk, a treasurer, and other officials.

A professional manager with expertise in municipal finance and management is commonly found in larger municipalities. A city manager provides functional and operational continuity. The manager is also relatively free of political pressures from residents. However, changes in the philosophy of elected officials can threaten a manager's security. A further disadvantage is the cost. A variation on hiring a manager involves appointing an administrator. The administrator's powers are not as broad as those of a manager, but the job tenure of an administrator is that of a regular employee.

A significant change affecting Illinois city government in recent years is the provision of home rule powers in the 1970 Illinois constitution.[31] As stated in Article VII,

> . . . a home rule unit may exercise any power and perform any function pertaining to its government and affairs including, but not limited to, the power to regulate for the protection of the public health, safety, morals and welfare; to license; to tax; and to incur debt.[32]

Home rule authority permits municipalities wide discretionary powers in adapting revenue sources to the local economy.

Although home rule powers have been construed liberally in accordance with a constitutional mandate, city officials have used them conservatively in order to avoid setting restrictive legal precedents. As a result of the recent increase in taxpayer resistance, home rule has been challenged in several large Illinois cities with home rule being removed in Rockford.

Home rule offers considerable flexibility in establishing a city's revenue structure and simplifies administration. However, relatively few cities have gained home rule authority through referendum. Dillon's rule still governs nearly 1200 cities in Illinois.

Within Illinois, wide diversity exists among municipalities in age, population, size, socioeconomic status, and economic base. On the north shore of Lake Michigan are several wealthy Chicago suburbs with limited industry providing caretaker services for their residents. At the other extreme are cities with relatively high percentages of minorities, low incomes, and declining tax base.[33] An outcome of these differences, of course, is wide variations in services provided and revenue instruments used to finance them.

School Districts

Education is one of the largest expenditures by local governments in the United States. The 1977 combined education expenditures of state and local governments represented 37.5 percent of the total outlay.[34] The financing arrangement for education is among the most complex because of the number of governments involved and the intrastate formulas needed to disburse state aid to schools on equity criteria. Sometimes a constitution requires a state government to assume a specified portion of the cost and in the Serrano-type decisions in California it appeared for a while that the courts were going to assume an increasing role in resource allocation.[35]

States differ significantly in responsibility for providing educational services. In some states education is provided by cities. In Illinois, there are over 1000 school districts responsibile for educating primary and secondary school children. In addition, there are numerous parochial schools receiving partial reimbursement from the state for textbooks and materials. At this writing, President Reagan has proposed allowing income tax relief for parents sending students to private schools.

Table 3.3 shows a major nationwide decline in number of school districts between 1967 and 1977. In Illinois 1063 school districts remained in 1977 with 160 school districts in Cook County alone. Bureau County has a population of 37,262 and thirty-seven school districts. School districts are coordinated through county and state offices and must meet minimum requirements in order to receive reimbursement. However, as is true in many states, school districts in Illinois are the largest users of property taxes.[36]

Governance Structure. School districts are governed by a locally elected board of education, usually containing seven members. The board meets regularly to discuss personnel, finances, curriculum, and other relevant issues. The Chicago School District and the Chicago Community College District boards are appointed by the mayor of Chicago with the consent and approval of the city council. Counties in Illinois are grouped into educational service regions with an elected regional superintendent. The Illinois State Board of Education often uses regional superintendent offices in program administration. There are eighty educational service regions in the state.

State statutes control the governance policies and procedures for each of the districts in the state. Including thirty-eight community college districts, total enrollment in all local school systems was 2,487,052 in 1977.

Table 3.11. Number, Type and Enrollment of Operating School Districts in Illinois

Total	Enrollment							
	25,000 or over	10,000 to 24,999	5,000 to 9,999	2,500 to 4,999	1,000 to 2,499	600 to 999	300 to 599	less than 300
	Elementary School Districts (K-8)							
436	0	2	7	38	101	58	73	158
	Secondary School Districts (9-12)							
125	0	2	12	18	34	16	12	31
	Unit School Districts (K-12)							
448	3	10	22	35	120	112	121	25
1,009	3	14	41	91	255	186	206	214

Source: Illinois State Board of Education, *21st Report of the Status of School District Organization in the State of Illinois* (Springfield, IL, 1983).

School Districts by Size. The size distribution of school districts in Illinois provides an interesting comparison in diversity. As shown in Table 3.11, three school districts had more than 25,000 pupils enrolled with one district reporting over 400,000 pupils and one district reporting seventy-three pupils. The median school district lies between 600 and 999 pupils, but 214 districts had fewer than 300 students. The thirty-eight community college districts bring the total number of school systems to 1047 in 1982.

A major factor affecting both number and location of school districts is student density. Administrators must balance cost savings that can be accomplished from larger schools with the travel time that students must spend and the transportation cost of collecting students and returning them to their homes. Especially in some rural sections of Illinois, the population density is very low and even districts encompassing large areas may have relatively few students.

Special Districts

In an early section in this chapter, types of special districts operating in Illinois were described. The number of districts and the diversity in authority and services provided makes a detailed description of district types almost impossible. However, a thorough study of the functions and powers of special districts and their taxing limits was undertaken in 1979 by Redfield and Brown.[37] A summary of their findings is provided in an appendix to this chapter.

A brief review of this material illustrates some useful points. Parks and sanitation districts maintain a police force. In fact, eight of the twenty-seven types of districts listed have authority to provide police services. Available information does not indicate number of districts that actually provide each service. However, it is not uncommon for residents to pay taxes to more than one district providing similar services. A study of the capital city of Springfield (population 99,637), revealed that a typical resident received services from "15 independent or semi-independent governmental organizations."[38] Eight were fully independent of other governments. Other governments were semi-independent, reporting to voters indirectly, and five were governed by appointed boards. Some districts do not completely cover the city's jurisdiction. Financing these districts with user charges and property taxes means that residents in one portion of the city receive the same services, but pay property taxes very different from those in other sections. It is easy for this to happen, especially when a city annexes territory while the boundaries of a special district do not change. This situation contributes to resentment by property owners toward property taxes as a method of financing local public services.

SUMMARY

Financing local public services in Illinois is a complex process. The number of independent units involved is 6620, and the majority operates largely independent of other governmental agencies. The purposes and scope of activities of all non-home rule units are tightly controlled by the state legislature either through authorizing legislation or tax rate limits. Nevertheless, there is no easy mechanism to eliminate governments that have outlived their usefulness. Attempts by the legislature to consolidate or eliminate units of government bring an outcry from officials and no response from the public.

There is disagreement concerning the impact of having numerous governments provide local public services. There can be little doubt, however, but that the governmental arrangement affects taxing and spending practices. Citizens have rebelled against property tax increases and have worked to tighten limits in Illinois and other states. A critical question is whether the structure of government matters with respect to the amount of monies spent on local public services and how they are financed. The next two chapters examine these issues.

APPENDIX

Structure of Special Districts in Illinois

Types of District and Number	Purpose and Power	Financing	Provisions for:			
			Annex	Disconnect	Consolidation	Dissolution
Community Services						
Fire Protection (762)	Prevention and control of fires, recovery of drowning victims, ambulance service.	Corporate tax limit of .125%, may increase levy to .30% by back door referendum. Special tax up to .30 may be authorized by referendum. Debt limit of 5%, referendum required.	X	X	X	X
Public Library (94)	To acquire and/or construct, equip, and maintain public libraries	Corporate tax rate of .15% by referendum: may increase to .40-also special rate .02% for buildings; .0833% for construction and reconstruction; .03% working case. No rate limit on G.O. bonds authorized by referendum.	X	X	X	X
Street Light (22)	To contract with any municipality lying adjacent to district, or with public utility for street lighting; may also contract for rental and installation of street lights, and for furnishing electricity.	Corporate tax rate of .125% may increase to 1.00 by referendum. Rate limit of .075% on G.O. bonds by referendum.	X	X		

Structure of Special Districts in Illinois *continued*

Types of District and Number	Purpose and Power	Financing	Annex	Provisions for: Disconnect	Consolidation	Dissolution
Cemetery (22)	To maintain public cemeteries.	Corporate tax limit of .06.				
Recreation *Parks-Counties* *Less Than 500,000 (314)*	Powers include, but not limited to: acquisition of land and management of parks; public street improvements construction and operation of recreational facilities, aquariums, museums, zoos; to provide sites for armories, landing fields and national guard; to maintain a police force.	Corporate tax rate of .10% additional rate of .05% by referendum. A number of other taxes with varying rates may be adopted by referendum. 2 1/2% debt limit on G.O. bonds. May be increased to 5% by referendum. Revenue bonds may be issued subject to referendum.	X	X	X	X
Parks-Chicago	Same as above with addition of power to construct and operate a harbor.	Corporate tax rate of .6% additional tax of .09% for aquariums and museums. G.O. bonds have 2% debt limit. Direct referendum of bond issuance raises debt about .75%. Revenue bonds have no limit.				

Structure of Special Districts in Illinois *continued*

Types of District and Number	Purpose and Power	Financing	Annex	Provisions for: Disconnect	Consolidation	Dissolution
Transportation Airport (27)	To establish and maintain airports; to make rules and regulations regarding aircraft, motor vehicles and facilities; to fix charges and fees for airport use; to maintain police and fire forces.	Corporate tax rate limit of .075%; debt limit of 2% on G.O. bonds, revenue may be issued.	X	X	X	
Port (13)	To establish and operate terminals, port facilities; to regulate structures within statutorily defined distance of navigable waters; to exercise police powers.	Chicago regional port district has no power to tax. All others have corporate tax limit of .05%, referendum required. Authority to issue G.O. bonds varies. All have authority to issue revenue bonds.	X			
Urban Transportation	To establish and maintain transportation systems.	Corporate tax rate limit of .10%. Debt limit of 5% on G.O. bonds.				
Local Mass Transit (6)	To acquire, operate, contract or subsidize public mass transit facilities.	Corporate tax rate limit of .25% with referendum	X	X	X	

Structure of Special Districts in Illinois *continued*

Types of District and Number	Purpose and Power	Financing	Annex	Disconnect	Consolidation	Dissolution
					Provisions for:	
Health						
Public Health (7)	To appoint a medical health officier and professional and technical personnel to equip and establish offices, facilities and labs. To enforce orders of the state department of public health and all state laws pertaining to public health.	Maximum corporate tax rate of .10%. G.O. bonds authorized by referendum.	X			
Hospital (24)	To establish, maintain and operate public hospitals.	Corporate tax rate limit .075% 5% debt limit on G.O. bonds if debt will exceed 1.5% of assessed valuation. Revenue bonds may be issued.	X	X	X	
Tuberculosis Sanitarium (2)	To offer care to persons afflicted with TB and other pulmonary diseases.	Corporate tax limit of .25%. Debt limit on G.O. bonds of .5%.				
Mosquito Abatement (20)	To exterminate mosquitoes and other insects; to abate insect breeding places; and if necessary to construct and maintain channels and levies.	Maximum corporate tax limit is .025%.	X	X	X	

Structure of Special Districts in Illinois *continued*

Types of District and Number	Purpose and Power	Financing	Provisions for:			
			Annex	Disconnect	Consolidation	Dissolution
Medical Center	To establish and operate hospitals or other medical facilities for research and treatment of illness.	Revenue bond debt limit of cost of the project.				
Sanitation						
Sanitary (153)	To provide collection, treatment and disposal of sewage and to provide for drainage to preserve water supply of the district. May also acquire and operate water works.	Corporate tax rate of .25% may be increased to .5% by referendum. .03% for sewage treatment, may be increased to .05% by referendum. G.O. bonds have debt limit of 5%. Revenue bonds authorized by referendum.	X	X	X	
Chicago Metropolitan Sanitary	To provide collection, treatment and disposal of sewage to protect the water supply; to remove obstructions in the Illinois and Des Plaines Rivers; to maintain a police force; to build bridges, channels and dams; to develop and sell electrical energy; to supply water and sewers to contracting municipalities; and to build and maintain highways.	Corporate tax rate limit of .46%. Additional tax of .26% for seres and sewage treatment facilities, .005% rate for reserve fund. 5% debt limit on G.O. bonds for corporate purposes. 3% limit on G.O. bonds for sewage treatment. Debt limit of cost of project for revenue bonds.				

Structure of Special Districts in Illinois continued

Types of District and Number	Purpose and Power	Financing	Provisions for: Annex	Disconnect	Consolidation	Dissolution
Solid Waste Disposal (0)	To collect and transport solid waste; to establish facilities for disposal, treatment or conversion of solid waste, and to exercise police power.	Corporate rate limit of .05%. Debt limit for G.O. bonds of .5%. Referendum required. Revenue bonds authorized.				
Drainage and Conservation Drainage (814)	To construct, maintain, or repair drains or levees for agricultural, sanitary or mining purposes.	Benefit assessment, revenue bonds authorized by resolution with debt limit of 90% of special assessment.	X	X	X	
Surface Water Protection (7)	To collect surface water and subsequent conveyance and disposal of such waters, and to provide protection from damage to lives and property from surface water.	Maximum corporate tax rate of .125%. May be increased to .25% by referendum. No rate limit on G.O. bonds, referendum required.	X	X		
River Conservancy (198)	To effectuate river and flood control, drainage, irrigation, conservation, sanitation, navigation, development of water supplies, sewerage systems, and protection of fish life.	Corporate tax rate of .083%, mayt be increased to .75% in districts of less than 25,000, and .375% in other districts, by referendum G.O. bond debt limit 5%, referendum required. Revenue bonds subjected to referendum.	X			

Structure of Special Districts in Illinois *continued*

Types of District and Number	Purpose and Power	Financing	Annex	Disconnect	Consolidation	Dissolution
					Provisions for:	
Forest Preserve Counties Less Than 3,000,000 (9)	To establish and operate forest reserves, develop recreational facilities, and to maintain a police force. Districts greater than 100,000 may operate botanical gardens; and districts greater than 150,000 may operate zoological gardens.	Corporate tax rate of .025%, .06% with referendum. A number of other taxes with varying rates may be adopted by referendum. Aggregate debt limit for G.O. bonds may not exceed 2%. Revenue bonds allowed in districts of greater than 100,000.	X			
Soil and Water Conservation (98)	To conduct surveys, investigations and research and to develop comprehensive plans for the conservation of soil resources and for the control and preservation of soil erosion, flooding, and sediment damage.	Subdistricts formed by referendum may tax not in excess of .125%.	X		X	X
Cook County Forest Preserve	To create forest preserves, develop recreational facilities, zoos, and botanic gardens, and to maintain a police force.	Corporate tax limit of .06%. A number of taxes with varying limits have been adopted. G.O. bond limit of .3%. Referendum required. Revenue bonds can be issued for development of recreational facilities.	X			

Structure of Special Districts in Illinois *continued*

Types of District and Number	Purpose and Power	Financing	Provisions for: Annex	Disconnect	Consolidation	Dissolution
Conservation (5)	To acquire, preserve, manage, and promote wildland and other open land. Must preserve the natural environment and resources of at least part of the district while having option to develop other portions.	Corporate tax limit of .1%. Debt limit of .5% on G.O. bonds. Revenue bonds may be issued with repayment solely from revenue derived from operation.				X
Water Supply Public Water (37)	To obtain and deliver water; and to construct and operate water works and sewerage properties.	Corporate tax limit of .02%. Referendum required. Levy limited to 10 years. Revenue bonds can be issued.	X	X	X	
Water Service (16)	To distribute water supply; may construct a distribution system and contract for water; no authority to own and operate water works.	Corporate tax limit of .125%. 5% debt limit on G.O. bonds. Referendum required.	X	X		

Source: House Democratic Staff (Kent Redfield and Dawn Brown) Special Services in Illinois, Vol. I, *Inventory of Special Districts: Powers and Numbers in Existence,* (Springfield, IL: Spring 1979).

NOTES

1. States vary with respect to the amount of control exerted over units of local government. Also, the legal requirements for establishing a new unit of government vary, sometimes by type of government within a state.
2. U.S. Bureau of the Census, *Governmental Organization*, (Washington, D.C.: Government Printing Office, 1978) GC 77(1)-1, Table 2.
3. In the 1960s, the term "governmental fragmentation" was used to describe the splitting of the tax base among many different governments. This term is used throughout subsequent analysis to describe the numbers and density of governments within a state or subregion. Governmental fragmentation is being used synonymously with governmental structure or arrangement to provide consistency in terms. No negative connotation is intended with the use of "fragmentation."
4. There is disagreement regarding the number of governments in Illinois. The Census of Governments found 6620 while the Illinois Department of Revenue counted 6630. However, there are instances where one district overlaps into another county causing double-counting. By the Illinois Department of Revenue count, there are 5609 local government taxing units including the 102 county governments. See *Illinois Property Tax Statistics, 1977* (Springfield: Illinois Department of Revenue, 1980), Table 1. For consistency, throughout this book the Census of Governments numbers are used.
5. The strong township states include Indiana, Kansas, Minnesota, Missouri, Nebraska, North Dakota, Ohio, South Dakota, and Illinois.
6. Includes "town" governments in the New England States. More detail can be found in *Governmental Organization*, Table 8.
7. See Robert B. Hawkins, Jr., *Self Government by District: Myth and Reality* (Palo Alto, CA: Hoover Institution, Stanford University Press, 1976), especially Chapter 3.
8. See John C. Bollens, *Special District Governments in the United States* (Berkeley, CA: University of California, 1957) for an extensive, but dated, study of special districts.
9. James T. Bennett and Thomas J. Dilorenzo, "Off-Budget Activities of Local Government: The Bane of the Tax Revolt," *Public Choice*, Vol. 39, No. 33, 1982, pp. 333–342 and Robert J. Cline and John Shannon, "Municipal Revenue Behavior After Proposition 13," *Intergovernmental Perspective*, Vol. 8, Summer, 1982, pp. 22–28.
10. See Donald Foster Stetzer, *Special Districts in Cook County: Toward a Geography of Local Government* (Chicago, IL: University of Chicago, Department of Geography, 1975).
11. Norton E. Long, "The Local Community as an Ecology of Games," *American Journal of Sociology*, Vol. 63, No. 3, November 1958, pp. 251–261.
12. Fisher claims that the property tax system is the only revenue system of those currently in existence which permits the duplicative, overlapping systems of local governments which operate. See Glenn W. Fisher, "The Property Tax and Survival of Independent Local Government," *Assessment Digest*, March/April 1980, pp. 2–7.
13. See Robert B. Hawkins, Jr., "Special Districts and Urban Services," in Elinor Ostrom, ed. *The Delivery of Urban Services: Outcome of Change* (Beverly Hills, CA: Sage Publications, 1976), pp. 171–188 for evidence on rural special districts.
14. Kalman Goldberg and Robert C. Scott, "Fiscal Incidence: A Revision of Benefits Incidence Estimates," *Journal of Regional Science*, Vol. 21, No. 2, May 1981, pp. 203–222.
15. Richard J. Cebula, "Voting with One's Feet: A Critique of the Evidence," *Regional Science and Urban Economics*, Vol. 10, No. 1, March 1980, pp. 91–100.
16. See Goldberg and Scott, 1981.
17. County governments have been studied extensively in the past. See, for example, Herbert Sydney Duncombe, *Modern County Governments* (Washington, D.C.: National

Association of Counties, 1977); Vincent L. Marando and Robert D. Thomas, *The For-gotten Governments* (Gainesville, FL: University of Florida Press, 1977); John C. Bollens, *American County Government* (Beverly Hills, CA: Sage Publications, Inc., 1969). An early history of counties in Illinois is available in Clyde F. Snider, *County Government in Illinois* (Springfield, IL: Illinois Tax Commission, 1943). Also, see Daniel R. Grant and H. C. Nixon, *State and Local Government in America* (Boston, MA: Allyn and Bacon, Inc., 1982), Chapter I, and Charles E. Whalen, *ABC's of County Government*, Circular 933 (Urbana, IL: Cooperative Extension Service, University of Illinois, 1966).

18. Carolyn B. Lawrence and John M. DeGrove, "County Government Services," *The County Yearbook, 1976* (Washington, D.C.: National Association of Counties and International City Management Association, 1976), pp. 91–129. Only 24 Illinois counties are reported in this survey. See also, ACIR, *Profile of County Governments* (Washington, D.C.: Advisory Commission on Intergovernmental Relations, 1972).

19. In 1980, state legislation mandated townships be grouped to provide assessment jurisdictions with at least 1000 people. Multitownship assessors are elected from these areas. As a result, the number of assessment districts was reduced from over 1400 to about 750.

20. Clyde F. Snider and Roy Andersen, *Local Taxing Units: The Illinois Experience*, Institute of Government and Public Affairs, (Urbana, IL: University of Illinois, 1968) pp. 17–18.

21. ILL CONST 1970, Art. VII, Sec. 8.

22. *Structure of Local Government in Illinois* (Springfield: Illinois Legislative Council, 1978), p. 14.

23. See Richard Cowen, "Township Government in Illinois," *Special Districts*, (Springfield, IL: Institute of Continuing Legal Information, 1977).

24. For additional information see Barbara W. Solomon and Norman Walzer, *Rural Roads in Illinois: Township Administration and Finance*; Institute of Government and Public Affairs, (Urbana, IL: University of Illinois, 1976).

25. For additional information on the duties of township officials, see Troy A. Kost, *Guide and Duties of Township Officials*, (Astoria, IL, Township Officials of Illinois, 1977).

26. The multidistrict assessment law changed the assessment responsibilities in some counties.

27. See, for example, Shirley R. Keller, "Abolish Townships? 'Yes'," and Lee Ahlswede, "Abolish Townships? 'No'," *Illinois Issues*, Vol. 1, No. 7, July 1975, pp. 208–209.

28. Home rule authority can be removed by a referendum and Rockford, the second largest city in Illinois, lost home rule in 1983. See Barbara W. Solomon and C. Allen Bock, *Home Rule in Illinois*, Circular 1146, Cooperative Extension Service, (Urbana, IL: University of Illinois, 1977) for a discussion of Illinois home rule.

29. U.S. Bureau of the Census, 1980 Census of Population and Housing, *Final Population and Housing Unit Counts*, PHC 80–V15 (Washington, D.C.: Government Printing Office, 1981), Table 2.

30. For a nontechnical discussion of legal requirements for city government see Louis Ancel and Stewart Diamond, *Illinois Municipal Handbook*, Springfield, IL: 1978). Also see Grant and Nixon, 1982, pp. 354–378.

31. For a review of home rule see Stephanie Cole and Samuel K. Gove, eds. *Home Rule in Illinois*, Institute of Government and Public Affairs, (Urbana, IL: University of Illinois, 1973).

32. ILL CONST 1970, Art. VII.

33. A detailed picture of the financing of the largest Illinois cities is available in Norman Walzer and Glenn Fisher, *Cities, Suburbs and Property Taxes* (Cambridge, MA:

Oelgeschlager, Gunn and Hain, Inc., 1981). The data base for this analysis was the 1977 Census of Governments.

34. U.S. Bureau of the Census, *Compendium of Government Finances* GC 77(4)–5 (Washington, D.C.: Government Printing Office, 1979), Table F.

35. Serrano v. Priest 487 P 2nd 1241 (1971).

36. David L. Chicoine and Norman Walzer, "Property Taxes and Public Education," *Illinois Research*, Vol. 23, No. 1, Winter 1981, pp. 12–13.

37. Kent Redfield and Dawn Brown, *Inventory of Special Districts: Powers and Numbers in Existence*, House Democratic Staff, (Springfield, IL: State of Illinois, 1979). Also see John Rehfuss and David Tobias, "Special Districts: The Little Governments Providing Specialized Services," *Illinois Issues*, Vol. 3, No. 9, September 1979, pp. 22–26, and Ed McManus, "1,214 Special Districts – Efficiency vs. Local Control," *Illinois Issues*, Vol. 5, No. 4, April 1979, p. 35.

38. Clarence H. Danhof, *Modernizing Springfield's Governments*, Center for Study of Middle-Size Cities, (Springfield, IL: Sangamon State University, 1977) mimeo.

Chapter 4

Revenue Administration

Property taxes, having weathered substantial criticism from many sources, remain the mainstay of local governments. This tax, for years, has been viewed as one of the most inequitably administered taxes and, until recently, has generally been considered regressive. Yet it persists as a major revenue source for most local governments. Over time, the importance of the property tax has declined as local governments broadened their revenue bases. Following Proposition 13, taxpayers have expressed renewed interest in tax rate limits. The full extent to which these limits will reduce the importance of property taxes as a revenue source for local governments remains to be seen.[1]

Because of its importance in financing local services, most of this chapter has been devoted to property taxes. Assessment of property and collection of taxes involves several units of local government, and perhaps no other revenue source is capable of supporting as many public agencies as the property tax. This chapter details the mechanics of the property tax and briefly identifies other important revenues used in financing services. In 1977, more than 5500 local governments had authority to collect property taxes in Illinois and most relied on this revenue source for a significant part of their financing. Although townships, counties, and the state government are involved in administering property taxes, each local government is responsible for determining the amount of taxes to be collected.

Following a discussion of property tax administration, a profile of its use by local governments is presented. Special attention is paid to changes by type of government. Reduction in reliance on property taxes has not been true for all governments. Those that have reported reduced emphasis have replaced property taxes with other revenues.

The final section examines factors and characteristics associated with variations in the reliance of areas on the property tax as a revenue source. Particular attention is paid to the role of government structure. Understanding the importance of local government organizational structure is necessary to appreciate the decisionmaking process surrounding property taxation and likely future changes.

PROPERTY TAXES AS A REVENUE SOURCE

Although the property tax historically has been one of the most disliked form of taxation in the United States, it has many characteristics attractive for financing local government. Several financial system criteria that are needed for financing a system of small, autonomous, independent governments are:

1. The tax must be capable of producing a large amount of revenue.
2. The base must be widely distributed among units of government to be financed.
3. The tax must be administratively feasible so that rates, tax bills, and amounts due to each unit of government can be computed.
4. The tax must be administratively feasible so that small units of government can collect the tax at a reasonable cost to government and the taxpayer.[2]

The property tax meets these overall criteria better than most other revenue sources. Real estate, the major tax base, is easily identifiable and immobile. The owner of record also can be readily ascertained. Since the tax is levied against property, unpaid taxes can be recovered through a tax sale if necessary. The collection costs of property taxes are reasonable and taxpayers do not experience major compliance costs.

The property tax also encourages political accountability by closely linking local services to tax prices faced by voter taxpayers. Tax levels are set by the same officials who decide on budget outlays. In this context, the property tax is the residual revenue source financing local services. The visibility of the tax and its direct link to service benefits encourages balanced local fiscal choices, service levels, and tax burdens. Property taxes are also readily amenable to annual adjustments through rate changes in response to changing service demands.

Finally, the property tax provides a stable revenue source. Although it does not have the revenue elasticity or responsiveness of an income tax, there are fewer fluctuations during an economic downturn. The property tax could be made more revenue responsive if the assessments were conducted annually, or at least more frequently than the usual four year intervals. This stability is important to local governments which are usually limited in their borrowing capabilities either by statute or interest costs.

The property tax has several characteristics that taxpayers find distasteful, however. A common complaint is the uneven assessment. While major strides in improving assessment practices have been made through the introduction of mass appraisal systems, the coefficient of dispersion, a measure of nonuniformity, remains at unacceptable levels. Since the assessment procedure is used to spread the property tax cost of local government services, poor assessment practices mean inequitable tax bills.

A second negative aspect of the property tax is the semiannual relatively large tax bill received by residents. The collection of property taxes in two installments makes the tax highly visible and burdensome. The withholding of the income tax and the small, frequent payments of the sales tax create less opposition than the few installments in which property taxes are paid. Switching to a monthly payment schedule might increase administrative costs for local governments but could lessen public resistance.[3]

A third distractive feature of the property tax is its alleged regressivity. The public finance cannon of ability to pay means that wealthy residents should pay relatively more for public services. Traditionally, however, the property tax was viewed as collecting proportionally more from the poor. Recently, relief programs for the poor and senior citizens have addressed this issue directly. The academic community has also changed its view about the incidence of property taxes by suggesting the tax may be proportional. This issue, however, is still subject to debate.[4]

Property taxes, like other revenue sources, have strengths and weaknesses. However, the system of local government and the property tax have evolved together, and local governments continue to rely heavily on it. It is essentially a tax that works. Although voters successfully limit the amounts of revenue that can be collected or the growth in the base, there are few other revenue sources that would support the array of small, independent, overlapping governments currently providing services as easily as the property tax. Not all types of local governments use property taxes to the same extent, however.

PROPERTY TAX ADMINISTRATION

To the uninitiated, property tax administration can be complicated and confusing. It spans several years, is legalistic and technical in operation, and involves several separate jurisdictions. The administration of the property tax involves five basic steps: assessment, equalization, levy determination, tax rate extension, and collection. Each step is described to illustrate the mechanics and the governments involved.

Assessment

Property taxation is based on the premise that residents benefit from public services in accordance with the value of property owned, and that property ownership is an acceptable index of ability to pay for public services, even though gross property wealth is an imprecise measure of income. However, collecting revenues through a combined system of income and property taxation spreads the cost of public services in accordance with accepted equity standards. The assessment procedure allocates the property tax costs of services among property owners based on the relative value of property owned. More specifically, each property owner's share of the total property tax receipts is proportional to his or her share of the local property valuation within the boundaries of the local government:

$$\text{Tax Bill} = \text{Total Property Taxes} \times \frac{\text{Assessed Value of Taxpayer's Property}}{\text{Total Assessed Value of Local Government}}$$

Property assessment procedures, however, are nearly always complicated by a lack of information on the value of property and, in practice, have led to significant inequities in distributing the costs of public services.

The determination of property values by a professional appraiser should not be confused with assessment for property tax purposes. In the former case, a trained professional uses current market information to determine the expected price of property, in light of its characteristics and location. Professional appraisals are costly and time-consuming. Assessing jurisdictions typically do not have the financial resources to conduct an appraisal of each property parcel for assessment purposes even at four year intervals. Rather, the mass appraisal of property for tax purposes involves estimating value based on rules and guides for condition, age, and other characteristics provided in an assessor's manual.[5] The assessor notes improvements, additions, or removals on property record cards. Detailed property record cards, while desirable, are not always available. During reassessment, the revised value is based on trends in sales prices for comparable properties. Over a long period, the assessment level and market value of property can diverge considerably, especially in areas where there are few sales and for types of property infrequently sold. Attempts by assessors to adjust assessments so that they conform to the legally required level of assessment or assessment ratio invariably meet with taxpayer appeals and usually assessment reductions.

Recently, state agencies and organizations of professional assessors have taken major steps to upgrade the assessment process. Training seminars are conducted and stipends are provided to assessors holding a professional designation. During 1977 the state of Illinois paid $180,000 to townships and $696,000 to counties for the improvement of assessment practices.

In addition to improving the human component of the assessment process, major efforts to develop more sophisticated procedures for mass assessing property are underway. Of particular significance is the introduction of mass appraisal systems in which the relationship between property characteristics and market value is estimated and used to determine the value of comparable property. By using an extensive file of property characteristics and sales prices, the marginal contribution of each property characteristic to the selling price is estimated using multiple regression techniques. Information is collected on size of lot, structural characteristics, siding, presence of garage, basement, heating system, number of rooms, and assorted other features that affect selling prices of residential property. With the average relationships between property characteristics and market value for a sample in a neighborhood, the assessor can quickly compute the estimated value of each property parcel for taxing purposes.[6]

Mass appraisal techniques are particularly useful in identifying properties with unexpectedly high or low assessments. Houses that have not sold for long periods may have assessment levels that differ markedly from the legal level. Local assessors may be reluctant to increase assessments in areas with rising housing prices because of possible protests. Mass appraisal techniques objectively identify property parcels that do not conform to historical patterns revealed by the sale of other properties.

Improvements in assessment practices are not always greeted with enthusiasm by property owners. For many residents, improved assessment practices result in property tax assessment increases and in higher tax bills. What this means is that these residents were not paying their fair share in recent years and higher taxes were being imposed on others. Disgruntled property owners have the option of appealing their assessments and quite often obtain relief. These changes, of course, defeat the purpose of the mass appraisal since they distort the relationship between property characteristics and assessed values.

Preferential Treatment

Homeowners and owners of farmland have been provided property tax relief in almost all states through preferential assessment programs. The most widespread form of relief for homeowners is the homestead exemption, which provides exemption from taxation of a specified amount of a home's assessed value. For example, if a home's assessed value is $20,000 and the homestead exemption is $3000, taxes will be paid on only $17,000. Homestead exemptions may be made available to all homeowners or limited to the elderly, veterans or some other group. Exemptions may also be granted for home improvements. For example, improvements to an existing home are exempt up to a total of $25,000 in actual value in Illinois. This exemption lasts four years or until the next reassessment, whichever is later. A twenty percent reduction in an Illinois county's residential assessments due to homestead exemptions is common.[7]

Homestead exemptions exist in thirty-seven states and in every state that does not have a circuit breaker program. A circuit breaker is a form of property tax relief in which benefits depend on both household income and property tax payments. When there is an overload of property taxes relative to income, as determined by statute, property tax relief is provided commonly through a refund check from the state after an application is filed and approved. Twenty-eight states provide a circuit breaker in some form. Regionally, circuit breakers are common outside the southern states. Most programs are only for elderly households, although nine have no age limit. The circuit breaker program in Illinois includes aged and disabled households.[8]

The differential assessment of farmland for property tax purposes is essentially universal in the United States. Following Maryland's lead in 1956, forty-eight states have adopted programs providing property tax relief to the owners of farmland and other specified open space lands. A common element of most state farmland property tax programs is that assessed values are well below comparable market assessments. The property tax programs embrace the valuation of eligible agricultural lands for taxation based on current use in farming or the use value of the land. Illinois first adopted a use value program for farmland in 1977.[9]

The rationale for the preferential treatment of farmland is: (1) the encouragement of particular types of land use and/or (2) the reduction of the tax burden on farmers. The aim is to forestall the conversion of farm land to urban uses by basing tax liability on farm value, which is less than the highest and best use value. Highest and best use value reflects gains from potential conversion to urban uses. The latter equity argument is based on the belief that taxes paid on farmland either are not appropriately related to the economic capacity of farm landowners, or that they are not closely associated with benefits received from local government expenditures.

Property tax use value programs focusing on the land use objective commonly include provisions for land use restrictions or conversion penalties. Conversion penalties generally require the payment of deferred taxes or tax recapture when the land is converted to an ineligible use. This complicates assessment administration by requiring both an application process and the dual assessment of enrolled lands. About thirty states have adopted deferred preferential assessment programs in pursuit of land use goals. Eighteen states have authorized pure preferential assessment schemes where no land use commitment is required to benefit from use value assessments. Illinois' use value assessment program follows the pure preferential approach.[10]

Equalization

The county board of review can alter assessments within a county but has no power to alter assessments outside the county. However, the need to ascertain that Illinois residents are assessed similarly regardless of location is important especially when the state provides financial assistance for education based on assessed valuations.[11]

The equalization process is carried out by the Illinois Department of Revenue using assessment-sales ratio studies. The information obtained from the ratio studies serves as a base for computing equalization factors or multipliers which, when applied to all nonfarm property in a county, brings median assessments to the level required by law. Under Illinois' fractional assessment system, the legal level of assessment for nonfarm property is 33 1/3 percent of fair cash market value. The application of the multiplier, by the county, does not affect the distribution of burden within the county. Thus, the equalization process corrects only disparities between counties. The appeals process at the county level, the state Property Tax Appeal Board, and the courts affect inequities among property owners within the county.

Only after the county multiplier has been certified can local governments be certain of the total assessed valuation available for taxation. The revised assessments, after the multiplier has been applied, are termed equalized and are used by the county clerk in extending the tax rates. The effect of the equalization process is to bring county assessments to the legally prescribed assessment level. The multiplier can be greater or less than 1.0, as shown in Table 4.1. Multipliers greater than 1.0 indicate that property was underassessed and those less than 1.0 that it was overassessed. A multiplier of less than 1.0 means a decrease in total assessed valuation for the governments in the county and has commonly been termed a "negative" multiplier. Local government officials seek a multiplier of 1.0, indicating that the assessment level on urban property is at the legal requirement and the expected revenues will be forthcoming. The practice followed is that a multiplier of 1.0 is assigned to counties whose actual level of assessment lies within one percent of the required level.[12] During 1977, this was the case in seventeen of Illinois' 102 counties.

A recent development allows a county board to request multipliers by township. This partially corrects assessment inequities within the county but not within a township. Without general assessment quality improvements, township multipliers will become more common in Illinois.

Tax Levies

Each local government collecting property taxes must follow specific procedures. Depending on statute, these requirements may involve passing appropriation and tax levy ordinances stating how the monies are to be spent and the amounts to be collected. The tax levy procedure is set out in the statutes and an incorrect tax levy ordinance permits property owners to challenge and delay the revenue collection process.

Because the tax levy procedure must be followed precisely, local governments commonly employ legal counsel to prepare the forms and ascertain that all requirements have been met. The Department of Revenue prepares standardized forms for use by local governments and answers requests for clarification. Unfortunately, rigid controls over the tax levy procedures have probably stifled innovative budgeting practices in local governments. Professionals are hired to prepare budget forms and related documents. These professionals are often trained as lawyers or accountants rather than managers. When the technical requirements have been met, local officials put the budget materials on the shelf and become involved in the daily operations of running the government. Ideally, the budget and tax levy process should be designed for management purposes, with possibilities for adjustments in the budget in response to changing needs.

The tax levy is virtually the only step in the property tax collection procedure in which each unit of local government must take an active role. Each governing agency must determine how much is to be collected from property taxes with only two restraints. First is the tax rate limit

Table 4.1. Property Tax Statistics

Counties	Average Assessment Level, 1974–1976	1977 Multiplier	Equalized Assessment Level
Adams	38.75	.8601	33.33
Alexander	12.54	3.0159	37.82*
Bond	26.30	1.2673	33.33
Boone	32.56	1.0236	33.33
Brown	29.07	1.1465	33.33
Bureau	33.52	1.0000	33.52
Calhoun	26.68	1.2493	33.33
Carroll	32.21	1.0348	33.33
Cass	32.32	1.0312	33.33
Champaign	33.23	1.0000	33.23
Christian	31.08	1.0724	33.33
Clark	22.23	1.4993	33.33
Clay	26.15	1.2746	33.33
Clinton	33.28	1.0000	33.28
Coles	30.53	1.0917	33.33
Cook	23.55	1.4153	33.33
Crawford	33.34	1.0000	33.34
Cumberland	28.16	1.1836	33.33
DeKalb	32.27	1.0328	33.33
DeWitt	25.60	1.3020	33.33
Douglas	31.75	1.0498	33.33
DuPage	28.19	1.1823	33.33
Edgar	29.08	1.1461	33.33
Edwards	22.37	1.4899	33.33
Effingham	21.60	1.5431	33.33
Fayette	21.09	1.5804	33.33
Ford	30.66	1.0871	33.33
Franklin	33.27	1.0000	33.27
Fulton	31.22	1.0676	33.33
Gallatin	24.87	1.3402	33.33
Greene	33.33	1.0000	33.33
Grundy	34.42	.9683	33.33
Hamilton	17.38	1.9177	33.33
Hancock	31.21	1.0679	33.33
Hardin	28.29	1.1782	33.33
Henderson	17.33	1.9233	33.33
Henry	19.51	1.7084	33.33
Iroquois	32.03	1.0406	33.33
Jackson	29.44	1.1321	33.33
Jasper	26.03	1.2804	33.33
Jefferson	28.23	1.1807	33.33
Jersey	27.57	1.2089	33.33
JoDaviess	27.24	1.2236	33.33
Johnson	34.03	.9794	33.33
Kane	33.31	1.0000	33.31
Kankakee	32.31	1.0316	33.33
Kendall	30.90	1.0786	33.33

Table 4.1. *continued*

Counties	Average Assessment Level, 1974–1976	1977 Multiplier	Equalized Assessment Level
Knox	33.02	1.0000	33.02
Lake	30.62	1.0885	33.33
LaSalle	28.31	1.1773	33.33
Lawrence	19.38	1.7198	33.33
Lee	35.88	1.0000	35.88*
Livingston	29.64	1.1245	33.33
Logan	28.62	1.1646	33.33
McDonough	33.69	1.0000	33.69
McHenry	27.59	1.2080	33.33
McLean	31.95	1.0432	33.33
Macon	34.84	.9646	33.61*
Macoupin	26.40	1.2625	33.33
Madison	33.35	1.0000	33.35
Marion	31.82	1.0475	33.33
Marshall	23.47	1.4201	33.33
Mason	25.55	1.3045	33.33
Massac	23.45	1.4213	33.33
Menard	30.40	1.0964	33.33
Mercer	30.06	1.1088	33.33
Monroe	42.59	.7826	33.33
Montgomery	24.57	1.3565	33.33
Morgan	36.03	.9251	33.33
Moultrie	25.07	1.3295	33.33
Ogle	33.98	.9809	33.33
Peoria	33.01	1.0000	33.01
Perry	27.88	1.1955	33.33
Piatt	35.97	.9266	33.33
Pike	33.88	.9838	33.33
Pope	13.71	2.4311	33.33
Pulaski	26.92	1.2381	33.33
Putnam	30.31	1.0996	33.33
Randolph	37.08	.8989	33.33
Richland	35.71	.9334	33.33
Rock Island	29.68	1.1230	33.33
St. Clair	29.88	1.1416	34.11*
Saline	30.92	1.0779	33.33
Sangamon	30.54	1.0914	33.33
Schuyler	30.48	1.0936	33.33
Scott	7.17	4.6485	33.33
Shelby	30.26	1.1015	33.33
Stark	36.32	.9177	33.33
Stephenson	33.65	1.0192	34.30*
Tazewell	37.99	1.0000	37.99*
Union	20.22	1.6484	33.33
Vermilion	30.77	1.0832	33.33

Table 4.1. *continued*

Counties	Average Assessment Level, 1974–1976	1977 Multiplier	Equalized Assessment Level
Wabash	33.50	1.0000	33.50
Warren	32.86	1.0000	32.86
Washington	25.02	1.3321	33.33
Wayne	14.07	2.3689	33.33
White	25.63	1.3475	34.54*
Whiteside	32.44	1.0274	33.33
Will	32.95	1.0000	32.95
Williamson	29.39	1.1341	33.33
Winnebago	37.04	1.1112	41.16*
Woodford	32.89	1.0000	32.89

Source: Assessment/Sales Ratio Study findings, Department of Revenue, (Springfield, IL: State of Illinois, 1977).

*Multiplier affected by provision in paragraph 627 (Ch. 120) that no multiplier should reduce the 1975 or 1976 county aggregate reviewed assessment below the 1974 total equalized assessed value.

imposed by the state statutes. Each type of local government is subject to maximum tax rate limits, some of which can be adjusted by referendum. A second, and sometimes more effective, limit is the local pressure applied by residents at election time. When many governments are involved, however, the marginal contribution to the total tax bill from each government's property tax levy is small and may go unnoticed.

The only really effective limit on property taxes is the state imposed rate limit. The creation of a new government, generally by referendum, automatically brings with it the maximum statutorily authorized taxing power. All the governing board must do is pass the levy and the taxes are collected automatically by the county. This ease in collection is amenable for citizens with limited technical background but a desire to increase services in which they are interested. It certainly accommodates small independent governments that can easily be incorporated into the property tax collection process.

The financial management process differs by level and size of government as well as by individual governments within each group. Large cities have extensive fiscal management programs, frequently with computer capabilities, that permit a careful monitoring of cash flow and other useful administrative indices. At the other extreme in small governments, it is common to find simplistic operating practices in which little effort is devoted to evaluating alternatives for providing services and discovering opportunities to take advantage of available efficiencies.

Tax Extensions

The process of calculating tax bills is a fairly routine procedure carried out by the county clerk. Local governments provide a tax levy to the county clerk, who determines whether the total levy can be collected within the legal tax rate limit. Next, the levy is divided by the equalized assessed valuation in the district to determine a tax rate which is applied to the equalized assessed value of individual tax parcels within the district. If the total tax levy cannot be collected, the county clerk then applies the maximum tax rate allowable and the levying government receives a smaller amount than requested.

Since local officials are uncertain of the equalized assessed valuation at the time the tax levy is prepared, a common practice is to request a higher levy than they expect to collect. If the equalized assessed valuation is higher than expected, the government receives a windfall. This common practice provides revenue for projects that otherwise might not be feasible.

In a state with a complex system of local governments like Illinois, it can be a complicated task for the county clerk to extend taxes since it involves determining the property contained in each taxing district. Taxing districts are oddly shaped with many overlaps. The county clerk must use taxing maps or other means such as tax codes to determine which tax rates apply to each property parcel. When a new taxing district is created, or one is eliminated, suitable adjustments must be made. In recent years the adoption of computer technology has greatly facilitated the tax billing process.

The outcome of the tax extension process can be equally confusing for taxpayers. Each fund used by a local government has a separate tax rate so that a property parcel could be subject to as many as twenty-five to thirty different rates and four or five different governments. Each rate is extended to the appropriate parcel so note must be taken of changes in the boundaries of each jurisdiction. Boundary adjustments are uncommon but with municipal expansions or the creation of new districts adjustments must be made.

Taxpayers who receive a bill accompanied by a list of rates can become frustrated when they are not sure in which district their property is located and lack information about the level of taxes collected in the previous period. Trying to identify the tax rates applying to the assessed valuation involves considerable effort and results in taxpayer confusion. Fortunately, in Illinois, this situation has been improving. Taxpayers now receive more organized tax bills showing which rates apply and the tax bill for each government unit. It is not uncommon for the tax increases to be noted also.

Tax Collection

The final step in the property tax administrative process is the payment of taxes to the county treasurer or collector. After receiving the payments, the county collector distributes the funds to each government in several installments.

Taxpayers may pay their taxes under protest if they suspect that legal or other requirements were not followed. In these instances, the funds are held in escrow until the challenge is resolved. In addition, there may be a few delinquent property owners who never pay their tax bills. After specific legal steps are taken, a tax sale of delinquent property allows the county collector to recover as much of the tax as possible. This sale delays the tax collection process but the delinquency rate on real property taxes is usually low. In a city such as Chicago, however, the problem is more significant. One estimate is that only about eighty-nine percent of the taxes are collected in the city. However, the delinquency problem was more serious for taxes on personal property where the collections as of December 1976 were running about sixty percent while real property collections were approximately 97.4 percent.[13] In Illinois, corporate and business personal property taxes were removed as of 1979 and replaced by an income tax adjustment.

In downstate counties the delinquencies, in most instances, are less than one half of one percent, but in certain counties, such as Alexander, the figure is as high as 12.5 percent of extensions. Saline County, with 5.3 percent delinquent extensions, was the second highest.[14]

The assessment and collection of property taxes in Illinois takes two years. The length of the collection process adds considerably to the confusion of citizens since assessments made early in 1976 serve as the basis for taxes collected in 1977. A schematic of the assessment and collection process is provided in Figure 4.1 for the 1978 assessment. In late 1977, the county clerk begins preparing the assessment books which are transferred to the county supervisor of assessments in early 1978. After the supervisor provides the books to the township assessors, the assessment process begins, taking several months, or until about June 1, to complete. During the next six months, the county supervisor reviews the books, the county board of review hears appeals, and the Illinois Department of Revenue issues a multiplier. By the end of 1978, the county clerk calculates the tax rates needed to raise the revenues requested by local governments and taxes are extended. In the first quarter of 1979, the county collector prepares the tax bills, and if everything is on schedule, the taxpayer receives a bill in May. The first installment is due on June 1 and the second installment on September 1, except in those counties with an accelerated billing system in which the payments are due on March 1 and August 1.[15]

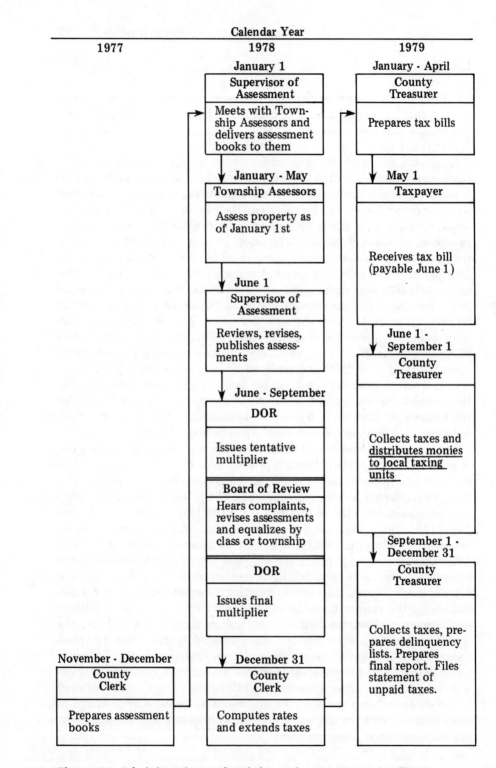

Figure 4.1. Administrative cycle of the real property tax in Illinois

Many factors may intervene to disrupt and extend the schedule. For example, a special district may lie in two counties, thereby delaying the data needed to extend the tax rate. Tax bills may not be mailed until the end of June or later, delaying tax receipts. In Illinois the first bill can be an estimate based on the previous year's bill. The second installment incorporates any corrections.

Delays in the tax collection procedure create difficulties for local governments which must issue tax anticipation warrants to raise working cash until tax revenues are received. While the issuing of anticipation warrants is not a complicated process, it involves interest costs which can be avoided if the payments are on schedule. In periods of high interest rates, these unnecessary costs are significant.

TAX COLLECTIONS BY LEVEL OF GOVERNMENT

A discussion of property tax administration naturally leads into an analysis of property tax collections by type of government. Taxpayers might be surprised to learn, for example, that school districts collected 57.8 percent of the total property taxes and that municipalities collected less than twenty percent. Counties and townships combined, as shown in Figure 4.2, collected less than twelve cents per dollar raised, with special districts receiving the remainder.

The interesting feature of this comparison is that although much attention and criticism is given to the 2745 special districts in Illinois, they represent a relatively minor portion of the aggregate property tax collections. Based on the 1977 fiscal year, parks, sanitary districts, and other special districts represented approximately twelve percent of the tax extensions. Given these figures, one might question whether consolidation or elimination of special districts would do much to lower property tax collections. However, later analyses show that number of governments is correlated with property tax dependence.

The relatively small role played by special districts in property tax collections should not be taken as a defense of special districts. Many factors should be considered in the delivery of services. Types of revenues used in financing may not be the most important. Coordination of services, efficiency in provision, and responsiveness to citizens' needs are very important.

An aggregate comparison of property tax collections, by type of government, does shed light on the governments to be affected by property tax relief involving limits, levies, or assessed valuation changes. Figure 4.2 shows that schools would be affected most by an across-the-board reduc-

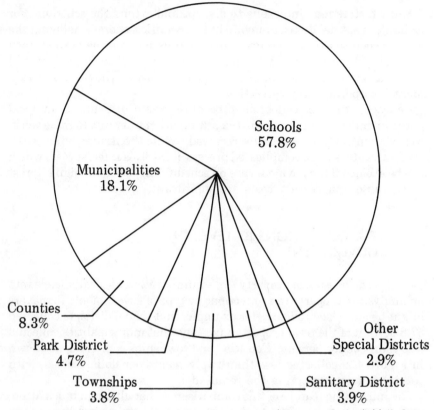

Source: 1978 Illinois *Property Tax Statistics,* Department of Revenue, (Springfield, IL: State of Illinois, 1978).

Figure 4.2. Percent of Total Taxes Extended, by Types of Taxing Districts, 1977

tion in rates or limits on increases. The relative importance of the various governments in property taxes has been shifting, however, with the share represented by special districts increasing. In 1966, for instance, special districts represented 9.3 percent of the extensions. An increase of 2.2 percentage points in a decade (to 11.5 percent in 1977) may not seem like much, but from a base of 9.3 percent in 1977, it represents a growth of twenty-five percent.

Except for home rule municipalities and Cook County, local governments in Illinois operate under tax rate limits imposed on most funds. These limits are statutory and are intended to exert control over revenues raised by local governments. While tax rate limits control property tax collections by the governments involved, they do not provide an overall limit on the amount of revenue that can be collected or spent. Some governments have access to sales taxes and income tax sharing programs; others make extensive use of fees and charges. The governments relying most heavily on property taxes obviously will be affected most by the property tax rate limits.

An examination of the property tax collections and percentage which they represent of total revenues collected by governments illustrates the importance of property taxes. These comparisons are facilitated by adjusting property taxes for population size of the government unit such as in Table 4.2 where per capita amounts are shown. These amounts reflect the aggregate collections by all governments in the county and do not pertain to only the county government. By including data on all governments, a better picture of the role played by property taxes in financing services is provided.

In 1977, local governments in Illinois collected an average of $315.69 per resident from property taxes. Twenty years earlier, the average was $92.35 for an increase by 241.8 percent. Not all of this increase, however, reflects growth in resources available to the public sector. Between 1957 and 1977, the Implicit Price Deflator for State and Local Government Purchases increased 184.6 percent.[16] Property tax collections by local governments in constant dollars were $171.01 per capita in 1977 representing an increase of eighty-five percent during the previous twenty years. Since price increases and population growth are extracted in these comparisons, the eighty-five percent increase mainly reflects extra resources for additional services.

The relative importance of property taxes among general revenues is also provided in Table 4.2. In 1977, property taxes represented an average of 40.1 percent of local government general revenues in Illinois, a substantial decrease from the 61.1 percent twenty years earlier. Within

Table 4.2. Aggregate Per Capita Illinois Property Tax Collections, by County Size

| | | 1977 | |
| | | *Per Capita* | *Percent of* |
County Population	*Number of Counties*	*Collections*	*Revenue*
TOTAL	102	$315.69	40.1%
1,000,000 plus	1	335.03	38.5
250,000 to 999,999	5	359.42	44.7
100,000 to 249,999	11	293.43	42.5
50,000 to 99,999	10	248.55	37.8
10,000 to 49,999	61	256.58	39.5
less than 10,000	14	207.44	31.9

Source: U.S. Bureau of the Census, *Compendium of Government Finances* (Washington, D.C.: Government Printing Office, 1978).

this time, a noticeable increase occurred in the intergovernmental assistance obtained by local governments.

The dependence on property taxes by size of county is also interesting. Except for Cook County, governments in the largest counties, those with populations between 250,000 and less than one million, were most dependent on property taxes with 44.7 percent obtained from this source in 1977. Dependence on property taxes declined with size of county with the exception of counties having populations between 10,000 and 49,999.

There are several explanations for this pattern. One of the most obvious lies with differences in the services provided. Larger counties are likely to be urbanized with more required, and possibly expensive, public services. Rural areas are less likely, for example, to have full-time police or fire departments. Environmental protection services such as waste water treatment may also be less expensive as are street maintenance costs.

Intergovernmental revenues, at least partly distributed by population, can also affect the need for reliance on property taxes. The state income tax sharing program, for example, provides revenues to municipalities and counties based on population. Motor fuel taxes are distributed to cities based on population and to counties based on number of motor vehicles registered. Motor vehicles may be correlated with population. Thus the state intergovernmental revenue program provides similar per capita amounts to large and small counties. It makes sense, then, that funds for additional services in urban areas are obtained from property taxes increasing the reliance on property taxes in more populous areas. A more detailed examination of factors associated with tax reliance is provided later.

In examining the role of property taxes in financing local services, changes by type of government are worth noting. Since 1957, have all types of governments reduced their reliance on property taxes to the same extent, or have certain types of government moved away from this revenue source while others became more dependent?

The relative importance of property taxes and the percentage changes in collections during the past two decades are shown in Table 4.3. In 1957, as noted earlier, property taxes financed 61.1 percent of local government services in Illinois. In 1977, the comparable figure was 40.1 percent. A more detailed comparison shows that each government type reduced its reliance on this revenue source but the magnitude of the reduction differs. Since 1957, townships and school districts have been most dependent on property taxes. However, townships dropped from 76.1 percent of their revenues derived from property taxes to 58.3 percent, and school districts dropped from 75.5 percent in 1957 to 48.8 percent in 1977. The school district case resulted from a greater role played by

Table 4.3. Illinois Property Taxes, by Type of Government

	1957		1977		1957–1977
Government Type	Amount (000)	Reliance	Amount (000)	Reliance	Percent Change
All Local Governments	$895,039	61.1%	$3,537,703	40.1%	295.3%
Counties	87,614	48.2	321,495	35.2	266.9
Municipalities	177,367	39.3	657,806	26.5	270.9
Townships	36,964	76.1	118,153	58.3	219.6
School Districts	501,146	75.5	2,126,275	48.8	324.3
Special Districts	91,948	71.7	313,974	36.3	241.5

Source: U.S. Bureau of the Census, *Compendium of Government Finances* (Washington, D.C.: Government Printing Office, 1978).

Illinois state government in financing public education through flat grant and resource equalizer formulas.

Special districts, as a group, experienced the greatest decline in dependence on property taxes with a drop from 71.7 percent to 36.3 percent during this period. However, the number of special districts during this period increased dramatically so that the types of districts changed markedly, effectively altering the method of financing services. Federal grants are available to water and sewerage districts, for example, or state funds are available for park district projects.

The two remaining general-purpose governments, municipalities and counties, both reduced the role which property taxes play in the financing of services by approximately the same number of percentage points. In municipalities, property taxes represent slightly more than one-quarter of their revenues and county governments obtain slightly more than one-third from this source. Intergovernmental revenues made up the difference in the financing of local services in most instances although user charges and fees have also increased in importance.

Table 4.3 also shows the relative change in property tax collections by type of government. These changes are measured in current dollars but have not been adjusted for population changes.[17] Consequently, part of the increase reflects changes in the number of residents served. Overall, the increase in property taxes collected by local governments was 295.3 percent since 1957. The largest percentage increase was reported by school districts with 324.3 percent. This growth is easily explained by the need to accommodate the baby boom population following the Second World War. The growth in property taxes for school purposes may be slower during the next decade and already has slowed down during the second half of the 1970s.

Municipalities and counties were similar in the percentage change in property tax collections. Collections from this source between 1957 and 1977 increased statewide, by 270.9 percent in the case of municipalities and 295.3 percent for counties. During this period, cities and counties took on a much greater role in providing services with federal and state mandated programs increasing in importance. Although special districts increased significantly in number, their percentage increase in property tax collections was the second lowest next to townships. The changing mix of special districts makes it difficult to conduct a detailed comparison of these changes.

During the 1970s the property tax collections of special districts increased faster than other governments. Between 1972 and 1977 the tax collections of special districts increased by 89.4 percent compared with 18.6 percent for counties, 32.2 percent for municipalities, 26.8 percent for townships, and 26.1 percent for school districts.

DETERMINANTS OF PROPERTY TAX RELIANCE

The discussion of property tax use naturally leads to an analysis of the extent to which local governments rely on property taxes in financing services. In this section a series of multiple regression equations are estimated to isolate the effects of governmental structure on the percentage of total local revenues obtained from property taxes.

Decision Model

In spite of some shortcomings, the basic model employed in many local public finance analyses involves the median voter approach. This model applied to property tax reliance assumes that the amount of local public goods is fixed and that the tax price faced by local residents varies with reliance on alternative taxes and intergovernmental aid arrangements. With the community as the unit of analysis, voters then select combinations of private goods consistent with the fixed level of local services and the combination of taxes maximizing their well-being, subject to a budget constraint. With this approach, the median voter becomes very important and his or her preferences become representative. The budget constraint restricts available resources to the sum of private good consumption and the local taxes collected. In addition, an identity equating total tax revenues and the expenditures for the fixed level of services must be met. Through this balanced budget requirement, given private good consumption and local government outlays, the levels of alternative tax rates become dependent. In a simple two tax case, selecting one rate automatically determines the second rate.

The maximization problem for individual voter (i) can be summarized in simplified terms as:

Max $U(x_i, h_i, G_0)$ subject to:

$$Y_i = P_1(x_i + x_i t_1) + P_2(h_i + h_i t_2),$$

where:

x_i = a composite private good excluding housing,
h_i = housing,
G_0 = local public good (assumed fixed),
Y_i = income,
P_1^i, P_2 = fixed prices of x and h set at \$1, and
t_1, t_2 = tax rates on private goods (x) and housing (h).

The local government identity, ultimately constraining voter choices, is that outlays for the fixed level of local public goods (G_0 when measured in dollars) must equal revenues from the consumption tax base ($t_1 X$) and the property tax base ($t_2 H$). Since the level of consumption and the amount of housing are themselves functions of the respective tax rates, the relationship between the tax rates and the fixed level of government spending or the tax rate constraint is not necessarily linear.

The choice facing taxpayers is to select from among alternative combinations of tax rates and private goods in order to maximize satisfaction while maintaining a balanced local budget and living within available resources. Assuming single-peaked preferences, majority rule and an odd numbered constituency, the median voter will determine the respective tax rates and thus the dependence of the community on any particular tax.

Variations in taxes among communities are due to (1) differences in the local government tax rate constraint and (2) differences in preferences. The tax rate constraint depends on the community's tax base. Important differences in the revenue raising possibilities are explained by tax exporting, level and distribution of income, and level of government expenditures. For example, greater reliance on property taxes is expected in communities with more opportunity to export the costs of local services out of the community. Similarly, communities with opportunities to export local service costs through other tax bases, such as retail sales, are expected to favor a tax composition biased in that direction. This would reduce reliance on the property tax.

The level and distribution of income are also driving forces behind variations among localities in the tax base components of the tax rate constraint, (X and H). Because marginal propensities to consume housing and other private goods vary with income, aggregate demand for both housing and other goods that comprise the community tax base will differ with different income distributions. Based on evidence showing that marginal propensity to consume housing and other goods are inversely and directly related to income, respectively, a community with a more equal income distribution will rely less on the property tax than a community with a similar level of income but a less equal distribution.

Also, because of the differences in the relationship between propensities to consume housing and income, and other private goods and income, the level of income will affect the tax bases of communities and thus the tax rate constraint. The positive relationship between the propensity to consume nonhousing private goods suggests that this tax base will be relatively larger than the housing tax base in higher income communities. More revenues would be available from the larger tax base with given rates. Thus, as incomes rise, communities will be more dependent on consumption or sales tax than on the property tax on real estate.

A larger local public sector requires more revenues and higher tax rates to meet the balanced budget requirement. The higher rates shift the tax rate constraint to a higher level. The impact of the higher tax levels on the tax composition chosen in otherwise similar communities is indeterminant because the effects of the higher tax rates on the respective tax bases is uncertain. The impact of variations in the size of the local government sector on property tax reliance could be positive or negative.

Differences in voter preferences can result in differences in the tax composition among governments. Income differences will likely favor one tax alternative over another. For example, the federal income tax deductibility of the property tax suggests that higher income areas might have a preference for property taxes over fee financed services. On the other hand, property taxes discriminate against those holding a majority of their assets in housing, notably the aged. Since communities with higher proportions of aged may have lower median incomes, the presence of this constituency reinforces the expectation that the greater the level of income in a community, the more favorably the property tax will be viewed.

Others have argued that by assuming the income elasticity of housing is smaller than the income elasticity of other private goods, an increase in income shifts median voter preferences in favor of the property tax. Note that this expectation is the reverse of the expected impact of the community income level in the tax rate constraint or balanced budget requirement previously discussed.

To summarize, a simple model of tax composition suggests several variables may account, at least in part, for differences among communities in property tax reliance. These factors are related to differences in the tax rate constraint or the balanced local budget requirement and voter preferences.

First, the possibilities of property tax and sales tax exporting from a community are expected to increase and decrease, respectively, the relative use of the property tax. Second, the more equal a community's income distribution, the less dependent the community will be on the property tax. Here the relative size of the tax base suggests the tax composition choice will favor nonproperty tax levies to finance local government outlays when a community's income distribution is flatter. Third, the level of public services, as reflected in expenditures, shifts the tax rate constraint as more revenues are collected. The precise implication of this shift regarding property tax reliance is indeterminant. No sign is therefore hypothesized for the relationship between expenditures and property tax reliance. One hypothesis is that community income operating through the tax bases and the rate constraint should result in a choice favoring nonproperty taxes. However, differences in community income, resulting in differences in preferences, suggest the opposite. Communities with higher median incomes would be expected to be associated with a greater property tax reliance.

Implicit in the tax composition choice is a generalized governmental structure. However, wide variation in local government institutions is more common. Most localities, as shown earlier, are served by a system of local governments comprised of general-purpose units and overlapping special purpose districts. The degree of territorial and functional inclusiveness generally depends on the extensiveness of single-purpose special districts. The impact, if any, of structural variation on the tax composition choice has not been determined conclusively. Critics of a fragmented governmental arrangement characterized by overlapping single-purpose districts claim voters are confused by the complex decisionmaking system that hampers collective choices. Other critics claim that information is more difficult to obtain, transaction costs of participation are higher, individuals with intense preferences may have undue influence, and public scrutiny is dimmed. If these criticisms are true, the local government system serving a community will affect reliance on property taxes.

The argument of the reformists is that large numbers of local governments lead to duplication, loss of identity, and waste in public spending. The obvious implication for present purposes is that property taxes in areas populated by many small, overlapping governments will be higher and the reliance on property taxes in the financing of aggregate local services greater than in counties containing fewer local governments.

Empirical Evidence

To investigate the factors influencing property tax reliance, data on property tax collections from all governments in 101 Illinois counties were examined. Cook County was excluded because of its size and atypical standing. Property tax collections for each government were summed and divided by total revenues to obtain tax reliance (P_{tax}). This approach suffers from the usual deficiencies including the implicit assumption that taxes are uniform throughout the country and that similar governmental arrangements exist in all parts of the community.[20]

The following OLS regression equation was estimated:

$$P_{tax} = a_0 + \sum_{i=1}^{7} a_i X_i + e.$$

P_{tax} is the ratio of property taxes to total revenues in 1977. X_1 and X_2 are measures of the extent of property tax exporting and sales tax exporting, respectively. Since data on actual tax exporting are not available, proxies were constructed. The proportion of the property tax base that is nonresidential was used as a surrogate for property tax exports. A location quotient measure based on per capita sales tax receipts was used to represent the exportability of other taxes. This variable was constructed for each county by subtracting the ratio of per capita state sales tax receipts to county per capita sales tax receipts from one. X_3 is the proportion of families below 125 percent of poverty and is the measure of income distribution. X_4 is 1977 county per capita income.[21] X_5 is per capita local government spending. X_6 is per capita intergovernmental assistance which is expected to reduce property tax dependence.

Three alternative measures of local government structure (X_7) are used. First is the number of taxing units per 10,000 residents. The number of administrative units within a county is the most direct measure of organization structure for public services. Since more heavily populated counties have more governments on average, the number of units was scaled to population. Second is the number of single-purpose districts per 10,000 residents. This measure more directly accounts for differences in functional fragmentation. Major differences exist among Illinois counties in number of single-purpose governments ranging from 1.32 to 27.16 units per 10,000 people.

A third measure of governmental structure is a structural index obtained from the industrial organization literature. The structural index is defined as:[22]

$$P_{tax} = \cfrac{1}{\left(\cfrac{1}{s_1}\right)^{s_1} \left(\cfrac{1}{s_2}\right)^{s_2} \left(\cfrac{1}{s_3}\right)^{s_3} \cdots \left(\cfrac{1}{s_n}\right)^{s_n}}$$

In industrial organization applications, s_i represents the relative share of the industry accounted for by the ith firm and n equals the number of firms in the industry. For a monopoly the structural index equals one. The less concentrated (more fragmented) an industry's structure, the lower the value of the structural index. The index is attractive because it provides a weighting system for the collective choice process inherent in the organizational structure of local government. Because of data limitations, the structural index was constructed using the number of the five respective major types of local governments within each county area.

The regression analysis results are presented in Table 4.4. Overall, the findings support the hypotheses discussed. Most coefficients are relatively stable across the three regressions.[23] The coefficient of the property tax export measure is positive in all specifications and significant in two, demonstrating that areas with more opportunities to export property taxes rely more heavily on this source of public revenues. The negative and significant sign of the coefficient for the sales tax export measure also supports the tax export argument. Communities with higher relative sales tax receipts rely more on this source of revenue and less on property taxes. These results are similar to those found in other studies of tax choice.[24] The coefficient of the income distribution variable is negative in all specifications and is significant. This is also consistent with expectations.

The positive significant coefficient for per capita income indicates that the effects of income operating through community preferences are dominant. Recall that this variable captures both the negative effects of higher income operating through the tax rate constraint as well as the dominant positive effects. The shift in the tax rate constraint to accommodate higher expenditure levels increases dependence on the property tax, as shown by the positive coefficient on the expenditures measure. However, this coefficient is not significantly different from zero in any of the equations.

The signs of the three measures of local government organization are consistent in the respective regressions and the coefficients are statistically significant. The negative sign on the index coefficient indicates that more complex, fragmented government structures (lower index value) are associated, on average, with a higher reliance on property taxes. The positive sign on the taxing units and special districts variables clearly demonstrates that more governments per 10,000 residents are associated with higher property tax reliance.

Table 4.4. Determinants of Property Tax Reliance[a]

Variable	Model A	Model B	Model C
Structural Index	− 33.931*	−	−
	(2.08)		
Taxing Units/10,000 pop.	−	.155*	−
		(2.05)	
Special Districts/10,000 pop.	−	−	.260*
			(1.92)
Property Tax Export	.185*	.100	.140*
	(3.52)	(1.44)	(2.40)
Sales Tax Export	− 5.468*	− 4.189**	− 4.716*
	(2.46)	(1.83)	(2.10)
Per Capita Income	.006*	.006*	.006*
	(3.93)	(3.79)	(3.61)
Percent Poverty	− .923*	− 1.090*	− 1.083*
	(3.65)	(4.33)	(4.30)
Expenditures	.002	.002	.002
	(.33)	(.29)	(.34)
Intergovernmental Aid	− .048*	− .036*	− .037*
	(3.67)	(2.68)	(2.79)
Constant	30.92	22.79	23.43
R^2 Adjusted	.71	.71	.71
F–Ratio	36.24	36.17	36.91
S.E.E.	6.05	6.06	6.07
N	101	101	101

[a] Dependent variable is ratio of property taxes to total revenue.
Absolute value of t statistics are in parentheses.
* Significant at 5% level
** Significant at 10% level

The statistical results shown in Table 4.4 strongly suggest that, when expenditures are considered, adding more governments increases reliance on property taxes. This should not be interpreted as a negative finding. Rather, it is consistent with the earlier finding that fewer tax rate limits are associated with fewer governments. Here more governments have been shown to be associated with higher property tax reliance. Also of interest is the finding that areas that are better able to export property taxes are more dependent on this revenue source. Intergovernmental aid appears to reduce the relative importance of property tax collections in the financing of local services in Illinois.

LOCAL NONPROPERTY TAX REVENUES

In addition to property taxes, local governments rely on a variety of other revenue sources such as utility taxes, sales taxes, licenses and fees, and intergovernmental aid from the federal and state governments. The importance of these revenues depends on the specific type of government, its revenue raising authority, and the economic base available for raising revenues. However, as noted, most of the local governments in Illinois use property taxes on real estate as an important revenue source. A complete understanding of financing methods and the impact of governmental structure on local finance requires a review of the nonproperty tax revenues. Three major revenue sources—local taxes, license fees/ user charges, and intergovernmental assistance are discussed below.

Local Taxes

The local taxes, excluding property taxes, collected by governments in Illinois are shown in Table 4.5. Counties collected an average of $6.71 per capita in 1977 compared with an average of $74.99 per capita by municipalities from local taxes other than those on property. In the case of municipalities the major contributors are sales taxes and utility taxes for those cities which have adopted this revenue source. The remaining governmental types are much less dependent on these taxes.

The use of charges and miscellaneous revenues including interest income and other minor revenues is more significant. The subdivision shown in Table 4.5 demonstrates that for each governmental type, the current charge for services is the dominant component in this category

Table 4.5. Per Capita Illinois Non-Property Tax Revenues, 1977

	Type of Government				
Revenue Source	Counties	Municipalities	Townships	School Districts	Special Districts
Own Revenue	$55.66	$249.38	$16.15	$228.08	$71.56
General Revenue					
From Own Source	52.66	187.20	16.03	217.17	51.33
Taxes, Excluding Property	6.71	74.99	0.01	0.19	–
Charges & Miscellaneous	17.24	42.27	0.81	27.09	23.28
Current Charges	11.90	24.70	0.05	19.04	19.94
Other	5.34	17.57	0.76	8.05	3.35
Utility Revenue	0.20	44.21	0.12	–	16.42
Intergovernmental Revenues	28.88	76.40	10.05	172.14	25.91
From Federal Government	8.94	40.21	4.03	2.32	20.16
General Revenue Sharing	4.17	14.54	3.77	–	–
From State Government	19.94	36.19	6.02	169.81	5.74

Source: U.S. Bureau of the Census, *Compendium of Government Finances*, (Washington, D.C.: Government Printing Office, 1979).

with the exception of townships. Statewide comparisons are limited because aggregate collections are divided by the number of residents in each governmental type. Since not all units of government use the same revenue sources, there tends to be a downward bias in the reported figures.

Of particular interest is the relative importance of current charges in the financing of special districts. The $19.94 per capita collected from this revenue source comprised more than twenty-five percent of the total own source revenues. This percentage is by far higher in special districts than for any other governmental type.[25] In the financing of services, however, major variations in reliance on charges and fees are found as shown in Table 4.6. Detailed information on the reliance on charges by type of district is not readily available but insight into the methods of financing services, independent of governmental type, is available from the data presented. The largest use of fees, compared with expenditures for services is found in airports and water transportation terminals. The information provided suggests that in 1967 and 1977, collected fees exceeded the expenditures for services. There are many possible explanations for this finding but the most logical is the timing of the receipts and expenditures. Airports, for example, that do not have outstanding debt may be collecting more in fees than they spend on operating expenses. It appears that hospitals recover approximately half of the outlay in fees and charges. In the case of education, on the other hand, relatively small proportions of the expenditures are recovered in fees for services. A more detailed analysis of these operations is needed before generalizations are warranted. The role of intergovernmental assistance, the timing of the construction and debt issuance, and the attitude of local

Table 4.6. Charges and Fees Revenue as Percent of Expenditures (Illinois)

Local Government Service	1957	1967	1977
Education	5.3%	6.1%	5.2%
Hospitals	42.9	41.4	52.0
Sanitation[a]	6.1	7.4	7.7
Parks and Recreation	10.8	13.4	20.8
Natural Resources	11.4	10.9	20.6
Housing and Community Redevelopment	27.0	33.1	25.8
Airports	54.8	112.7	129.5
Water Transportation and Terminals	2.1	170.2	118.5
Parking	b	115.7	87.8

Source: U.S. Bureau of the Census, Compendium of Government Finances, (Washington, D.C.: Government Printing Office, 1979).

[a] Other than sewage services
[b] Not reported in 1957

officials about subsidization of the activity all affect the extent to which
user fees are employed in financing services.

Intergovernmental Revenues

In 1977 Illinois local governments received over $761 million in federal
revenues and more than $2.5 billion in state revenues compared with
approximately $4.3 billion from their own tax revenues. Some revenues
are formula-based while others are provided through competitive grants.
Local discretion in the use of intergovernmental revenues also varies
among sources.

Although direct federal revenues distributed to local governments can
be traced to the Depression, federal funds became a permanent component of local government revenues during post World War II years when
major program expansions occurred. The grants were used to stimulate
urban development and redevelopment by emphasizing physical capital projects. They often required an extensive application and approval
process, often failed to appropriately weigh recipient needs, and contained
many federal restrictions on local spending.

The 1960s brought a complex system of federal categorical grant programs.[26] The complex structure of the funding programs fostered a
cadre of "grantspeople" skilled in obtaining funds from the system. The
receipt of direct federal-local revenues became directly linked to the skills
of local personnel often with little relationship to need or fiscal capacity of the recipient governments. Areas and localities with sufficient
resources to bear the startup costs of acquiring staff knowledgeable about
the federal grant system were favored by the system.

The availability of grant funds for specific purposes with requirements
of local matching funds were often at odds with the desires of locally
elected officials. The attraction of low cost programs financed with federal funds skewed the preferences of local officials in favor of these
programs.

During the 1960s, pressure mounted to establish a revenue sharing
program for general-purpose governments with minimum strings on the
expenditure of the funds and to consolidate categorical grants into block
grants allocated among all eligible recipients. The main thrust was to
distribute funds based on prearranged formulas. The rationale was to
encourage state and local services to be provided at least at a basic level
with average local fiscal effort. The intent of the block grants was to
reduce the complexity of the federal grant system and to bypass burdensome application procedures.

In 1972 the State and Local Fiscal Assistance Act was passed providing general-purpose governments funds based on a formula that included

population, relative income and relative tax effort. One-third of the funds was initially distributed to state governments and two-thirds to local governments, although the renewal in 1976 removed the state portion.[27] Block grant programs in the areas of housing and community development, manpower development and job training, health, and criminal justice were developed and authorized.

Intergovernmental revenues from state government are classified as either grants from state appropriated funds or shared taxes. The former require annual appropriations and are distributed to local jurisdictions using a formula while the latter are specified portions of tax yields. The rationale for the latter is that states are generally better equipped to efficiently collect certain taxes, especially when distributions to local governments can be accomplished at low cost. Shared taxes have varying degrees of state controls regarding expenditures.

Shared taxes in Illinois include state motor fuel taxes provided to counties, municipalities, and townships, and one-twelfth of the state income tax receipts distributed to counties and cities. Beginning in 1979 with the elimination of the corporate personal property tax, replacement revenues from an increase in state income taxes were provided. Motor fuel taxes are allocated to counties, municipalities, and townships for road and street purposes. Municipalities receive allotments based on population. County allotments are based on motor vehicle registrations and townships receive funds according to road mileage maintained. These allocation elements have implications that may not be initially clear. Little weight is given to existing local fiscal capacity to provide services. Equalization is not a primary objective of the program. Some redistribution may occur, especially when population is a key element of the distribution formula, since poorer communities receive the same per capita amounts as wealthy areas. However, because of a close relationship between population and vehicle registration, population in incorporated areas may be counted twice in the calculations of county and municipal government motor fuel tax allocations. Counties with a large proportion of their population living in incorporated areas may be favorably treated since they have a high incidence of vehicle registrations and few county roads.

Finally, the use of road mileage to compute township revenues fails to consider a major cost factor and encourages possible misallocations of resources. Township motor fuel tax receipts do not reflect traffic loads and basing them on road mileage provides no incentive to eliminate unneeded roads in sparsely populated rural areas. In fact, the incentive is to retain or expand road mileage to increase state intergovernmental revenues.

Expenditures of motor fuel tax monies are closely monitored and regulated by the Illinois Department of Transportation. A main objective of the regulation process is to coordinate local road design standards and quality. This is particularly important in urban areas where high volume local streets of contiguous jurisdictions feed into one another. The close monitoring by the state government meets with considerable resistance by local governments.

One-twelfth of the individual and corporate state income tax receipts is shared with counties and municipalities on the basis of population. There are no restrictions on use as long as the local governments have authority to spend their own funds for the purpose. The income tax sharing program provides counties and municipalities with a revenue source that is sensitive to both real and inflationary changes in income. The flat rate structure in Illinois results in less revenue elasticity than would be the case with a system of progressive rates. Redistribution will occur to the extent that the tax receipts from a municipality or unincorporated county area differ from the revenues shared based on population.

To replace the revenues foregone by local units of government with the abolishment of the corporate personal property tax in 1979, the Illinois legislature adopted a state collected replacement tax program. The replacement program in effect increased the corporate income tax rate, placed a tax on trust, corporate, and partnership incomes, and imposed a levy on the invested capital of utilities. The revenues from the levies are distributed to local units on a replacement basis.

For local governments the implications of intergovernmental revenues from this source are related to the amount of funds generated by the replacement package and the rate at which the funds change over time. Some stability may be lost because of the reliance on income taxes but revenue growth may be greater because of the higher elasticity of the base.

In addition to shared taxes, local governments are eligible for state grants available on a project or a formula basis and are reimbursed for services performed. The largest formula grant program is intergovernmental revenues for education. Since education is provided by single function government units, these funds are allocated to school districts. State grant funds are also available for selected public facilities including waste-water treatment plants. Some of these funds are derived from federal programs operating through states. County governments are partially reimbursed for providing services including criminal justice and the courts. Some of the state grant revenues are distributed based on indices of need. For example, educational aid is allocated on the basis of fiscal capacity, local tax effort, target student populations, and numbers of students.

A profile of the intergovernmental revenues received by type of local government is provided in Table 4.5. The largest amount of intergovernmental aid went to school districts which received an average of $172.14 per capita statewide. The majority of this revenue was provided by the state with only an average of $2.32 per capita derived directly from the federal government. Of course, much of the state intergovernmental revenues provided to schools is derived from federal sources. The units of government with the second largest per capita receipts are municipalities which received an average of $76.40 per capita, of which $36.19 per capita was from the state and the remainder from the federal government.

Of some interest is the relative importance of federal intergovernmental revenues to special districts. An average of $20.16 per capita was received in 1977 from federal sources compared with an average of $5.74 per capita from the state government. These figures are difficult to compare, however, since special districts differ widely in type and size. A few large, specific districts can make large differences in the averages reported. The Metropolitan Sanitary District of Greater Chicago is a prime example.

A more complete profile of the state aid to local governments by public service is shown in Table 4.7. Education stands out clearly as the leader with 70.02 percent of the total in 1977. The growth in dollar amounts for education during the twenty year period shown far exceeds the growth for any other purpose. While it was not possible to determine in each case whether the funds are provided to special districts directly or to general-purpose governments, the information in Table 4.7 provides a reasonable picture of the role of state government in financing local services.

The relationship between governmental structure and intergovernmental assistance is complex. The fact that special districts qualify for federal and/or state funds independently of general-purpose governments may provide a reason for their existence. A similar case was created when the federal general revenue sharing program was implemented. Eliminating townships may have meant fewer federal dollars coming to local governments in Illinois. Many townships qualified for the minimum distribution amounts and these funds might not otherwise have been allocated to the county or municipal governments in the area. Thus, a definite incentive was provided not to reorganize governmental structure in highly urbanized areas even though the need for these governments might be questioned.[28]

Since many different types of governments obtain intergovernmental assistance from alternate programs, the problem of coordinating services is difficult. Local taxes may not be needed and the public has very little say in the distribution of the funds. General-purpose governments may

Table 4.7. State Intergovernmental Aid by Government Service (Illinois)

	Amount			Percent of Total		
Category	1957	1967	1977	1957	1967	1977
Education	$119,348	$463,842	$1,975,012	48.46%	66.43%	70.02%
Public Welfare	25,673	79,365	105,116	10.42	11.37	3.73
General Support and Planning Aid			149,621			5.53
Highways	88,228	146,705	251,287	35.82	21.01	8.91
Health and Hospitals	10,708	3,608	32,266	4.34	.52	1.14
Public Safety			31,541			1.12
Sewage			80,484			2.85
Public Transportation		277[b]	149,784		.04	5.31
Assessment Improvements			876			.03
Libraries		2,863	10,431		.41	.37
Manpower Development			6,416			.23
Outdoor Recreation			7,235			.26
Soil and Water Conservation			404			.01
Housing and Urban Redevelopment			397			.01
Tourism		359[a]	1,794		.05	.06
Airports	2,203	752	2,612	.90	.11	.09
Disaster Aid		306	4,490		.04	.16
Fairs and Expositions	119[c]	117[c]	10,705	.06	.02	.38

Source: U.S. Bureau of the Census, *Compendium of Local Government Finance,* Washington, D.C.: Government Printing Office, 1979).
[a] Includes all forms of business and economic development.
[b] Port development.
[c] County veterinary services.

have little knowledge or involvement if the review process is limited. Thus it is conceivable for two units of government to receive intergovernmental assistance for essentially similar programs with minimal coordination of effort. The extent to which this is occurring cannot be documented without more micro data and personal surveys.

Debt Structure

Local governments are also able to raise revenues through borrowing. The per capita debt by type of government is shown in Table 4.8. Local debt is typically classified as either long-term or short-term and as full faith and credit or nonguaranteed. Long-term is generally reserved for issues with a maturity of more than one year. Full faith and credit obligations have the taxing power of the issuing government behind them;

Table 4.8. Per Capita Debt of Illinois Local Governments, 1977

Debt Type	Total	Counties	Municipalities	Townships	School Districts	Special Districts
Total Debt Outstanding	$736.78	$35.91	$308.75	$3.44	$217.68	$171.00
Long Term	643.21	25.66	283.16	3.43	177.90	153.06
Full Faith & Credit	352.67	21.53	88.91	3.43	177.90	60.90
Nonguaranteed	290.54	4.13	194.25	–	–	92.16
Short Term	93.58	10.24	25.59	0.02	39.78	17.95

Source: U.S. Bureau of the Census, *Compendium of Local Government Finance,* (Washington, D.C.: Government Printing Office, 1979).

the debt will be retired with tax dollars whereas the nonguaranteed debt is retired from the proceeds of the project being financed. Since the taxing powers of the borrowing government are not available to lenders of nonguaranteed issues, the interest rates on these obligations are typically higher than for full faith and credit debt. However, state debt limits usually do not pertain to nonguaranteed obligations and residents may be more willing to accept increased debt if they understand that taxes will not be increased to retire the issue, and that the users of the facility will be paying the costs of financing the project directly.

Many approaches to raising capital for local projects can be found. In some instances, a full faith and credit approach will be used with the intention of retiring the debt using proceeds from the project. The attraction of the guaranteed debt is the lower interest rate while the use of revenue proceeds means that tax rates are not increased. Of course, the tax base is available to lenders if the need should arise.

The comparison of debt by type and length of maturity in Table 4.8 shows that municipalities and school districts are the leaders with an average of $308.75 and $217.68 per capita, respectively. Special districts ranked third with an average of $171.00 per capita. The main difference among types of government arises in type of debt. In the case of municipalities, the dominant share of the debt was nonguaranteed. In recent years many municipalities have become involved in assisting economic development in their communities by financing industrial parks, transportation facilities, and parking garages. Most of these facilities are financed with user charges.

School districts, on the other hand, reported that all of their long-term debt was in the form of full faith and credit obligations. The main factors underlying the difference in debt structure are the state restrictions on the debt usage by type of government and the types of activities being financed.

The importance of governmental structure on debt analysis arises from two facts. First, all government units have access to the same tax base. When many overlapping governments are involved, large borrowing programs can create a situation in which the amounts of property taxes that would have to be collected to retire the debt simply would not be accepted by taxpayers. Situations in which this is likely to occur with existing debt practices in Illinois are very rare.

Second, separate units of government can be developed to borrow funds, construct the facility, and lease it to another government. This use of building commissions means that the debt does not appear in the records of the governmental agency using the facility. The rent paid is treated as an expense. These types of arrangements make a careful analysis of debt structure much more difficult than usual.

SUMMARY

Raising revenues to provide local services is a complicated and time-consuming process that is little understood by the average citizen. Numerous governments rely on property taxes to provide a multitude of services that are known to relatively few citizens. Local officials decide on budgets and service levels with little direct input from citizens and with little coordination with other governments that may be providing similar services. While this maze of governments collecting revenues frustrates many scholars and public interest groups, citizens seem to have little interest in reducing the number of taxing units on a selective basis. They have tried to impose statewide tax rate limits with no consideration for the differences among governments regarding access to other revenue sources.

In a previous chapter, evidence was provided to support the idea that tax limits provide an incentive to create additional governments with additional taxing authority. The findings in this chapter further these results and suggest that additional governments per 10,000 residents raise the reliance on property taxes for the same overall expenditure for services. There are many possible explanations for this finding and not all are based on duplication or inefficiency. However, in an era of taxpayer resentment to property taxes, increased governmental fragmentation and higher property tax dependence will exacerbate taxpayer resistance. Based on the findings in this study, one might hypothesize that tax limits can stimulate the growth of additional governments which in turn increase property taxes and possibly trigger additional tax limits.

The reason for collecting revenues is to provide public services. The level of services, furthermore, is of paramount interest to residents. Local governments are created in response to citizen requests and presumably a new government means that the existing structure was not adequately meeting needs. The important question to be asked concerns the effects of governmental structure or fragmentation on service levels and expenditures. Many hypotheses have been raised. The next two chapters examine the importance of governmental structure on expenditures for services and how citizens perceive the services provided.

NOTES

1. Werner Z. Hirsh, "Local Government's Painful Choices," *Journal of Contemporary Studies*, Vol. 4, No. 3, Summer 1981, pp. 71–78 and Dick Nitzer, "Does the Property Tax Have a Future?" in C. Lowell Harriss, ed. *The Property Tax and Local Finance* (New York, NY: Academy of Political Science, 1983), pp. 222–236.
2. Glenn W. Fisher, "The Property Tax and the Survival of Independent Local Government," *Assessment Digest*, March/April 1980, pp. 2–7.
3. A good review of the advantages and disadvantages of the property tax is found in Marvin B. Johnson, "The Property Tax is Here to Stay," *Economic Issues* (Madison, WI: University of Wisconsin) No. 32, April 1979.
4. Henry Aaron, *Who Pays the Property Tax?* (Washington, D.C.: Brookings Institution, 1975) and Peter M. Mieszkowski, "The Property Tax: An Excise or a Profits Tax?" *Journal of Public Economics*, Vol. 1, No. 1, April 1972, pp. 73–96. Also see Steven D. Gold, *Property Tax Relief* (Lexington, MA: D. C. Heath Co., 1979).
5. For example see Illinois Department of Revenue, *Illinois Real Property Appraisal Manual* (Springfield, IL: State of Illinois, December 1980).
6. Charles C. Cook, "Computers in Local Property-Tax Administration," in C. Lowell Harriss, ed. *The Property Tax and Local Finance* (New York, NY: Academy of Political Science, 1983), pp. 95–107.
7. *Illinois Tax Facts* (Springfield, IL: Taxpayers' Federation of Illinois, September–October 1982), pp. 2–3 and Gold, 1979.
8. Gold, 1979, pp. 55–59.
9. Richard W. Dunford, "A Survey of Property Tax Relief Programs for the Retention of Agricultural and Open Space," *Gonzaga Law Review*, Vol. 15, No. 3, pp. 675–699. For details on Illinois' program as amended in 1981 see David L. Chicoine and John T. Scott, Jr., "Agricultural Use-Valuation Using Farm-Level Data," *Property Tax Journal*, Vol. 2, No. 1, March 1983, pp. 1–12.
10. The merits of preferential tax treatment of agricultural lands are not universally accepted. See, for example, N. A. Roberts and H. J. Brown, eds. *Property Tax Preferences for Agricultural Land* (New York, NY: Universe Books, 1980). For a historical review of farm property taxation, see Jerome M. Stam and Ann G. Sibold, *Agriculture and the Property Tax: A Forward Look Based on a Historical Perspective*, AER 392, ERS-USDA (Washington, D.C.: Government Printing Office, November 1977). Empirical investigations have pointed out weaknesses in preferential taxation arguments. See David L. Chicoine, Steven T. Sonka and Robert D. Doty, "The Effects of Farm Property Tax Relief Programs on Farm Financial Conditions," *Land Economics*, Vol. 58, No. 4, November 1982, pp. 516–523.
11. David L. Chicoine and Norman Walzer, "Property Taxes and Public Education," *Illinois Research*, Vol. 23, No. 1, Winter 1981, pp. 12–13.
12. This function is currently carried out by the Department of Revenue. To preserve

consistency with the operations in effect in 1977, the discussions will be current as of that time.

13. *Debts/Taxes/Assessments, The Major Chicago Area Governments for Calendar Year Ending December 31, 1976*, (Chicago, IL: The Civic Federation, 1977), Bulletin No. 882, p. 3. Individual personal property was excluded from the Illinois property tax base in 1969.

14. A listing of the counties and delinquency rates is available in *Illinois Property Tax Statistics, 1975*, Department of Local Government Affairs, (Springfield, IL: State of Illinois, 1978), Table XXVI.

15. The only two counties currently following this schedule are Cook and DuPage. In these counties the first payment is an estimate computed as one-half of the previous year's tax bill.

16. The Implicit Price Deflator for State and Local Government Purchases is commonly used to depict price increases of goods and services purchased by state and local governments in the production of public services.

17. Population data are not available for school districts and special districts because of irregular boundaries.

18. One of the early models using this approach to financial analysis is David L. Sjoquist, "A Median Voter Analysis of Variations in the Use of Property Taxes Among Local Governments," *Public Choice*, Vol. 36, No. 2, 1981, pp. 273–285. The analysis reported in this section is based on an earlier paper, David L. Chicoine and Norman Walzer, "Factors Affecting Property Tax Reliance: Some Additional Evidence," (unpublished manuscript, 1983).

19. X is the consumption tax base and is the community's aggregate demand for these goods. H is the property tax base if the community contains no other type of taxable property than housing and is the aggregate demand for housing. The local government identity or balanced budget requirement is $G_0=t_1X+t_2H$ if the relationship between t_1 and t_2 is linear.

20. An alternative is to trace out each taxing unit serving residents in a particular government, such as a municipality and then determine the amount of property tax collections which occur within the city. This procedure is very time consuming and not feasible for more than a relatively few observations. It was undertaken for a sample of large Illinois cities and the results were consistent with those reported later in this paper. See Norman Walzer and Glenn W. Fisher, "Property Taxes in Cities and Suburbs: An Empirical Inquiry," paper presented at the Atlantic Economics Association Meetings, London, August 1981. Also see Ray Bahl, Jesse Burkhead and Bernard Jump, Jr., eds. *Public Employment and State and Local Government Finance* (Cambridge, MA: Ballinger Publishing Company, 1980), pp. 97–101.

21. The conceptual discussion suggested both the level of community income and the income of the median voter will impact the tax configuration choice but in opposite directions. Since the median voter's income, represented by median family income, and the average income level are highly correlated, only one income variable is included to avoid multicollinearity problems. This, however, makes an unambiguous interpretation of the results difficult.

22. See George J. Stigler, *The Organization of Industry* (Homewood, IL: Richard D. Irwin, Inc., 1968), Chapter 4, pp. 29–38. Measures of concentration from the industrial organization literature have been used in earlier empirical public finance studies. For examples, see Richard E. Wagner, "Revenue Structure, Fiscal Illusion and Budgetary Choice," *Public Choice*, Vol. 25, No. 1, 1976, pp. 45–61; Werner E. Pommerehne and Friedrich Schneider, "Fiscal Illusion, Political Institutions, and Local Public Spending," *Kyklos*, Vol. 31, No. 3, 1978, pp. 381–407 and Charles T. Clotfelter, "Public Spend-

ing for Higher Education: An Empirical Test of Two Hypotheses," *Public Finance*, Vol. 31, No. 2, 1976, pp. 177–195.

23. In a cross-sectional study such as this, multicollinearity is always potentially problematic. For example, the simple correlation coefficient between per capita income (X_4) and percent poverty (X_3) is $-.72$. However, excluding one of these potentially collinear variables from the equation did not substantially alter the coefficient or standard error of the other. Also, the simple correlation coefficients between P_{tax} and the respective dependent variables are of the same sign as the coefficients in Table 4.4.

24. David L. Sjoquist, "A Median Voter Analysis of Variations in the Use of Property Taxes Among Local Governments," *Public Choice*, Vol. 36, No. 2, 1981, pp. 273–285.

25. This is consistent with other findings. See Paul B. Downing and Thomas J. Dilorenzo, "User Charges and Special Districts," in R. Aronson and E. Schwartz, eds. *Management Policies in Local Goverment Finance* (Washington, D.C.: International City Management Association, 1981), pp. 184–210.

26. See ACIR, *Categorical Grants: Their Role and Design* (Washington, D.C.: Advisory Commission on Intergovernmental Relations, May 1978).

27. For more information see R. P. Nathan, A. D. Manuel and S. E. Calkins, *Monitoring Revenue Sharing* (Washington, D.C.: The Brookings Institution, 1975), Norman Walzer and David Ward, *General Revenue Sharing in Large Illinois Municipalities* (Springfield, IL: Illinois Municipal Problems Commission, March 1975), and Norman Walzer and Barbara Solomon, "Revenue Sharing in Illinois Counties and Townships – A Regional Comparison, " *Illinois County and Township Officials*, April 1976, pp. 34–38.

28. For example see Marvin B. Johnson, "Recognizing the Competitive Nature of General Revenue Sharing," *Southern Economic Journal*, Vol. 44, No. 2, July 1977, pp. 143–147 and Andrew M. Isserman and Karen L. Majors, "General Revenue Sharing: Federal Incentives to Change Local Government," *Journal of the American Institute of Planners*, Vol. 44, No. 3, July 1978, pp. 317–327.

Chapter 5

Expenditures for Public Services

Local public officials provide a set of public services reflecting the demands of residents, determined by the public choice process. This chapter examines local government expenditures and employment used in providing these services. Special attention is paid to changes in levels and composition of expenditures. A major issue is whether differences in governmental structure affect either the aggregate expenditure for public services or expenditures for a particular service. The competition among governments in a decentralized system and constraints on local public decisions are studied as key factors in accounting for differences in expenditure levels.

LEGAL BASIS FOR EXPENDITURES

Before a local government can provide a service, it must have either a statutory or constitutional basis. Although this grant of authority is much broader for home rule cities and counties, such is not the case in the majority of local governments in Illinois. The restrictive Dillon's Rule interpretation of local government authority has meant relatively slow changes in the delivery of services. Before initiating a new program, hours are spent researching statutory and case law to find authority for spending funds in a new area or a precedent for other policies. If a legal basis is not found, then the legislature must be petitioned for additional authority. Of course, these legal obstacles also provide stability to local government and a sense of continuity which, in itself, may be desirable.

A possible undesirable outcome, however, is that changes in the delivery of local services are not made consistently. Public officials in one region of the state who face a special problem develop a unique solution and petition the legislature for authority to act. However, the same solution may not be useful in another part of the state. A third, more general solution, might not be considered. Legislation affecting local governments often occurs on a needs basis with little time spent on long-term planning or study of the impact of the legislation on other governments.

Tight state controls on local governments' powers also may perpetuate existing service delivery systems beyond their useful lives. There is no automatic mechanism for evaluating, dissolving, combining, or otherwise changing the numbers and types of local governments providing services. When changes are attempted at the state level, representatives of local governments feel threatened and fight to block passage of these changes even when possibly advantageous to taxpayers. As shown in Chapter 2, restrictive tax rate limits and controls over local governments may be a factor causing more complex government structures.

The result is a local government system slowly responding to shifts in population and economic activities. Financing arrangements change infrequently when the state legislature grants additional revenue raising authority or when existing revenue sources are altered.

The fact that the local government structure changes slowly does not mean that local government expenditures and employment have changed at the same pace. In practice, local government expenditures and employment have increased substantially since the Second World War, often with financial support and mandates from federal and state governments.

While many studies of local government are designed to examine the efficiency of alternate government types and sizes, empirical investigations, based on theories of private sector operations applied to the public sector, have met with little success. A major limitation in public sector expenditure analyses is the lack of information about service delivery. Many services are difficult to measure. Police protection, in its truest sense, protects residents from crimes that would have occurred had there been no protection. Fire protection is aimed at preventing fires. In both instances, the challenge facing analysts is to measure or quantify those crimes which were not committed and fires which were prevented.

In addition to these problems is the fact that governmental accounting systems do not yield cost information. Appropriations and expenditures are organized by fund, making an examination of costs related to a particular service difficult. Within the fund, line item expenditures frequently cross several activities so that personal costs, for example, cannot be disaggregated to each service. Attempts to disaggregate expenditure summaries and reassemble them by service are usually met with considerable frustration even by those knowledgable about government accounting practices.

As a result, many studies use expenditures per capita as a measure of public output or an indication of the cost for public services. This approach provides the basis for analyses in this chapter.[1]

EXPENDITURES BY GOVERNMENT TYPE

The importance of local governments in the provision of services is shown by an examination of expenditures and employment. Table 5.1 compares total expenditures and employment, by type of government, for 1977 with the percentage which each represents of the aggregate. Combined Illinois local governments spent $9,650,300 thousand in 1977 or an average of $861.14 per resident. School districts reported the largest expenditure—44 percent of the total. Cities followed with 30.8 percent and an average of $310.70 per resident. Collectively, special districts represented 12.9 percent of the total expenditures by all local governments but, given the wide array of governments, a detailed analysis by district type is difficult.

The growth in expenditures by local governments in Illinois during the past twenty years is clear. Local governments spent $1,841.9 million in 1957 and, by 1977, total expenditures had increased 5.24 times. In relative importance by government type, counties increased from 9.7

Table 5.1. Total Illinois Local Government Expenditures, 1977

	Expenditures		Employment	
Government Type	Amount (000)	Percent	FTE	Percent
Total Local Government	$9,650,300	100.0%	376,797	100.0%
Counties	1,011,477	10.4	41,983	11.1
Municipalities	2,922,142	30.8	91,371	24.2
Townships	181,455	1.9	5,305	1.4
School Districts	4,270,866	44.0	202,589	53.8
Special Districts	1,250,682	12.9	35,549	9.4

Source: U.S. Bureau of the Census, *Compendium of Government Finances*, and *Compendium of Public Employment*, (Washington, D.C.: Government Printing Office, 1978).

percent to 10.4 percent, municipalities decreased from 34.8 percent to 30.8 percent, townships declined from 2.5 percent to 1.9 percent, school districts increased from 37.2 percent to 44.0 percent, and special districts went from 16.0 percent to 12.0 percent. These shifts reflect both changes in service demands and changes in the system for delivering local services. They also reflect shifts in available revenues, particularly regarding intergovernmental aid. Differences in revenue structures, because of varying revenue elasticities, alter the rate at which the expenditures of each government type can change.[2]

The importance of each government type is also shown by employment patterns. Table 5.1 shows full-time equivalent employment for each government type. Two interesting points result from this employment comparison. First, while school districts account for forty-four percent of the expenditures, they represent 53.8 percent of the full-time equivalent employment. Municipalities spend 30.8 percent of the total but they employ only 24.2 percent.

Second, one of every thirty residents in Illinois works for local government. If part-time employment is included, then one in every 24.5 residents works for local government and one in every nineteen is employed by a state or local government in Illinois. These figures compare with the U.S. average of one person in every seventeen working for state or local government.

Differences in local government expenditures and employment, by size of county, are also interesting. For comparison, employment has been converted to full-time equivalents (FTE) and expenditures are per capita (Table 5.2). A U-shaped pattern is evident in employment ratios. Cook County, with more than one million residents, employed 363.4 FTE per 10,000 residents compared with an average of 336.2 statewide. However,

Table 5.2. Direct Illinois Local Government General Expenditures, 1977

County Size	Expenditures		Employment	
	Amount (000)	Per Capita	Number	Per 10,000
All Local Governments	$8,622,886	$769.46	376,797	336.2
1,000,000 or more	4,591,408	855.12	195,131	363.4
250,000 to 999,999	1,371,443	761.54	55,994	319.2
100,000 to 249,999	1,204,074	671.62	54,542	304.2
50,000 to 99,999	447,241	665.49	19,732	293.6
10,000 to 49,999	944,446	640.45	47,610	336.0
Less than 10,000	64,274	664.83	3,254	336.6

Source: U.S. Bureau of the Census, Compendium of Public Employment, (Washington, D.C.: Government Printing Office, 1978).

Cook County is highly urbanized. Substantially more services are provided in this region because of the higher population density. The employment ratios decrease with each population size category until the 50,000 to 99,999 class reporting 293.6 FTE per 10,000 residents. The small counties are similar with 336.0 and 336.6 respectively.

The analytical value of employment figures is limited because they represent only one component in service delivery. However, labor inputs are superior to expenditure comparisons because wage variations are eliminated. Productivity differences among public employees, however, do complicate comparisons of employment data. A definite pattern can be found among labor inputs in counties having various population sizes. Public services in middle size counties, 50,000 to 99,999, employ nearly one-third fewer employees per 10,000 people than either larger or smaller counties. However, clear statements about efficiency in service delivery cannot be made with these data alone.

EXPENDITURES BY FUNCTION

A basic understanding of local fiscal behavior requires detailed information on the functions provided, the amounts spent, and the number of employees employed by each type of government. Such detail, unfortunately, is not available for each service type. Expenditures and employment consequently provide the best bases for comparisons.

In making expenditure comparisons, per capita data must be used to adjust for population differences. Two computational methods are available. First is an unweighted average in which expenditures summed across governments of a certain type are divided by the population receiving services. The second is an average in which per capita expenditures are computed by government and then averaged across governments. The former average depicts the outlay for a service per taxpayer while the latter shows the experience of the average governmental unit. To show service expenditures from the taxpayer's perspective, per taxpayer averages are reported in Table 5.3.

Aggregate averages computed in this manner have disadvantages, however, especially when not all governments of a particular type report expenditures for each service. With existing published information, a count of the number of governments reporting is not available. To adjust for this, data from the Census of Governments data tapes were used to calculate per capita expenditures by type of government considering only governments reporting outlays. An expenditure of zero caused a government's population not to be considered in the per capita computation. The figures in Table 5.3 thus will not sum to the values shown in Table 5.2.

Table 5.3. 1977 Public Safety Expenditures

Function	Counties			Municipalities			Townships			Special Districts	
	Amount (000)	Per Capita	Percent	Amount (000)	Per Capita	Percent	Amount (000)	Per Capita	Percent	Amount (000)	Percent
Police Protection	$55,311	$8.20	9.0%	$545,266	$29.17	88.6	$14,751	$24.28	2.4%	–	–
Fire Protection	7	.36	–	222,383	18.04	85.1	3,477	7.02	1.3	$35,580	13.6%
Corrections	60,280	2.48	98.8	708	1.36	1.2	–	–	–	–	–

Source: Aggregate expenditures are obtained from U.S. Bureau of the Census, Compendium of Government Finances, (Washington, D.C.: Government Printing Office, 1978). Per capita data were obtained from the 1977 Census of Governments tapes.

In the following discussions services have been grouped to facilitate comparisons. Six classifications are employed: public safety, transportation, environment and housing, social services, governmental administration, and education. Not all governments provide each of these services and the delivery systems vary by region in the state.

Public Safety

The three main public safety expenditures include police protection, fire protection, and corrections. Responsibility for these services rests with three general-purpose governments – counties, municipalities, and townships. Special districts, one of the most common being park districts, also provide policing services. Although park districts can provide security service directly, they also contract with a local municipal police department or county sheriff department. In rural areas containing a state park, the security function is commonly provided by state park rangers so that the full cost of police protection does not rest with local governments. Also state police, while primarily responsible for highway patrolling, assist local police agencies on special occasions.

Police Protection. Table 5.3 shows that municipalities have the greatest police protection expenditures. In 1977, cities spent $545,266,000 for police – 88.6 percent of the total by the three general-purpose governments. When compared with the population served, cities spent an average of $29.17 on police services, excluding corrections. Counties were second with 9.0 percent of the total or $8.20 per resident. These expenditures were for sheriff departments, including law enforcement activities and serving court orders and related tasks. Sheriff departments often patrol communities that are too small to efficiently provide police protection. The sheriff department traditionally provided the only law enforcement for rural residents but townships have recently become more active in financing this service.

Townships spent $24.28 per resident for police protection. This average is misleading, however, because only 342 of the 1435 Illinois townships reported police protection expenditures. Much of this spending was revenue sharing funds and represents contracts with other government agencies. No township reported expenditures for corrections. Overall, townships accounted for only 2.4 percent of police protection expenditures.

Corrections. Correction expenditures include outlays for confinement as well as pardon, probation, and parole activities. In some areas, the county houses prisoners, or when a county facility is inadequate, prisoners are housed in neighboring counties. Some of the correction expenditures at the county level may represent costs reimbursed by cities. The extent of these arrangements could not be determined with existing data. On average, counties reported expenditures of $2.48 per resident and cities reported $1.36 per capita for correctional activities.

Fire Protection. Another major component in public safety services is fire protection. Expenditures for fire protection in Illinois are made by counties, cities, townships and/or special districts. It is not uncommon to find more than one government providing these services in one municipality. Large cities may be served by a fire protection district and a municipal department. Fire protection districts based on volunteer service are common in rural areas. This method is the only viable way to provide fire service to farms and low density rural regions.[3]

Fire protection expenditures vary greatly by governmental unit. Municipal fire departments often have a full emergency medically trained paramedic rescue unit. Injured parties are stabilized at the scene of an accident before being transported to the hospital. In other cases, the emergency health and transport services are provided by funeral directors or community volunteer rescue squads. Ambulance service provided by funeral directors is rapidly disappearing. Hospitals often maintain an emergency transport service and the fire department is not directly involved, while in other communities this service is provided by the private sector. Other than emergency care facilities, fire departments carry out inspection activities, educational programs, and other preventive services.

The majority of fire protection services in Illinois are provided by municipalities. In 1977, cities spent an average of $18.04 per capita–85.1 percent of total fire protection expenditures. Counties averaged only 36¢ per resident. Although townships spent $7.02 per capita for this service, only 200 townships reported and their aggregate expenditures represented 1.3 percent of the total. Over fourteen percent of fire protection expenditures were by fire protection districts which are mainly volunteer services.

During the past two decades, expenditures for public safety have grown, with increases in number and types of services provided. In 1957, for instance, per capita expenditures for police protection, including corrections, were $9.30 per resident for all local governments combined. By 1977, the average expenditure had increased to $54.50 per resident, a growth of 486 percent. This comparison does not begin to tell the complete story, however. When price increases for inputs purchased are removed, the 1977 expenditure, in 1957 dollars, was $19.16 per resident or an increase of 106.0 percent during the twenty year period. Part of these expenditure increases can be traced to court mandates covering the treatment of prisoners and the gathering of evidence for use in prosecution.

Fire protection expenditures in 1957 were $4.58 per resident and had grown to an average of $23.16 per capita twenty years later. However, when the effects of reductions in purchasing power are considered, the 1977 expenditure, in 1957 dollars, was reduced to $8.14 for an increase of 77.7 percent during the two decades.

These comparisons also take no account of changes in the types and amounts of services provided. There are few who would argue that police or fire protection in 1977 is the same as twenty years ago. There is greater focus on protecting citizens' rights in arrest and trial proceedings, for instance. Firefighters in many instances have assumed responsibility for providing medical treatment in emergency cases. This is a relatively recent phenomenon that broadens fire service responsibilities and requires more training, better equipment, a quicker response time, and greater expenditures.

Transportation Facilities

A second major type of local public service is the construction and maintenance of transportation facilities.

Roads and Highways. The greatest share of transportation expenditures goes to roads, although municipalities sometimes provide bus services. Expenditures for transportation services are not all locally financed since the state provides significant assistance through a sharing of the state tax on motor fuels purchased in Illinois. However, local revenues are a major factor in financing road services.

Expenditures for roads and highways, by type of government, are provided in Table 5.4. Municipalities represented approximately half of the total spent for roads and highways with an average expenditure of $26.43 per resident. Counties spent 36.3 percent and averaged $40.76 per capita while townships spent an average of $43.80 per capita and represented 11.5 percent of the aggregate.

The importance of the motor fuel tax in financing transportation expenditures is shown in a brief comparison of the amounts received by each type of government in 1977. Counties averaged $8.10 per resident, municipalities received $12.11 per capita and townships (road districts) received $4.84 per person.[4]

Highway expenditures went from $24.08 per capita to $47.11 per resident, an increase of 95.6 percent from 1957 to 1977. In constant dollars, however, quite a different picture is presented. Removing the effects of

Table 5.4. 1977 Transportation Expenditures

Function	Counties Amount (000)	Per Capita	Percent	Municipalities Amount (000)	Per Capita	Percent	Townships Amount (000)	Per Capita	Percent	Special Districts Amount (000)	Percent
Roads and Highways	$193,194	$40.76	36.3%	$277,311	$26.43	52.1%	$61,266	$43.80	11.5%	$ 85	*
Airport	539	1.38	.9	44,617	4.55	77.5	9	.67	*	12,437	21.6

* Less than 0.1 percent

Source: Aggregate expenditures are obtained from U.S. Bureau of the Census, Compendium of Government Finances, (Washington, D.C.: Government Printing Office, 1978). Per capita data were obtained from the 1977 Census of Governments tapes.

inflation lowers the 1977 expenditure to $16.56 per capita, a decrease in real terms of 31.2 percent. The GNP Implicit Price Deflator for State and Local Government Purchases probably underestimates the price increases for road construction and maintenance materials. The price increases in oil-based materials, used extensively for transportation services, led other price increases during this period.

Airports. A second transportation expenditure category includes airport construction and operations. In Illinois, airports are financed using several approaches involving state and local governments. Cities such as Chicago and Galesburg operate municipal airports. Airports in other regions of the state are operated by park districts. A separate airport authority, operating as a special district, provides services in other cases. In Champaign-Urbana, the state operates the airport through the University of Illinois. In the Census of Governments survey, eight counties reported expenditures for airport facilities.

Airport expenditures in 1977 are shown by type of government in Table 5.4. Throughout Illinois, thirty general-purpose governments reported expenditures for airports—eight counties, twenty-one cities, and one township. The average expenditure reported by municipalities was $4.55 per resident representing 77.5 percent of the aggregate airport expenditures within the state. The eight counties reporting expenditures averaged $1.38 per resident and less than one percent of the aggregate amount spent. In addition to general purpose governments, special districts or airport authorities spent $12,437,000 on airports, 21.6 percent of the total. Because detailed population data are not available for special districts, these expenditures cannot be expressed per capita.

Environment, Recreation, and Library Services

There is a group of local services that can be conveniently termed environment, recreation, and library services. They are offered under a wide array of financing arrangements and at many levels of performance.

Sewerage Treatment and Disposal. The treatment and disposal of sewerage offers excellent opportunities, especially in metropolitan areas, for economies of scale. This is particularly true when a central location is available to house the treatment facility and many governments can establish feeder lines to the main treatment plant. In these instances an opportunity for effective use of sanitation districts exists. Sewerage treatment and disposal services are provided by at least four different types of governments in Illinois although detailed information on financing arrangements is not readily available.

Expenditures for sewerage treatment and disposal are shown by type of government in Table 5.5. A majority of the expenditures involved special districts but this is easily explained by the Metropolitan Sanitary District of Greater Chicago (MSD). Of the $294.1 million spent by sanitary districts, the MSD represented $219.4 million or nearly seventy-five percent. This district serves Chicago and a majority of the municipalities in Cook County.

In arrangements where sanitary districts provide services, municipalities commonly maintain feeder lines within the city limits to connect with the collection system maintained by the special district. Thus, city government expenditures in some instances represent maintenance of the collection system and are not direct expenditures for sewerage treatment.

Municipal expenditures for these services averaged $25.47 per resident in 1977 and represented approximately 33.2 percent of expenditures by local governments for sewerage treatment and disposal. Eighty-one townships reported an average expenditure of $2.46 per capita. In very small communities it is still possible to find residents with a septic tank system although these systems are less common as federal and state environmental protection policies become more stringent about water pollution.

In 1957, local governments in Illinois spent an average of $6.89 per resident for sewerage related services. By 1977, the average expenditure statewide was $39.61 per capita, an increase of 474.9 percent. However, removing the effects of price increases brings the 1977 figure, in 1957 dollars, to $13.92 per resident for an increase of 102 percent.

Increases in expenditures for sewerage treatment arise from several factors, including a need for additional lines resulting from urban development and increases in treatment capacity involving urban population growth. Environmental protection mandates have also accounted for the increases. Concern about air and water pollution within a growing industrial society has caused more stringent requirements for the treatment of waste. It is no longer acceptable to dispose of untreated sewerage in lakes or rivers because another city downstream may find its drinking water polluted. The extra steps involved in processing the sewerage are costly but the federal government, through the state, frequently provides partial funding for upgrading treatment plants. However, there are instances when local public officials and residents resent what they feel is interference by federal and state governments in local service provision. Small towns, in particular, find the costs involved in meeting the federal and state mandates difficult to finance. The point reflected in the increases in outlays for sewerage treatment and disposal is that the quality of this service has increased drastically during the past twenty years.

Table 5.5. 1977 Environment, Recreation, and Library Expenditures

Function	Counties			Municipalities			Townships			Special Districts	
	Amount (000)	Per Capita	Percent	Amount (000)	Per Capita	Percent	Amount (000)	Per Capita	Percent	Amount (000)	Percent
Sewerage	$ 1,613	–	.4%	$148,307	$25.47	33.2%	$3,094	$2.46	.7%	$294,059	65.8%
Sanitation Other Than Sewerage	1,130	$ .91	.8	133,318	32.11	97.3	1,708	7.22	1.2	925	.7
Parks and Recreation	40,339	2.81	13.3	49,281	8.69	16.5	774	.83	.3	211,906	70.0
Libraries	48	.42	.1	61,076	8.44	80.1	647	.51	.8	14,472	19.0

Source: Aggregate expenditures obtained from U.S. Bureau of the Census, *Compendium of Government Finances*, (Washington, D.C.: Government Printing Office, 1978). Per capita data were obtained from the Census of Governments tapes.

Other Sanitation. In addition to sewerage treatment, local governments must dispose of solid wastes. Increasing amounts of waste disposal and past conflicts with policies regarding air quality make it a major problem for local governments in Illinois and in other states. Trash formerly was burned openly. This lowered the waste disposal volumes which had to be dealt with by local governments. Open, privately owned garbage dumps were maintained.

However, the disposal of waste through open burning and garbage dumps represents potential health hazards. Rodents were common and offered the potential for disease in populous areas. Open burning contributed to air pollution and the water runoff from these areas posed a threat to nearby water sources.

Although the elimination of open burning and the requirement that refuse in landfills be covered daily may have contributed significantly to the reduction of air and water pollution, these changes imposed significant costs on local governments as solid waste services dramatically changed. Solid waste accumulates at a staggering rate and involves large amounts of land to compact and bury it. Under severe penalties, fairly strict controls have been imposed by the Illinois Environmental Protection Agency over landfills and the disposal of solid wastes.

Stricter state and federal policies on solid waste have increased the costs of solid waste services. In addition, the complexities of administering this service have increased as local governments must deal with state-imposed requirements. While the environment has improved, it clearly has been at higher costs.

As expected, municipalities in Illinois accounted for nearly all the expenditures for sanitation other than sewerage treatment and disposal. Specifically, cities spent an average of $32.11 per resident for solid waste disposal and street cleaning, representing 97.3 percent of the aggregate expenditures. Expenditures were reported by 125 townships averaging $7.22 per capita but represented only 1.2 percent of the total. Three counties reported expenditures amounting to less than one percent.

Between 1957 and 1977, expenditures for sanitation services other than sewerage treatment and disposal rose from $6.89 to $39.61 per capita, an increase of 222 percent. Eliminating the price increases during this period reduces the 1977 expenditure, in 1957 dollars, to $4.27 per resident or an increase of 13.3 percent.

Parks and Recreation. Shorter workweeks and an increase in leisure time have prompted local governments to respond to demands for more recreational programs and facilities. Crowds at beaches and campgrounds on weekends demonstrate the importance and the shortage of these programs. Parks and recreational activities are provided through many governmental arrangements in Illinois, the most common including municipal park departments and park districts. Park districts offer an opportunity to tap the tax base outside a municipality to provide park services and permit differences in park services within a city when residents in certain sections desire additional or different services. Special districts offer an opportunity for local governments facing tax rate and debt limits to raise revenues for additional services and for all those benefiting from the service to be included in the park district. These districts also may originate because a group of interested residents desire service expansions without competing with other demands on the city budget. Park districts may be coterminous with cities and both governments levy taxes for park and recreation services.

Financing park services through a single-function district creates inequities in tax burdens. If the park district is not coterminous with the city, or does not encompass park users, some residents pay for services used by others who do not pay. This benefit spillover may cause the underprovision of local parks. One rationale is that a majority of the property taxes are paid by middle and upper income groups but parks are used by poorer residents outside the taxing jurisdiction. A desirable income transfer may result. Research suggests, however, that this is not necessarily the case. Although wealthy residents are more prone to use private entertainment sources such as country clubs and fraternal lodges, a positive relationship exists between income levels and use of parks.[5]

Parks and recreation expenditures are presented in Table 5.5. The majority were special district expenditures. Specifically, seventy percent were made by park districts. Municipalities spent the second largest amount with 267 cities reporting an average of $8.69 per resident. Only one of every five municipalities reported park or recreation outlays. Twenty-three counties reported spending $2.81 per resident for parks and recreation, representing 13.3 percent of the total.

Park-related services vary widely across Illinois. Golf courses, swimming programs, senior citizen activities, organized youth and adult sports activities, and summer day camps are just a few of the services provided. Services have greatly increased in recent years, reflected in increased expenditures. In 1957, for instance, local governments in Illinois spent an average of $6.27 per capita compared with $26.83 twenty years later, an increase of 327.9 percent. In constant dollars, however, the 1977 expenditure was $9.34 representing a real increase of 50.4 percent. More leisure time has increased pressures on recreational facilities. With higher travel costs, the demands on local parks and recreational facilities immediately surrounding population centers will increase disproportionally.

Libraries. A service similar to the parks and recreation service in method of finance is libraries. These services are provided by counties, townships, municipalities, and library districts. Library services are also provided by governments cooperating in a distribution center and receiving state grants to purchase books and educational materials.

Library expenditures by local governments are presented in Table 5.5. Four-fifths of the statewide library expenditures are by municipalities averaging $8.44 per resident. The remaining nineteen percent were library district expenditures. Eleven counties reported expenditures of forty-two cents per resident and twenty-four townships reported expenditures of fifty- one cents per capita. However, these two government types combined represented less than one percent of the aggregate expenditures.

During the past twenty years, libraries have upgraded collections and staffs in response to service demands. In some areas there are regularly scheduled events for children. Other libraries have expanded their audiovisual materials as well as their traditional book and newspaper collections. The concept of a library as a leisure and educational center is clearly gaining acceptance. In 1957, local governments spent an average of $1.14 per resident for library services. In 1977, the expenditures were $6.75 per capita, a change of 492.1 percent. When price increases have been removed, the 1977 expenditure is $2.37 per resident making the expenditure growth, in real terms, 248.5 percent during the twenty years. In amounts spent, library services represent a small proportion of local government services.

Social Services and Income Maintenance

A set of services are provided by state and local governments which might be termed social services and include hospitals, health services, and income maintenance programs. Governments exhibit major variations in types and amounts of services provided in these programs and the programs are provided differently throughout Illinois.

Hospitals. Hospitals are maintained by counties, municipalities, special districts or authorities, and private agencies. In a few cases, contributions are made by township governments for hospital related services. Cities commonly establish a hospital board acting as a quasi-independent agency although the city council may approve the hospital budget. Borrowing is from revenue bonds and grants from outside agencies support part of the operations and capital expansions.

Public expenditures for hospital services by type of government are shown in Table 5.6. Few general-purpose governments reported expenditures for hospitals although, as a percentage of the aggregate public hospital expenditures, outlays by general purpose governments repre-

Table 5.6. 1977 Social Services and Income Maintenance Expenditures

	Counties			Municipalities			Townships			Special Districts	
Function	Amount (000)	Per Capita	Percent	Amount (000)	Per Capita	Percent	Amount (000)	Per Capita	Percent	Amount (000)	Percent
Public Welfare	$ 41,107	$10.21	54.8%	$16,139	$ 6.22	21.5%	$17,708	$3.20	23.6%	—	—
Hospital	168,049	50.60	50.6	17,621	262.39	21.6	9	.63	*	$92,624	27.9%
Health	36,655	4.65	36.3	62,061	2.23	61.5	5	8.61	*	2,225	2.2

* Less than .1 percent

Source: Aggregate expenditures obtained from U.S. Bureau of the Census, *Compendium of Government Finances*, (Washington, D.C.: Government Printing Office, 1978). Per capita data obtained from Census of Governments tapes.

sented approximately seventy-two percent of the total with special districts or hospital authorities accounting for the remainder. Some communities are served by private hospitals exclusively or in addition to public facilities. It is not our purpose to present total hospital expenditures, including both private and public sources, but rather to report the level of public hospital activity measured by expenditures.

Sixteen counties reported expenditures for hospitals averaging $50.60 per resident and twelve cities reported average expenditures of $262.39 per capita. The county share of the total expenditures was 50.6 percent, the municipal share was 21.6 percent, and single-function districts or authorities spent 27.9 percent of the total.

Hospitals obtain much of their operating revenues from fees for services charged patients. They also obtain gifts and grants from private and public sources. Thus, the expenditure of $262.39 per resident by municipalities is not entirely tax financed. Rather, the hospital operates as an enterprise and may be virtually self-supporting.

During the past twenty years, hospital expenditures in current dollars increased by 383.6 percent from $6.09 per resident in 1957 to $29.45 per resident, statewide, in 1977. However, the price increases in recent years for medical supplies have been dramatic as new technology and drugs are developed. According to the GNP Deflator for State and Local Government Purchases, not directly reflecting the price increases in drugs and related equipment, the 1977 expenditures in constant dollars are $10.36 per capita, an increase of 70.1 percent. Using the health care price increases shown in the Consumer Price Index makes the 1977 expenditure in constant dollars $10.51, an increase of 72.6 percent.

Health Services. In addition to hospitals, local governments also provide a group of health-related services. Included among these programs are inspections of businesses and eating establishments, water testing, and immunization programs intended to combat the spread of disease. Many large city governments have a health department as do many counties. Many counties also maintain nursing homes.

Ninety-seven counties reported an average expenditure of $4.65 per capita for health related services representing 36.3 percent of the expenditures by local governments for this service. Expenditures were reported by 251 municipalities averaging $2.23 per municipal resident and 61.5 percent of the aggregate expenditures. Only two townships reported expenditures for this service and special districts represented 2.2 percent of the aggregate expenditures.

Public Assistance. Most government units contain residents who, for one reason or another, are unable to provide for their own welfare.

There are reasons for local government public assistance programs. Sickness, poor skills, old age, and pregnancy are but a few reasons for residents to seek public assistance. The welfare expenditure category used by the Census Bureau in presenting data includes traditional cash assistance programs in addition to nursing homes, medical care, and hospital payments made for the needy.

In Illinois, locally-supported public assistance programs (cash assistance payments) are largely under the direction of townships. The township supervisor is responsible for administering the pauper assistance program, subject to approval by the township trustees. Unfortunately, there are state-wide differences in award standards and eligibility conditions. The State of Illinois, through the Department of Public Aid, works with townships in financing the pauper assistance programs. If a township government's funds become exhausted, the state government will finance the remainder of the program provided that the township levies at least one mill (10¢ per $100 assessed valuation). However, when townships receive funds from the state, they must follow certain guidelines and practices. Township supervisors, not receiving state funds, are responsible for establishing their own standards and carrying out the assistance program.

Public welfare expenditures by counties represented more than one-half of the total outlay. In fact, counties accounted for 54.8 percent of the aggregate expenditures with an average of $10.21 per capita reported by seventy-nine counties. The seventy-nine cities reporting welfare related expenditures averaged $6.77 per capita or 21.5 percent of the aggregate expenditures. When all welfare expenditures are considered together, townships account for 23.6 percent or about $3.20 per township resident. The townships account for only slightly more when only cash assistance payments are examined. However, there are numerous other cash assistance payments and welfare programs which are handled through the county government. These programs are federal and state supported.

There is great national concern over the rising costs of welfare and related programs. Examples of misuse, graft and abuse are often cited. While these factors have contributed to massive growth in the program, much of the increase stems from expanded program coverage at the federal level. In Illinois, the local government expenditure data do not reveal a large increase. Expenditures by local governments in 1957 averaged $5.46 per resident and twenty years later had increased to $6.64 per capita, a growth of 21.6 percent. Given the rise in consumer prices, the growth in constant dollars is negative. Local government expenditure growth, however, masks much of the change in public assistance outlays. Additional programs initiated by the federal government and those administered by state governments must be considered also. Township public assistance programs, for instance, are viewed as only temporary relief until a resident can qualify for a state or federal program. Also, much of the pressure that would have been imposed on local governments for senior citizen assistance and low income medical relief has been diverted by expansions in the federal and state financed medicare or medicaid programs.

States differ in the extent to which local governments are required to fund welfare programs. There is little dispute that local governments in Illinois benefited from the diversion of responsibility for income assistance to state government. In other states the weight of the welfare programs on local governments is staggering.

Governmental Administration

A necessary part of providing public services is administering the daily activities of governments involved. Programs must be formulated and implemented, budgets prepared, revenues collected, and bills paid. These activities are implicit in providing services and go unnoticed by the average citizen or taxpayer. They must nevertheless be carried out if the public's affairs are to be managed smoothly. Administering a public agency is a complicated business. Many federal and state intergovernmental revenues require detailed records of expenditures for auditing purposes. These extra records often require additional highly trained accountants and electronic data processing equipment. In recent years courts have imposed requirements for hiring practices and dismissals so that public agencies must follow specific procedures to avoid lawsuits claiming unequal or unfair treatment. Reporting requirements have mushroomed as mandates for greater public participation in the decisionmaking process increased. These activities all require additional personnel, often specialists.

Many of these operating requirements are not understood by the taxpaying public. The efforts of a new management team to increase services and lower costs simply gets lost when discussions about increases in property taxes occur. Innovations in public service production and provision are not commonly discussed in the public forum just as the impact of inflation on resources available to provide public services is not commonly recognized by taxpayers. What is recognized, however, is an increasing trend in the number of public employees and, correctly or incorrectly in the minds of constituents, many of these employees are assigned to governmental administration.

The Census Bureau reports expenditures for administration in two main categories—financial administration and general control. Financial administration includes expenditures for tax assessment and collection, accounting, auditing, budgeting, purchasing, custody of funds, and other central finance activities. General control includes expenditures for the governing body, courts, and office of the chief executive. Outlays for central staff services and agencies concerned with personnel administration, law, recording, and planning and zoning are also included in general control. While respondents to the census survey receive detailed instructions about what elements to include, there are likely to be many inconsistencies when the data are reported. Differences in public organization charts suggest that variations in the way services are administered will make any distinction between financial administration and general control imprecise. Consequently, expenditures for these two functions are combined in Table 5.7.

General Control. A comparison of local government expenditures for general administration and financial control is interesting. According to the available information, approximately thirty-one percent is spent by counties for an average of $16.08 per capita. Cities spent sixty-seven percent with an average expenditure of $16.52 per resident and townships spent 2.2 percent of the total amounting to $33.47 per resident. No separate expenditures for general administration and financial control for either school districts or special districts are reported in the Census of Governments, although, of course, such expenditures do occur. Because the data for special districts and school districts are organized by type of district rather than by functional category within governmental units, it becomes impossible to estimate the administrative expenses incurred.

In a subsequent analysis, the issue of whether additional governments raise the administrative costs of providing local government services is examined. Duplicative efforts, more complex intergovernmental relations, and the failure to take advantage of the complementarity of many public services could increase administrative costs in fragmented governance systems. In fact, higher administrative costs might be the strongest case raised for attempts to reorganize the delivery system for local public services, at least through cooperative agreements.

While increases in administrative bureaucracy and employment in local governments are often criticized, the data for the past twenty years in Illinois do not support these criticisms. In 1957, local governments spent an average of $6.63 per resident on financial administration and general control activities. By 1977, the expenditure had increased to $21.39 per resident for a growth of 222.6 percent. In constant dollars, the 1977 expenditure was $7.52 per resident for a growth in real terms of 13.4 percent during the past twenty years.

Table 5.7. 1977 Governmental Administration

Function	Counties Amount (000)	Per Capita	Percent	Municipalities Amount (000)	Per Capita	Percent	Townships Amount (000)	Per Capita	Percent	School Districts Amount (000)	Percent	Special Districts Amount (000)	Percent
Financial Administration and General Control	$ 55,150	$16.08	30.7%	$120,372	$ 16.52	67.1%	$ 3,901	$33.47	2.2%	–	–	–	–
General Public Buildings	68,599	3.25	28.2	72,527	6.26	71.6	176	.49	.2	–	–	–	–
Interest on General Debt	17,445	1.76	5.9	80,839	5.87	27.3	–	–	–	$128,007	43.2%	$69,753	23.6%
Other and Unallocable	106,275	13.54	18.3	412,666	208.31	70.9	62,389	22.44	10.7	–	–	928	.2

Source: Aggregate expenditures obtained from U.S. Bureau of the Census, *Compendium of Government Finances,* (Washington, D.C.: Government Printing Office, 1978). Per capita data obtained from Census of Governments tapes.

Public Buildings. In addition to general administrative costs, information is also available on expenditures for the construction and maintenance of general public buildings. These expenditures vary widely due to the relative importance of construction costs. Counties reported an average expenditure of $3.25 per capita compared with an average of $6.26 per resident in cities and 49¢ per capita for township residents. Expenditures in this category increased substantially during the twenty years under study from $1.57 per resident to $8.97 per capita in current dollars. In real terms, the expenditure increase was from $1.57 per capita to $3.15 per resident, a growth rate of 100.6 percent.

General Interest. The final general expenditure shown in Table 5.7 is for interest on general debt. Details are not available on the reasons for incurring debt so a sophisticated analysis is not possible. However, it is quite clear from even a brief examination of the data that school districts and special districts account for a majority of the outstanding debt of local governments in Illinois. Combined, municipalities and counties represent only one-third of the general interest expenditures.

It must be understood in comparing debt figures that local governments incur two types of debt. General obligation debt is repaid from property taxes or other revenue sources available to the local government incurring the debt. Nonguaranteed debt, a term applied to debt which does not have the full faith and credit of the government, is repaid with fee proceeds of the financed governmental enterprise. It is likely that municipalities represent a much greater portion of the nonguaranteed debt than is depicted in Table 5.7. In fact when only nonguaranteed debt outstanding is considered, municipalities constitute 62.9 percent. Repayment of this debt, however, does not obligate the taxing powers of the respective cities.

Education

In Illinois, educational services are provided almost exclusively by single-function districts, namely elementary, secondary, and unit districts for the common schools and community college districts for post-secondary education. These expenditures do not include those by private and religious affiliated groups which, in some areas, represent major segments of the educational community.

Among expenditures by public agencies, school districts spent $4.1 billion or an average of $1,704 per student in 1977 as revealed in Table 5.8. This expenditure represented 99.5 percent of the total for local governments in Illinois. These expenditures are not restricted to local revenue sources but also include state payments to school systems. In

1977 school districts collected $2.1 billion in property taxes while, as shown in Table 5.8, they collectively spent $4.1 billion. The difference between property taxes and expenditures mainly reflects state aid. School districts received $1.9 billion in state aid and an additional $26 million from the federal government.

Educational services are provided by several types of school systems. Some provide services for elementary grades only, others serve secondary grades only, still others educate both age groups, and community colleges provide two year post-secondary education. A profile of the relative importance of each type of school system is shown in Table 5.8 along with an estimate of per pupil outlays. The most expensive education is provided in the secondary grades which is not unexpected given the educational programs required for this age group.

Outlays for education in Illinois have risen considerably during the past two decades. In 1957 local governments were spending an average of $69.12 per capita (not per pupil) for education compared with an average of $362.57 in 1977. When the effects of inflation are removed, the 1977 expenditure in constant dollars was $127.49 per resident. During this period, however, the number of students to be educated increased markedly so that the per capita comparisons are not as meaningful as for other services. Converting the educational expenditures to per pupil provides a somewhat better comparison of the rising expenditures for educational services. In 1957, the statewide average was $327 per pupil compared with $1704 twenty years later for an increase of 421.1 percent during the period. In real terms, the 1977 expenditure was $599, an increase of 83.2 percent.

Table 5.8. 1977 Educational Expenditures by Illinois Local Governments

Governmental Unit	Amount (000)	Per Student	Percent
Total	$4,092,659	$1,704	100.0%
Counties	2,780	na	.1
Municipalities	17,513	na	.4
Townships	51	na	–
School Districts	4,072,315	1,704	99.5
Elementary Grades Only	817,612	1,547	
Secondary Grades Only	632,319	2,226	
Both Elementary and Secondary	2,422,954	1,720	
College Grades Only	327,725	1,339	

na = not applicable

Source: U.S. Bureau of the Census, 1977 Census of Governments, *Finances of School Districts,* and *Compendium of Governmental Finances,* (Washington, D.C.: Government Printing Office, 1978).

Local public services in Illinois are provided through many arrangements of local governments. It is thus difficult to summarize responsibilities for services. School districts provide virtually all educational services. Counties are relatively more important in coordinating welfare functions, providing hospitals and corrections, and maintaining the legal, judicial, and election systems. Municipalities are dominant in providing police and fire protection, highways, sanitation services, libraries, and other local services. Special districts provide a majority of the sewerage treatment and disposal functions, parks, and control over the use of natural resources. In Illinois, residents have a broad range to choose from in finding a community with the types of services desired under the preferred governmental arrangement. They also have opportunities to alter the local governance system in their communities to reflect their tastes for tax and service levels and organizational form.

DETERMINANTS OF EXPENDITURES

The impact of structural variation on local government budgetary behavior can be investigated using the expenditure approach. As reviewed in Chapter 2, this approach, generally following the median voter framework, has been employed to study political competition among governments, efficiencies or inefficiencies of alternate organizations, and the effects of benefit spillovers on expenditures. The use of expenditures lessens the difficulty of directly measuring local government services.

To consider variations in local governance structure, aggregate expenditures at the county level are studied. This approach captures the full outlay for available services, not just the services provided by a particular unit of government. If residents are served by park districts, fire protection districts, library districts, townships and counties, the complete outlay for public services is examined. The disadvantage in this approach is that not all residents in the county receive the same service and, because of intracounty variation in governmental structure, not all can participate in the public choices regarding service levels and budgetary commitments. However, the regional approach facilitates the inclusion of alternate governmental structures in the analysis. Does it make any difference, for example, if park services are provided mainly by a few general-purpose governments or by a mix of park districts and multipurpose governments?

Previous studies of expenditures and the structure of the local governance system comment on the efficiency with which local services are provided under alternate political organizational arrangements.[6] The efficiency issue relates to cost per unit of service provided. However, since information on service levels is not available, any relationship between expenditures and structure directly indicates little about cost levels in local political systems. At best what has been determined by these analyses and is investigated here is whether structure or number of taxing units affects how much is spent for public services. To what extent, if any, do additional local governments serving a community affect aggregate budget outlays?

Expenditure Model

To study this question the following reduced form public expenditure model is estimated with county area data from Illinois.

$$E_i = a + b_1 Y_i + b_2 T_i + b_3 G_i + \sum_{j=4}^{h} b_j X_{ji} + e$$

where:

E_i = per capita expenditures in county i, including outlays by county governments, municipalities, townships and special districts,

Y_i = income, measured by per capita, in county i,

T_i = tax price in county i,

G_i = government structure in ith county,

X_{ji} = vector of independent, socio-economic, taste and preference variables for county i,

a,b = constant term and vector of coefficients to be estimated, and

e = error term.

Using regression analysis, the model is estimated first with general per capita expenditures as the dependent variable and then for per capita expenditures on financial control, libraries, park and recreation services, local roads and streets and education.[7]

Expenditure-demand analyses of local government fiscal behavior have demonstrated the conceptual and empirical importance of income (Y_i) and tax price (T_i) in analyzing public expenditure variation across communities.[8] The competitive spirit underlying this approach assumes that any government that disregards the preferences of its constituents will soon be driven from office by an opposition that proposes to more closely adhere to the wishes of the electorate.

Since local public services, in general, can be described as normal goods, localities with higher incomes (Y_i) will demand more from local governments and have higher per capita expenditures.[9] Supply of local public services is financed by some combined revenue system comprised of property and nonproperty local taxes, aid from higher levels of government and service fees, particularly for enterprise services. The property tax, of course, plays a major role in this system. The higher the price that must be paid by residents in taxes, the fewer the public services. An indication of the median tax price (T_i) facing residents in the respective Illinois counties is the ratio of the taxable value on the median valued house to the total property tax base in the county. While this surrogate for the property tax share of the median household is crude, particularly for a regional analysis focused on the effects of local government structural variation, data limitations prevent the use of more refined measures.

To account for diversity in preferences and differences in outside aid (X_{ji}) which are expected to have an effect on local public expenditures, this analysis considers per capita intergovernmental revenues, percent rural population, percent school aged children, and population size. Of central concern with intergovernmental aid is its effect on local spending. Aid results in a substitution of federal and state money for local funds if the estimated relationship between aid and per capita outlays is greater than zero but less than unity.

Aggregate outlays capture not only service quantity but also service quality. Adjusting for service quality is difficult. As a proxy, the number of workers employed is included in the reduced form public expenditure model. To correct for productivity differences among public employees and regional wage variation, average earnings are also included.

Three measures of governmental structure (G_i) are used to investigate the relationship between per capita expenditures and local governance organization. The most direct measure of political structure is the number of administrative units. However, because more populous counties have a larger absolute number of local governments, the number of taxing units is scaled to population. A second measure of the local governance system is a structure index used in studies of industrial organization.[10] The larger the index value the fewer the number of political units and the more concentrated the governmental structure. To more directly investigate the implications of special districts in public service provision, the number of special districts per 10,000 population is the third measure of structure.

Finding a statistically significant negative association between measures of the local political structure and per capita expenditures has been viewed as supporting the notion that political competition among jurisdictions constrains choices made by elected officials and induces cost effectiveness in the provision of local public services. Symmetrically, this behavioral factor, operating on the demand side of local budgetary choice, implies that centralized government structures have higher expenditures because of monopoly power. These empirical findings are consistent with the interjurisdictional competition claim that political competition, like competition among firms in an industry, restricts a bureaucrat's ability to pursue policies that do not reflect the desires or preferences of taxpayers and to shirk the monitoring of public service provision.[11]

Concomitantly, political responsiveness in a fragmented governance system characterized by more homogeneous units may lead to an increased number of higher valued services. This would require greater outlays and would result in an inverse relationship between smaller, decentralized structures and observed budget commitments. As a demand factor emanating from the preference aggregating function of local political organizations, political responsiveness may offset the interjurisdictional competitive pressures expected to show fragmented governments with lower outlays.

Complementarities in the provision of public services may cause administrative inefficiencies and higher expenditures in fragmented, decentralized systems of local government. To directly test for the possible impact of this public service supply phenomena, the public expenditure model is estimated with administrative outlays as the dependent variable.

While increased responsiveness by public agencies may lead to gains in taxpayer satisfaction, and economic efficiencies with a decentralized local government structure characterized by many small units, such phenomena are not directly studied with the expenditure-demand approach. However, a fragmented governmental system could cause higher expenditures because: (1) citizens with intense preferences have an undue influence in setting service and expenditure levels, and (2) transaction and information costs facing voters in a decentralized system are higher. Structural illusion causing confusion and reduced political accountability as well as encumbering voter's perception of tax prices, may free a fragmented government structure to incur expenditures beyond the demands of residents.

There are some deeper issues involved. While one group of residents may wish only selected services, it is to their advantage to cause others to pay a share of the cost. When the group demanding and benefiting from the service is wealthier than the average taxpayer financing the service, there can be negative income transfers. An example might be an improved library system or airport facility where a special district is formed to provide the services. If the district covers the entire community and draws its tax revenues from throughout the municipality, but the incidence of service benefit favors the wealthy who make most extensive use of libraries and airports, then poorer taxpayers are disproportionally financing public services for the wealthy. There has been evidence suggesting that this occurs with locally financed airports, public boat marinas, libraries, nature preserves, tennis courts and golf courses, zoos, and park and recreation programs.[12] Unfortunately, available data do not permit a detailed examination of these possibilities, statewide.

Empirical Analysis

The empirical results of estimating the reduced form public expenditure model using data for 101 Illinois counties are presented in Table 5.9. Total local government per capita expenditure, as reported in the 1977 Census of Governments, is the dependent variable. Cook County was excluded because of its size and complexity.

Table 5.9. Determinants of Local Public Expenditures[a]

Variable	Model A	Model B	Model C
Average Earnings	0.0605*	0.0610*	0.0607*
	(16.91)	(17.15)	(17.37)
Per Capita Income	0.0474*	0.0481*	0.0459*
	(2.59)	(2.64)	(2.51)
Employees Per 10,000 Pop.	1.6640*	1.6876*	1.6830*
	(13.16)	(13.38)	(13.59)
Intergovernmental Revenues	0.3804*	0.3416*	0.3394*
	(2.95)	(2.66)	(2.71)
Population	−0.0002	−0.0002*	−0.0002
	(1.59)	(2.05)	(1.57)
Tax Price	−16.8921	−13.8127	−8.1335
	(0.90)	(0.76)	(0.44)
Taxing Units Per 10,000	0.0048	—	—
	(0.01)		
Special Districts Per 10,000	—	−1.6764	—
		(1.18)	
Structure Index	—	—	−325.1890**
			(1.77)
Constant	−845.91	−839.73	−750.85
R² Adjusted	.81	.81	.82
F-Ratio	62.32	63.45	64.86
S.E.E.	68.34	67.83	67.22
N	101	101	101

[a] Absolute value of t statistics are in parentheses. Dependent variable is per capita aggregate expenditures for the county.
* Significant at the 5% level
** Significant at the 10% level

For the most part, the findings of the analysis are as expected. Income and tax price are positively and negatively associated with per capita expenditures, respectively. Governments in counties with a per capita income $100 above average spend about $5 per capita more for public services. The coefficient for tax price, however, is not statistically different from zero. This likely reflects the crudeness of the measure for county level analyses. Intergovernmental revenue causes increases in local government spending although it does not stimulate more spending from local revenue sources. An additional dollar in per capita aid was associated, on average, with an increase of thirty-four to thirty-eight cents per capita in local spending. This suggests sixty-two to sixty-six cents were provided in local tax or debt relief for every one dollar in aid. Intergovernmental revenue clearly finds its way into additional expenditures, but not dollar for dollar.

Population size usually is not statistically associated with higher public expenditures. A significant positive association was found between full-time equivalent employees per 10,000 residents and level of public spending. On average, an additional full-time employee per 10,000 residents adds approximately $1.67 per person to the aggregate expenditures in the county. Similarly, an additional $100 in average public earnings by government workers causes expenditures to rise, on average, $6 per capita. Because average earnings are computed at the county level, wide intracounty variations in pay scales among jurisdictions causing large differences in expenditures are not captured in the intercounty analysis.

The coefficients for taxing units per 10,000 residents and special districts per 10,000 residents are not statistically different from zero. Thus, as measured by these characteristics, local government structure is unrelated to per capita aggregate spending levels in Illinois counties. The structure index, which is the more inclusive measure of political organization is, however, significantly related to outlays at the ten percent probability level. The index value approaches one when the number of governments in a county declines. The negative sign on the coefficient for the index therefore signifies that fragmented governance systems are associated with higher levels of per capita aggregate spending. This indicates that in Illinois, the efficiencies that may be available from a more centralized local political structure and the possible expenditure enhancing political responsiveness and control in fragmented systems outweigh and dominate the higher spending monopoly behavior potential with fewer competing jurisdictions. This finding warrants more attention.

This result does not support the demand driven spillover hypothesis where more resources would be expected to be allocated to public services if jurisdictions are spatially more centralized, causing greater fiscal equivalence between service costs and benefits. A positive relationship between expenditures and the structure index would support this hypothesis. This, however, is not the case.

The analyses in Table 5.9 are not unanimous regarding the impact of local government structure on expenditure behavior. They do suggest, however, that the richness of alternate governmental organizations are better captured by more complex, comprehensive measures of structure. In this case, the mean value of the structure index is .2783 with a standard deviation of .0381. A reduction in local government fragmentation increasing the index by one standard deviation from its mean is associated with a reduction in aggregate outlays of $12.39 per capita on average.

The variables account for approximately eighty-one percent of the variation in public spending. To investigate further the implications of governmental structure on local fiscal behavior, the public expenditure model is estimated for administrative control outlays and expenditures for four major service categories.

Administration. Because of the complementarities among many local services in their provision, a larger number of governments providing services to a community, particularly when special districts are involved, may cause higher spending because of required duplication and the discontinuities of many inputs. For example, one dispatcher may effectively handle police, fire, and emergency medical calls. Without cooperation when these services are provided by separate governments, more than one dispatcher is employed, thereby increasing outlays.

The regression estimates, with per capita financial control expenditures as the dependent variable, are provided in Table 5.10. These results are consistent with those shown above. Intergovernmental revenue increases of $100 per capita, on average, cause slightly more than a $1 per capita increase in financial control expenditures countywide. This reflects the accounting and reporting requirements commonly required of recipient governments. Of course, this increase is spread over many governments and does not reflect the actual variation in both aid dollars and increased control outlays among governments within a county.

Income is an important determinant of control outlays. Counties with $100 more income per capita, on average, spent sixteen to seventeen cents more on these functions. The inclusion of employees scaled to population to account for personnel related control expenditures resulted in a coefficient not significantly different from zero. This result may mask major intracounty variations among taxing units and may be a result of data aggregation.

Of particular interest is the impact of taxing unit organizational struc-

Table 5.10. Determinants of Financial Control Expenditures[a]

Variable	Model A	Model B
Intergovernmental Revenues	0.0114*	0.0104*
	(2.19)	(2.01)
Per Capita Income	0.0017*	0.0016*
	(2.48)	(2.31)
Percent Rural	0.032	0.056*
	(1.47)	(3.14)
Employees Per 10,000 Pop.	0.0030	0.0035
	(0.58)	(0.68)
Taxing Units Per 10,000 Pop.	0.1211*	—
	(3.15)	
Special Districts Per 10,000 Pop.	—	0.2025*
		(2.98)
Constant	− 8.39	− 7.71
R^5 Adjusted	.25	.24
F-Ratio	7.66	7.39
S.E.E.	3.13	3.15
N	101	101

[a] Absolute value of t statistics are in parentheses. Dependent variable is per capita aggregate expenditures for financial control.
* Significant at the 5 percent level
** Significant at the 10 percent level

ture on financial control spending. A significant positive relationship is reported between number of taxing units as well as number of special districts and aggregate outlays for these purposes. An additional taxing unit per 1000 residents was associated with $1.21 per capita higher financial control spending while an additional special district per 1000 residents was related to $2.03 more in per capita control expenditures. These results reinforce the notion that fragmented political systems fail to capture possible efficiencies associated with complementarities in the provision of public services.

While the analysis in Table 5.10 is useful in understanding the role of local governance organization in outlays for administrative functions, only twenty-five percent of the variation in these expenditures were associated with the variation in the determinants. Many other factors not considered here play a major role in determining outlays for financial control in a locality.

Parks and Libraries. Park districts are among the most numerous special districts in Illinois representing seventy percent of total local outlays for parks and recreation. Library districts, on the other hand, provide very specialized services and have been one of the faster grow-

Table 5.11. Determinants of Local Library and Park-Recreation Expenditures[a]

Variable	Library Services		Park-Recreation
	Model A	Model B	
Average Earnings	0.00003	0.00003	0.0001
	(0.28)	(0.23)	(0.23)
Per Capita Income	0.0023*	0.0022*	0.0058*
	(3.11)	(3.44)	(3.03)
Percent Rural	−0.0683*	−0.0680*	−0.1053**
	(3.00)	(3.03)	(1.82)
Library Employees Per 10,000 Pop.	−0.2019	−	−
	(0.43)		
Park Employees Per 10,000 Pop.	−	−	0.6869*
			(2.01)
Tax-Price	−2.1002	−2.0225	−5.6064
	(1.33)	(1.31)	(1.59)
Library Districts Per 10,000 Pop.	4.1682*	4.1816*	−
	(2.34)	(2.39)	
Park Districts Per 10,000 Pop.	−	−	3.1484
			(1.55)
Constant	−5.31	−5.07	−13.67
R² Adjusted	.67	.68	.45
F-Ratio	11.61	14.32	10.14
S.E.E.	1.78	1.76	7.41
N	33	33	67

[a] Absolute value of t statistics are in parentheses. Dependent variables are per capita aggregate expenditures for library and parks and recreation services, respectively.
* Significant at the 5 percent level
** Significant at the 10 percent level

ing types of single-purpose local governments. The determinants of park and recreation spending and library spending are shown in Table 5.11. In these models percent of population that is rural was included to adjust for preference variation among Illinois localities for park and library services, respectively. In both cases, only counties containing these types of governments and reporting expenditures for these services were studied (thirty-three counties for libraries and sixty-seven counties for park expenditures).

Library and park districts may both reflect demands by residents for more and better services, as well as the interest to not compete for revenues within a general-purpose government's budget. There may also be requirements to bypass tax limits in order to raise additional resources if service demands are to be met. On the other hand, the creation of a district may effectively match the beneficiaries of services and taxpayers.

This may be the case, for example, when demanders of the service reside outside municipal boundaries.

The importance of income in explaining variations in both park and library services is evident from the results in Table 5.11. Counties with per capita income $100 above the mean spent an additional twenty-two cents per capita on libraries in 1977 and fifty-eight cents more per capita on park and recreation services. This is consistent with the heavier use of these services by higher income families.[13]

Average public employee earnings were not significantly associated with per capita outlays for either library services or park and recreation services. This suggests that employment in these services may not reflect the mean county public wage scale because of the part time nature of many jobs in these agencies. Rural areas spent less on libraries and parks, indicated by the significant negative coefficient for percent rural population. For each ten percent increase in rural population, on average, sixty-eight cents less was spent on library services, and $1.05 less per capita were spent on park services. Park employment increased outlays, on average, $6.87 per capita for every additional employee per 1000 residents over the range of employment in Illinois localities. Library employment, however, was not statistically related to per capita spending for libraries.

The tax price variable had a negative coefficient significantly different from zero at the eleven percent level of confidence for park services. Higher tax prices were associated with lower park outlays. The coefficient for tax price was negative but significant at only the nineteen percent confidence level for library services. The small sample size and the lack of refinement in the measurement of tax prices for regional analysis likely prohibit a stronger relationship between tax price and spending on libraries and parks.

The results in Table 5.11 indicate higher per capita expenditures for libraries with more library districts. While park districts per 10,000 people had a positive coefficient, it was significant at only the twelve percent confidence level. An additional library district per 10,000 people was associated, on average, with approximately an additional $4.16 per capita spent for library services. If park employees are a proxy for recreation services, then the high outlays associated with more park districts suggests jurisdictional fragmentation in park services may cause services to be more costly. More sophisticated data and analyses are needed to confirm this hypothesis. Higher outlays with relatively more library districts may simply mean more and better library services.

Considered together, the determinants in Table 5.11 accounted for approximately fifty percent of the variation in park outlays among Illinois counties and two-thirds of the variation in library expenditures.

The ability to generalize the findings of the library service analysis may be reduced by the relatively small sample of counties studied.

Roads and Streets. Local roads and streets are provided by municipalities, counties, and road districts or townships. In Illinois, about fifty-five percent of the total public road mileage is the responsibility of townships. Much of this mileage has low traffic volumes and serves farms and rural residents.

To estimate the effects of governmental structure on aggregate expenditures for local roads and streets, the reduced form public expenditure model was derived using per capita local highway expenditures as the dependent variable. The results are shown in Table 5.12.

Counties with higher incomes spent more on local roads and streets. On average, counties $100 per capita above the average level of income spent about seventy cents more per capita for highway services. The coefficient for the tax price was negative and significantly different from zero in two of the three equations in Table 5.12. The higher the ratio of the assessment on the median-valued house in the county to total county assessment, the less the spending on local roads and streets.

The percentage of people residing in rural areas was positively

Table 5.12. Determinants of Local Road and Street Expenditures[a]

Variable	Model A	Model B	Model C
Average Earnings	0.0006	0.0006	0.0001
	(0.87)	(0.89)	(0.20)
Per Capita Income	0.0072*	0.0063*	0.0094*
	(2.46)	(2.13)	(3.42)
Tax Price	−9.1062*	−4.5834	−9.5707*
	(2.27)	(1.28)	(2.35)
Percent Rural	0.2644*	−	0.1890**
	(2.32)		(1.73)
Governmental Units Per 10,000 Pop.	2.6827*	3.2470*	2.7240*
	(7.61)	(12.41)	(7.61)
Highway Employment Per 10,000 Pop.	−0.5961*	−0.3727	−
	(2.03)	(1.31)	
Constant	4.96	12.79	04.08
R^2 Adjusted	.62	.60	.61
F-Ratio	28.37	31.51	32.17
S.E.E.	13.55	13.86	13.77
N	101	101	101

[a] Absolute value of t statistics are in parentheses. Dependent variable is per capita aggregate expenditures for roads and highways.
* Significant at the 5 percent level
** Significant at the 10 percent level

associated with per capita road and highway expenditures at the ten percent level. The per capita outlays to maintain road systems are higher in low density rural counties where greater distances have to be traveled.

The negative significant coefficient for local highway employment is unexpected. However, a closer look at the interaction among the explanatory variables raises doubt about the validity of this finding. The correlation coefficient for highway employment and percent rural population is .6124. Excluding percent rural population from the estimate (Model B) reduces the size of the coefficient for highway employment by forty percent. The coefficient is no longer statistically different from zero. Model C replaced local highway employment with percent rural population.

The relationship between the measure of government organization for highway services and associated aggregated budget outlays is important. The structural measure is the total road and street providing units of government (the sum of townships, municipalities and the county) per population of 10,000. As evidenced by the positive significant coefficient for street units per 10,000 residents, a more fragmented system for providing local highway services was associated with higher per capita spending on average. Expenditures increased about $2.70 per capita for each additional unit per 10,000 people. In general then, Illinois township counties spend more per capita for road and street services than nontownship counties because of political organization. The higher outlays may be associated with administrative and control inefficiencies that possibly characterize a more decentralized, fragmented local government structure for highway services. Service quality also may be greater with fragmented systems as preferences for services are more accurately articulated. The verification of these implications is beyond the scope of this analysis.

The determinants of local road and street expenditures performed well with approximately sixty percent of the expenditure variations for local highways associated with the determinants. The coefficients for the structural variables are reasonably stable across the alternate specifications. Possible multicollinearity problems restrict the interpretation of the analysis to some degree, suggesting caution in policymaking.

Education. The final service selected for expenditure analysis is of particular significance. Educational outlays represent a substantial proportion of local government expenditures and are supported by about sixty percent of all Illinois property taxes collected.[14] The public expenditure model estimated for education is presented in Table 5.13.[15]

A significant determinant of per capita spending on local schools is the school aid received from state and federal sources. State involvement

Table 5.13. Determinants of Public School Expenditures[a]

Variable	Model A	Model B
Average Earnings	0.0028	0.0028
	(1.23)	(1.24)
School Aid	0.4718*	0.4596*
	(4.14)	(3.98)
Tax Price	−19.9253**	−19.0847
	(1.66)	(1.57)
Per Capita Income	0.0420*	0.0489*
	(3.90)	(3.68)
Percent School Aged	13.6702*	14.5684*
	(7.08)	(7.83)
Teachers Per 1,000 Pupils	2.5290*	2.5389*
	(4.80)	(4.77)
School Districts Per 10,000 Residents	7.0385*	−
	(2.04)	
School Districts Per 1,000 Pupils	−	10.0520
		(1.47)
Constant	−413.89	−421.56
R^2 Adjusted	.60	.59
F-Ratio	21.45	20.72
S.E.E.	46.42	46.91
N	98	98

[a] Absolute value of t statistics are in parentheses. Dependent variable is per capita aggregate expenditures for education.
* Significant at the 5 percent level
** Significant at the 10 percent level

in local school finance has increased in the post World War II era as judicial and legislative actions have sought to provide all children equal access to educational opportunities. Most state aid programs are redistributional and are aimed at weakening or severing the link between school district property wealth and school expenditures.[16] For every dollar increase in per capita school aid, on average, school outlays across Illinois counties increased about sixty-seven cents per capita.[17]

Average public sector earnings were positively, but not significantly associated with per capita school spending. Communities with higher income levels budgeted larger educational outlays. An additional $100 in per capita income was associated with a more than $4.00 increase in per capita school expenditures. Expectedly, the greater the proportion of population in the school years, the larger the expenditures for education. On average, a one percent increase in the relative number of school children was associated with about a $14.00 increase in outlays per resident.

The negative and significant (at the ten percent level) coefficient for tax price signifies an inverse relationship between the price of education faced by local taxpayers and the level of expenditures. More teachers per 1000 pupils increased school spending. On average, for every additional teacher per 1000 students, outlays increased by $2.50 per citizen.

Also important is the effect of school system organization on local education budget outcomes. The two alternative measures of structural variation used to analyze these effects are number of school districts per population of 10,000 and number of school districts per 1000 pupils. The findings show a positive relationship between both the number of districts scaled to population and pupils, only the former having a coefficient significantly different from zero at or above the ten percent level of probability. The pupil scaled measure of structure was statistically significant at only the fourteen percent confidence level.[18]

Although not as strong, these results provide evidence that larger per capita expenditures are associated with a more fragmented system of local school political organization. More districts are associated with higher average per capita school spending. Specifically, an additional district per 10,000 population was associated, on average, with an increase of $7.04 per capita. Administrative and control inefficiencies could explain this finding. Furthermore, a fragmented political structure may more accurately reflect the preferences of citizens so higher expenditures are tolerated. Unfortunately, available data do not allow a distinction to be drawn between these possible explanations.

As a group, the independent factors were associated with about sixty percent of the variation among Illinois counties in per capita spending on education. A number of other factors not captured in this analysis contribute to the determination of educational expenditures. These include, but are not limited to, the qualitative dimensions of primary and secondary education which are difficult to quantify.

SUMMARY

Local government expenditures were examined in detail in this chapter with a focus, first, on describing expenditures by type of government and function and, second, on analyzing the effects of differences in local government structure on fiscal behavior in the aggregate and for several individual services. One finds, for example, that school districts represent forty-four percent of all outlays by Illinois local governments. Park districts are responsible for seventy percent of park and recreation expenditures. Perhaps the most significant finding of the descriptive comparisons is the major differences in the responsibilities for providing particular services. For example, special districts are very important in providing parks and sewerage. Cities assume major responsibility for police protection. The responsibilities for services closely follow population, and police or fire protection needs are probably best served by municipal departments.

Analyzing the effects of local government structure on expenditures indicates that political structure is an important consideration in local public finance. The challenge in empirical analyses is to design a quantitative measure of governmental structure. The analysis of aggregate expenditures, using a reduced form public expenditure model, did not yield unanimous conclusions about structure and fiscal behavior but provided a strong suggestion that counties with more fragmented political organizations are associated, on average, with higher per capita spending. This finding was generally reinforced in the separate analyses of administrative financial control spending and local government expenditures for libraries, local roads and streets, and education. For each service, politically fragmented local governance systems were associated with higher per capita spending after adjustments for income, tax prices, and other independent factors had been considered. For example, each additional school district per 10,000 residents causes spending increases of $7.40 per capita. For roads and streets the comparable amount is about $3.00 per capita. The study of administrative financial control suggests one reason for these findings. Here more units per citizen caused spending for these functions to increase. These findings indicate that efficiencies available from more centralized governance systems may be more important in setting spending levels than possible expenditure-increasing monopoly behavior of officials and bureaucrats in larger, more centralized organizations. This is but one possible explanation for these results. The evidence, however, is consistent in its support of lower spending levels by larger and more centralized systems of local governments in Illinois.

The primary function of local governments, of course, is to provide services to residents. Expenditures on services, while indicating a level of activity, can be viewed as measures of inputs rather than as a consequence of local fiscal behavior. More direct measures of local public services are the perceptions of residents and their satisfaction with the performance of local government. The relationship between citizen perceptions of local services and other measures of local sector output and local government organization are examined in the following chapter.

NOTES

1. See Roy Bahl, Marvin Johnson and Michael Wasylenko, "State and Local Government Expenditure Determinants: The Traditional View and a New Approach," in Roy Bahl, Jesse Burkhead and Bernard Jump, Jr., eds. *Public Employment and State and*

Local Government Finance (Cambridge, MA: Ballinger Publishing Co., 1980), pp. 65–119 and J. E. Fredland, *Determinants of State and Local Government Expenditures: An Annotated Bibliography* (Washington, D.C.: The Urban Institute, 1974).

2. See Thomas J. Dilorenzo, "Tax Elasticity and the Growth of Local Public Expenditure," *Public Finance Quarterly*, Vol. 10, No. 3, July 1982, pp. 385–391.

3. See, for example, William L. Manz and Fredrick J. Hitzhusen, "Costs and Financing of Volunteer Emergency Ambulance Services in Rural Ohio," RB 1110 (Wooster, OH: Ohio Agricultural Research and Development Center, April 1979). Also see Thomas F. Stinson, "Household Allocation of Voluntary Labor in the Production of Fire Protection: Minnesota Evidence," *American Journal of Agricultural Economics*, Vol. 60, No. 2, May 1978, pp. 331–337, and Thomas F. Stinson and Jerome M. Stam, "Toward an Economic Model of Volunteerism: The Case of Participation in Local Government," *Journal of Voluntary Action Research*, Vol. 5, No. 1, Winter 1976, pp. 52–69.

4. Counties are allocated motor fuel tax funds based on number of vehicles registered, road districts (townships) receive allocations based on miles of roads maintained, and municipalities receive funds based on population. The Illinois motor fuel tax rates and license fees were increased in 1983 to increase funds available for transportation.

5. Kalman Goldberg and Robert C. Scott, "Fiscal Incidence: A Revision of Benefits Incidence Estimates," *Journal of Regional Science*, Vol. 21, No. 2, May 1981, pp. 203–221.

6. For example see Thomas J. Dilorenzo, "Economic Competition and Political Competition: An Empirical Note," *Public Choice*, Vol. 40, No. 2, 1983, pp. 203–209.

7. Efforts to estimate the reduced form public expenditure model for fire protection were unsuccessful. Extensive use of volunteers in providing fire protection, particularly in smaller towns and rural areas, could explain our lack of success. One study, for example, reported 1976 fire protection outlays of $890,000 in Winona, Minnesota, a community of 20,000. In Bare Lake, Minnesota, also a community of 20,000, fire protection expenditures in 1976 were $165,000. The Bare Lake Fire Department was volunteer while the Winona Fire Department was a full-time professional department. See Thomas F. Stinson, "Volunteers: Part of Rural America's Lifehood," *Rural Development Perspectives*, USDA, Washington, D.C., November 1978, pp. 18–19. Also see Stinson, 1978.

8. The interested reader should refer to Thomas Romer and Howard Rosenthal, "The Elusive Median Voter," *Journal of Public Economics*, Vol. 12, No. 2, October 1979, pp. 143–170 and Werner W. Pommerehne, "Institutional Approaches to Public Expenditure: Empirical Evidence from Swiss Municipalities," *Journal of Public Economics*, Vol. 9, No. 2, April 1978, pp. 255–280 for conceptual and empirical treatments of the expenditure-demand approach to local fiscal behavior in a median voter framework.

9. See Goldberg and Scott, 1981, for evidence on the incidence of local public service benefits by family income class.

10. See George J. Stigler, *The Organization of Industry*, (Homewood, IL: Richard D. Irwin, Inc., 1968), Chapter 4, pp. 29–38. This index is expressed as:

$$\frac{1}{\dfrac{1}{S_1} S_1 \ \dfrac{1}{S_2} S_2 \ \dfrac{1}{S_3} S_3 \ \cdots \ \dfrac{1}{S_n} S_n}$$

where S_i represents the relative share of the ith organization. Due to data constraints the index was constructed using the relative number of five major types of local governments within each county area. Dilorenzo, 1983, constructed a concentration ratio similar to the four-firm ratio of industrial organization theory. The analysis was also conducted with government structure measured by a Herfindahl Index. These results were comparable to those reported here. See Stigler, pp. 30–33, for a description of the Herfindahl Index.

11. See Charles Tiebout, "A Pure Theory of Local Expenditures," *Journal of Political Economy*, Vol. 64, No. 5, October 1956, pp. 416–424. For a theoretical critique of "voting with one's feet" see Joseph E. Stiglitz, "The Theory of Local Public Goods" in M. Feldstein and R. Inman, eds. *The Economics of Public Services*, (London: The McMillan Press, Inc., 1977), pp. 274–333. For a review of empirical studies of this phenomena, as evidenced in migration patterns, see Richard J. Cebula, "Voting With One's Feet: A Critique of the Evidence," *Regional Science and Urban Economics*, Vol. 10, No. 1, March 1980, pp. 91–107.

For a property value maximization approach to local public sector analysis, see Jan K. Bruckner, "A Test For Allocative Efficiency in the Local Public Sector," *Journal of Public Economics*, Vol. 19, No. 3, December 1982, pp. 311–331.

12. Goldberg and Scott, 1981.

13. Goldberg and Scott, 1981.

14. David L. Chicoine and Norman Walzer, "Property Taxes and Public Education," *Illinois Research*, Vol. 23, No. 1, Winter 1981, pp. 12–13.

15. For earlier studies on the determinants of educational spending see, as examples, Walter W. McMahon, "An Economic Analysis of Major Determinants of Expenditures on Public Education," *Review of Economics and Statistics*, Vol. 52, No. 31, August 1970, pp. 244–338, and Arthur T. Denzau, "An Empirical Survey of Studies on Public School Spending," *National Tax Journal*, Vol. 28, No. 2, June 1975, pp. 241–249. A good critique of these studies for policy purposes is provided in G. Alan Hickrod, "Local Demand for Education - A Critique of School Finance and Economics Research Circa 1959-1969," *Review of Educational Research*, Vol. 41, No. 1, Winter 1971, pp. 35–49. More recent reviews are presented in William F. Fox, "Relationships Between Size of Schools and School Districts and the Cost of Education," 1621, Economic Research Service (Washington, D.C.: U.S. Department of Agriculture, 1980) and Brady J. Deaton and Kevin T. McNamara, *Education in a Changing Environment: Impact of Population and Economic Change on the Demand and Cost of Public Education in Rural America*, SRDC Series No. 17 (Mississippi State, MS: Southern Rural Development Center, 1984).

16. See Terry G. Geske, "Educational Finance Policy: A Search for Complementarities," *Education Evaluation and Policy Analysis*, Vol. 5, No. 1, Spring 1983, pp. 83–96, Walter W. McMahon and Terry G. Geske, eds. *Financing Education*, (Urbana, IL: University of Illinois Press, 1982), and Roe L. Johns, Irving J. Goffman, Kern Alexander and Dewey H. Stollar, eds. *Economic Factors Affecting the Financing of Education* (Gainesville, FL: National Educational Finance Project, 1970).

17. For analyses of the impact of commercial/industrial property on local school spending see Helen F. Ladd, "Local Educational Expenditures, Fiscal Capacity and the Composition of the Property Tax Base," *National Tax Journal*, Vol. 28, No. 2, June 1975, pp. 145–158, Michael C. Lovell, "Spending for Education: The Exercise of Public Choice," *Review of Economics and Statistics*, Vol. 60, No. 4, November 1978, pp. 487–495, and F. Howard Nelson, "A Note on the Effects of Commercial and Industrial Property in School Spending Decisions," *National Tax Journal*, Vol. 37, No. 1, March 1984, pp. 121–126.

18. This result is consistent with the one study of structure and school spending found in the literature. See Barbara S. Burnell, "The Effects of School District Structure on Education Spending," paper presented at the Mid-Continent Regional Science Association Meetings, Chicago, IL, May 5, 1984.

Chapter 6

Political Organization and Public Service Performance

Accurately measuring quantity and quality of local public services is a perplexing problem in an analysis of local government behavior. To assess the comparative productivity of alternatively organized local governance systems, inputs must be related to service outputs in light of factors such as differences in institutional arrangements that may affect productivity. However, the intrinsic nature of these services, and the reason they are in the public sector, limits the direct measurement of local government output. Routine transactions between providers and taxpayer/consumers about levels of production, preferences of residents for more or different mixes of services, or the value citizens place on local public sector output cannot be observed. The difficulties in measuring the output of local governments are intertwined with an analysis of the extent to which governmental structure affects local government performance.

Expenditures have been used as proxies for local government output. A frequent assumption is that expenditures are the primary determinants of performance—the greater the expenditures, the better the service. The amount spent by a government, however, does not always correspond directly with benefits perceived by constituents. Expenditures should consequently represent indicators of effort or measures of input.

The focus of this chapter is to isolate the effects of differences in organizational structure on local government behavior. Several measures of local output, including objective and subjective estimates of performance, are introduced. A review of service measures is presented first, followed by the findings of prior research on the importance of governmental structure on local public sector performance. Performance, here, is indicated by nonexpenditure service measures. Using evidence from Illinois localities, empirical analyses on the relation between political organization and subjective or objective estimates of performance are presented. As a prelude to subsequent analyses, the decisionmaking environment for local public services is described using number of local public officials involved in deciding on service levels and expenditures.

PUBLIC OFFICIALS AND GOVERNMENTAL STRUCTURE

Local public services are determined by elected officials in response to constituency demands for services within constitutional and legislative constraints. While the number of governments in a county or serving a community offers one indication of the complexity of local collective choices determining public sector output and performance, additional insight is gained by examining the number of officials. Particularly important is the fact that in some special districts only one or two policymakers and a small budget are involved while other districts have a professional staff and large budget outlays. In addition, some governments rely substantially on volunteerism to provide services. Some services involve multiple governments with possible duplication of effort.

In a complex local government system such as in Illinois, a detailed description of all officials and arrangements for making decisions would be voluminous. The Bureau of the Census reported 39,920 elected Illinois local government officials in 1977. Of course, these officials are not evenly distributed throughout the state. There were 7815 local officials in the six county Chicago metropolitan area or about 1303 officials per county. The ninety-six downstate counties had an average of 334 local officials per county.

Adjustments for population change the degree of political representation. Table 6.1 presents the average number of citizens per elected official in the 102 Illinois counties grouped by population. Statewide, there was one official for each 281 residents. Of course, in addition to elected officials, there are countless advisory boards and administrative agencies involved in policy development.

In general, there are more citizens per local official in the more populous urban counties in Illinois than in the rural counties of the state. In the eight counties with populations of at least 200,000, there were

Table 6.1. Degree of Political Representation by Size of County

County Population Size	Number of Counties	Mean Population Per Elected Official
200,000 and over	8	570
100,000 to 199,999	8	197
50,000 to 99,999	11	150
25,000 to 49,999	23	100
10,000 to 24,999	38	79
less than 10,000	14	60
Illinois	102	281

Source: U.S. Bureau of the Census, *Popularly Elected Officials*, (Washington, D.C.: Government Printing Office, 1979).

570 citizens for each elected official. In the small population sizes, the number of officials increases relative to population causing a decline in citizens per official. For the fourteen Illinois counties with fewer than 10,000 people there were sixty residents for each elected official.

Measured by elected representatives per capita, the degree of political representation is 9.5 times as great in the fourteen least populous Illinois counties compared with the eight most populous counties. By contrast, the degree of representation in the smaller counties is only 3.3 times greater than the local representation in counties with populations of 100,000 to 199,999. If political representation is linked with responsiveness and provision of local services in line with citizens' preferences, the local public sector in smaller communities, with relatively more units of government and officials, may be preferred. A fragmented structure with more elected positions may afford greater citizen input into local decisions.

Overlapping governments and many local officials may seem to contribute to coordination problems and unnecessarily expensive local government. Local boards and advisory groups, however, often receive no compensation and may not even be fully reimbursed for expenses.

Broad citizen governance may encourage specialization. Through special districts and fragmentation, residents become involved in activities offering a special service and/or in which they possess special knowledge and skills. Fragmentation may ultimately lead to better or more specialized services. Expenditures could be higher in these cases. Serving on a governing agency, however, also allows persons with a special interest and strong service preferences an opportunity to increase service levels and associated expenditures above the level preferred by the average taxpayer.

The numbers of elected local officials, by type of government, are shown

Table 6.2. Elected Local Officials in Illinois by Type of Government

Local Government	Number of Officials	Number of Governments	Officials Per Government
Total	39,920	6,620	6.03
Counties	2,933	102	28.75
Municipalities	12,014	1,274	9.43
Townships	12,463	1,436	8.68
School Districts	7,316	1,063	6.88
Special Districts	5,194	2,745	1.89

Source: U.S. Bureau of the Census, *Popularly Elected Officials*, (Washington, D.C.: Government Printing Office, 1979).

in Table 6.2. The three general-purpose governments—counties, municipalities, and townships—represent 27,410 elected officials (68.7 percent). School districts had 7316 elected officials. Another 5194 were responsible for administering special districts. These comparisons are not adjusted for time worked. Township boards, for example, do not meet as often as a city council or county board.

The complexity of local decisionmaking is reflected, in part, in the number of elected officials associated with each type of local government. The average local government in Illinois had 6.03 elected officials. The largest, per government, is county government with an average of 28.75 and the least is special districts averaging 1.89 elected officials per special district.

The 6.88 officials for school districts reflect the common seven member school boards. Selected types of schools have five member boards. Of course, only elected officials are reflected in these ratios. Appointed officials, advisory boards, and public employees also vary by government type.

MEASURING LOCAL SERVICES

Analyses of local government services have relied on per capita expenditures as a measure of public services produced. The amount of services produced, however, is the result of a process which translates inputs (outlays for labor, materials, etc.) into the product desired.[1] The benefits received by residents of a jurisdiction, measured with citizen surveys or by objective measures, are not always related to expenditure data. For example, pupil performance on standardized test scores and dropout rates, as measures of school output, have been found not to be related to spending for education. These findings suggest that expenditures on local education may not be an accurate indicator of educational services produced.[2]

Local Public Output

Identifying inappropriate measures of local government output or performance is an easier task than crisply defining local public services. The question is whether value lies in a service itself as captured by the intrinsic, quantifiable characteristics of a service, or in the satisfaction produced by the service and perceived by citizen taxpayers. Is the best performance measure of a service its intrinsic properties or people's perceptions of them? The measurement and relationship between public service inputs measured by public spending and performance is a critical area of considerable political importance in times of major budgetary readjustments.[3]

Objective Measures. Output measures either draw on the objective characteristics of a service or estimates of subjective performance. Objective measures reflect quantifiable service outputs while subjective measures provide citizens' qualitative evaluations of services. For example, library books per capita would be considered an objective measure of library service, while citizens' opinions about the adequacy of local libraries represent a subjective performance measure.[4] Subjective indicators of service satisfaction are more consumer oriented measures of local government services.

In a review of the literature on measures of local public services, Fisk and Winnie concluded:

1. most large governments (cities above 50,000 population and counties above 100,000) collect some data on objective performance criteria;
2. few jurisdictions consistently evaluate performance using subjective survey techniques; and
3. the measurement type varies dramatically with service and program area but with few comparative analyses across services and jurisdictions. Reasonably good objective performance measures exist for engineering, capital intensive services (such as water and sewage facilities or solid waste disposal). For other services, objective measures are poor or entirely lacking.[5]

Survey Measures. Policymakers and researchers are often uneasy about relying on data collected from a survey of residents' perceptions. Citizens are viewed as uninformed and unable to give reliable perceptions, opinions, and evaluations of local government services. However, objective measures gathered from agency records or census material provide limited information on the level of satisfaction perceived by taxpayer consumers. There is, however, some evidence that subjective and objective measures of performance are closely related. Close relationships between objective measures and perceived quality measures have been reported for road repair, street lighting, parks, and law enforcement.[6] Residents seem to be fairly accurate in their perception of some services. Citizen perceptions collected through surveys may serve well as performance measures of local government activities for those areas where no or limited objective measures of output exist.

Public employment is an alternative to the expenditures proxy for local government output. Because the public sector is labor-intensive and heavily service-oriented, public employment may be roughly proportional to public output and could be a proxy for output in analyses of community preferences for collectively provided services.[7] As a basis for policy, the employment approach to measuring local government output may yield more information than the traditional expenditure-demand approach because it disaggregates spending into wage rates and employment. For example, the positive effect of income on expenditures can be more easily separated into higher employment or higher wages in wealthier localities.

Analytical Framework

In assessing the extent to which structure affects the performance of local governments, the relationships outlined in Figure 6.1 serve as a

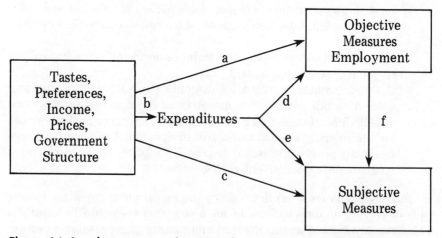

Figure 6.1. Local government inputs and outputs: A causal framework.

guide.[8] Expenditures are seen as indicators of effort or inputs. Objective measures of performance and employment as well as subjective measures are related to community taste and preference factors, income levels, tax prices and most importantly, local government structure. The correlation of objective measures, subjective measures, and expenditures is an empirical question. Within this framework, the importance of local government organizational arrangements for performance, measured objectively and subjectively, can be studied. The available empirical evidence employing this framework is reviewed in the next section.

LITERATURE ON LOCAL GOVERNMENT STRUCTURE AND PERFORMANCE

Several empirical studies have followed the path of inquiry identified as c in Figure 6.1 using case studies. Focusing on government structure, comparable localities are examined to control for taste, preference, and income differences. These analyses are summarized in Table 6.3.

A study by Christenson and Taylor is not included in Table 6.3 because structural arrangements were not explicitly included in their analysis. However, the authors investigated:

1. the impact of taste, preference and income factors on expenditures, objective performance measures, and perceptions of service quality;
2. the effect of expenditures on objective measures and subjective perceptions; and
3. the relationship between objective and subjective performance measures.

They concluded that input measures such as per capita expenditures should not be equated with output due to lack of a strong relationship with either objective or subjective output measures. Education, law enforcement, medical services, libraries, and parks were studied in North Carolina counties. Objective measures for only parks and law enforcement were strongly related to subjective measures of perceived service performance collected through a citizen survey.[9]

Studies of local government structure and service performance have commonly involved a single service and considered only metropolitan areas. A most-similar systems design is used in case studies. Following this methodology, McArthur surveyed the urban fringe residents of the Nashville, Tennessee area after a metropolitan city-county consolidation was approved by voters.[10] A main finding of the survey was that 58.1

Table 6.3. Empirical Evidence on Local Government Structure and Service Performance

Study	Unit of Analysis	Structural Variable	Major Hypothesis	Findings
McArthur (1971)	Nashville-Davidson Co., TN urban fringe area	metro consolidation	services are better after adoption of metro	surveyed citizens felt services did not change
Ostrom and Whitaker (1974)	Police services in Chicago area	size of department	large police departments perform better	citizens served by large departments didn't rank services better
Rogers and Lipsey (1974)	Nashville-Davidson Co., TN police, fire, garbage, street and park services	size of community	larger, fewer governments perform better	citizens in small cities more satisfied with services
Ostrom (1976)	Police services in a) Indianapolis, b) Grand Rapids, and c) St. Louis area	size of departments	large police departments perform better	citizens served by large departments didn't rank services better
Hawkins (1976)	California communities	size of community	services are perceived better in larger cities	citizens in small towns had higher level of satisfaction
Birgersson (1977)	Swedish communes	size and population density of community	larger communes offer better services, citizens satisfaction with services higher in larger communes	citizens in small, less urban communes had higher level of satisfaction
Christenson and Sachs (1980)	North Carolina county areas	no. of employees, no. of employees per capita, no. of employees per government, no. governments, no. of governments per capita	size increases perceived quality, centralization increases perceived quality	higher service quality with larger governments, lower service quality with decentralization (fragmentation)

percent of the respondents evaluated local services as essentially the same after the city-county consolidation. Approximately thirty-four percent said services had improved with consolidation and only seven percent indicated that services had deteriorated with the structural change.

Ostrom has reported case studies of police services in Chicago, Indianapolis, Grand Rapids, and St. Louis.[11] Each study was designed to elicit, among other things, the public's perception of police services provided by large and small police departments. The general finding is absence of a significant increase in perceived service quality with comparatively larger police departments.

Rogers and Lipsey evaluated citizen perceptions on police, fire, garbage, street, and park services under alternate structural arrangements within the Nashville-Davidson County, Tennessee metropolitan government.[12] Citizens in small independent communities reported greater satisfaction with services, causing the authors to conclude that consolidationist claims about higher service levels and efficiency being associated with larger units of government are unfounded.

Based on survey data from California communities, Hawkins concluded that citizens in smaller communities and those served by fragmented governance systems with special districts generally reported higher levels of service satisfaction.[13] This finding was for schools, street maintenance, police protection, zoning, and parks and recreation.

Studying thirty-six Swedish communes, the unit of local government in Sweden, Birgersson posed two questions: (1) Do larger communes generally offer a "better" standard of local government service than the smaller communes? and (2) Are the citizens more satisfied with local government service in the communes where service levels are highest? With citizen surveys and objective output measures, twelve general service sectors were analyzed. The sectors ranged from town planning and libraries to waterworks and sewage. Using objective measures of local government performance, higher levels of services were found to be provided in the larger, more populous communes. However, subjective measures of citizen satisfaction with public services were inversely related to commune size. The highest levels of service satisfaction were recorded in the smallest size communes.[14]

Based on multivariate analyses of county area data from North Carolina, Christenson and Sachs report higher perceptions of service quality for localities served by larger more centralized governance systems.[15] A scaling technique was used to combine citizens' perceptions about the quality of individual services into a comprehensive subjective measure. No relationship was found between per capita expenditures and constituents' perceptions.

The findings of the studies on the relationship between local government structure and public sector output as measured by subjective citizen evaluations are not unanimous. The general conclusions of the case studies suggest that larger governments are not associated with higher levels of service as perceived by citizens. However, a more comprehensive statistical study at the county area level supports the opposite conclusion. Higher levels of service satisfaction were reported by residents in communities having more centralized, larger political organizations.

PERFORMANCE AND STRUCTURE IN ILLINOIS

The importance of governmental organization in local public services must be evaluated considering the different measures of public performance. Consumer satisfaction from local public services may arise not from intrinsic service characteristics but consumers' perceptions of these properties. The evidence reported in studies of consumer satisfaction with local public services and government structure is ambiguous about whether fragmented local government systems (more governments per capita) are characterized by higher or lower perceptions of service quality. Three possible relationships were outlined in Figure 6.1:

1. the relationship between objective service measures, subjective service evaluations and per capita expenditures;
2. the effect of tastes, preferences, and income on subjective perceptions of local services; and especially
3. the relationships between local government size and structure and residents' perceptions of service quality.

These relationships are examined using evidence from Illinois counties.

Service Perceptions

A subjective evaluation of public services was obtained from a 1978 statewide mail survey conducted in 102 Illinois counties. The survey sample was drawn to obtain one usable questionnaire for each 1000 adults. A proportionate sampling technique was supplemented with an oversample to obtain sufficient respondents from each county. An average of eighty-one respondents in each county returned usable questionnaires for an overall response rate of 68.6 percent.[16]

Evaluative statements for twenty-five common public services were

Table 6.4. Subject Evaluation of Selected Public Services

County Population Size	Local Service						
	Education	Roads/Streets	Parks	Library	Police	Fire	Sanitary Sewer
	Mean Likert Score[a]						
200,000 and above	2.95	2.28	3.14	3.49	3.43	3.67	3.00
100,000-199,999	3.02	2.32	3.24	3.60	3.42	3.72	2.98
50,000-99,999	3.06	2.30	3.31	3.48	3.43	3.67	3.00
25,000-49,999	3.01	2.44	3.22	3.51	3.42	3.72	2.94
10,000-24,999	2.97	2.45	3.30	3.51	3.44	3.53	2.98
less than 10,000	2.92	2.15	2.97	3.29	3.29	3.19	2.83
all counties	3.01	2.37	3.22	3.48	3.41	3.57	2.95

[a] Likert Scores range from 1 = low to 4 = high. The scores reported are the averages of the county scores for the counties in each size category.

provided allowing respondents to rate the services. Likert scores were aggregated to produce a mean score of the collective experience of the citizenry for each county. The scales are from a four point system with one being low and four being high.

Table 6.4 presents the average Likert score for seven selected local public services summarized by county size. While aggregate means disguise much of the actual intracounty variation, several trends are evident from the average scores. First, for certain services the residents in the smallest and largest population counties reported generally lower levels of satisfaction than residents in middle-size counties. This pattern was particularly strong for education, roads and streets, and parks, but less evident for fire, police, and sewer services. In fact, the lowest satisfaction levels for each of the services listed in Table 6.4 were reported by residents in counties with fewer than 10,000 inhabitants. The lack of capacity within local government to adequately meet service demands may cause residents of less populated counties to be less satisfied. For police, fire and sanitary sewer service, the residents from the most urbanized counties expressed satisfaction levels close to the highest mean Likert score for the county size categories. Factors related to variation in service preference levels are investigated in more detail later.

Objective Service Measures

Several objective indicators of output were studied. In addition to full time equivalent employment, these indicators are per capita acres of public park and recreational lands (parks), number of books per capita (public libraries), and pupil-teacher ratios (education). Table 6.5 lists the aver-

Table 6.5. Objective Indicators of Public Sector Output

County Population Size	Local Service					
	Education		Parks		Library	
	Pupil Teacher Ratio	Employment Per 1,000 Pupils	Acres Per Capita	Employment Per 10,000 Residents	Books Per Capita	Employment Per 10,000 Residents
200,000 and above	14.14	101.38	.06	321.15	1.68	3.27
100,000-199,999	14.42	99.01	.05	287.76	1.86	3.42
50,000-99,999	14.61	99.56	.23	294.46	1.84	2.65
25,000-49,999	14.22	99.74	.19	306.40	1.77	2.33
10,000-24,999	14.30	102.64	.43	344.90	2.15	2.18
less than 10,000	13.61	107.12	1.77	335.05	1.87	1.79
all counties	14.21	101.88	0.50	323.08	1.93	2.40

age objective measures of public performance and average public employment for education, park services and libraries grouped by county population size. The pupil-teacher ratio ranged from a high of 14.61 in counties with 50,000 to 99,999 residents to a low of 13.61 in counties with fewer than 10,000 inhabitants. Instructional employment per 1000 students averaged 8.2 percent more in counties with fewer than 10,000 people, compared to counties with populations between 100,000 and 199,999 which had the lowest level of reported instructional employment.

There is some indication in park services that as counties increase in population size, acres of park lands per capita and park employment, adjusted for population, decrease. In the most sparsely populated counties, an average of 1.77 acres per capita was reported with park employment of 335.05 per 10,000 residents. Counties with populations between 100,000 and 199,999 indicated the lowest park acreage and employment. The acreage in park use unfortunately includes lands held by the state and federal government. This accounts, in part, for larger acreages per capita of park land in the rural, low population counties. The presence of federal and state park lands, however, does not explain the relatively higher park employment in the smaller size counties.

The third service studied is libraries. These services are provided by municipalities, special library districts and in some cases townships. The measures of library services reported in Table 6.5 indicate greater differences among county size categories in library employment than in books per capita. Generally, the larger the population, the more library employees per 10,000 residents. For all Illinois counties, there were 2.4 library employees per 10,000 people and 1.93 books per capita. The tendency for higher library employment in the more populous counties suggests that library services in larger communities reach beyond the provision of a repository of books and include programs with many dimensions. Audio-visual collections, community education programs, services for special populations such as preschoolers and the aged are offered through local libraries. These activities are labor intensive, and require additional employees. Factors underlying variation in book volume and employment measures of library services are studied later in this chapter.

Factor Analysis

As an analytical tool, factor analysis is a data reduction technique for identifying underlying common traits or dimensions implicit in empirical observations. For example, factor analysis of perceptual data on service quality from the survey of citizens provides evidence on the commonality of the underlying structure or traits among services perceived by residents.[17] The larger the numerical value a service's factor loading is, the greater the similiarity of underlying traits with those of other services with similar value loadings. The terminal pattern matrix from an oblique rotation factor analysis in Table 6.6 indicates that the attitude data on service quality across Illinois communities can be reduced to six factors. The table lists the factors in the order they emerged from the factor analysis. Similarly, the rows of the table are arranged so that the services with heavy loadings on factor one are shown first, then the loadings for factor two and so on. All factors are reported as evidence of the structure underlying Illinois citizens' perceptions of service quality. The factor loadings indicate that there are groups of services sharing a common underlying dimension that is stronger than the commonality across groups.[18]

The loadings of the services across factors indicate that factor one captures the commonality of the perceived quality of nine services ranging from cultural opportunities to bridges. The first factor is the most general as evidenced by the larger number of substantial loadings. The underlying dimension of the second factor is housing services—low cost and senior citizen housing. None of these services loaded heavily on any of the other factors.

The third factor contains the highest loadings for education. Both elementary schools and high schools loaded highest on this factor. Community zoning and local roads and streets both loaded heavily on the fourth factor. The commonality among water and sewer service quality including storm sewers underlies the fifth factor. Ambulance and emergency health service loaded heaviest on factor six. Including police protection, factor six takes on the character of the quality of emergency health and safety services. Police and park services were most heavily loaded on factor six and factor one, respectively.

The results of the factor analysis can be interpreted in several ways. First, more than ninety-five percent of the total variation among the service attributes as perceived by residents can be patterned into six factors. This finding indicates that the twenty-five service attitudes can be represented quite well by the six dimensions or underlying structural commonalities. Second, Table 6.6 demonstrates that most services fit within a group of services with high loadings (correlations) on one factor, but are associated only weakly or not at all with the other six, a pattern which facilitates substantive interpretation.

The first group, loading on factor one, is comprised of a potpourri of services signifying the general commonality of a wide range of local government activities. The second dimension consists of housing services—both low income and elderly. Education characterizes the third dimension with both primary and secondary schooling loading on this

Table 6.6. Factor Coefficients for Perceptions of Community Service Quality[a]

Service	Factor Loadings					
	ONE	TWO	THREE	FOUR	FIVE	SIX
Cultural Services	.8460	−.0583	.1193	.0390	−.2693	−.0477
Libraries	.6286	.0599	.0351	−.2330	.0906	.1105
Hospitals	.5801	−.0541	−.0612	.3431	.0035	.3968
Youth Recreation	.5446	.0222	.0007	−.0269	−.1505	.2016
Planning	.5311	−.0364	−.3301	−.1915	−.1393	.0293
Local Buses	.4844	.0484	.0186	−.0539	.0610	−.0553
Solid Waste	.4545	.0829	−.3999	.1331	−.0262	−.1450
Fire Protection	.4478	.0532	−.2163	−.0107	.0701	.3338
Bridges	.4359	.0612	−.2564	.0530	.2189	.1562
Housing for Aged	−.1659	.8098	.0845	−.1212	.0362	.1789
Low Cost Housing	.1016	.7270	−.2409	.0726	−.0092	−.3511
Grade Schools	−.1013	.0122	−.9308	−.0074	−.0966	.0170
High Schools	−.0700	.0423	−.6457	−.1228	−.1458	.0486
Zoning	.1135	.0471	−.0446	−.6665	−.1558	−.0798
Roads/Streets	.1471	.0556	−.3925	−.5461	.2523	.2107
Storm Sewers	.0762	.1351	−.1911	−.1146	−.6743	−.1536
Water	−.0293	−.0140	−.1080	−.0122	−.5044	.2439
Sewer	.1244	.2842	−.1247	−.0284	−.4310	.0647
Ambulances	.1234	.2799	−.2078	.0510	.0932	.4682
Emergency Health	.4169	.0264	−.1864	.4036	−.0218	.4537
Police	.0187	.0776	−.0525	−.0552	−.1883	.3848
Parks	.3379	.1060	−.1348	−.1881	−.2515	.2474
Income Assistance	.0350	.3041	−.0586	−.2884	−.1172	.0479
Mental Health	.3262	.2504	−.1886	.2092	−.1721	−.0420
Senior's Recreation	.1203	.3503	.1037	−.1468	−.1700	.0726
Percent of Variation						
Common	59.6	15.9	7.2	6.9	6.1	4.3
Cumulative	59.6	75.5	82.7	89.6	95.7	100.0
Eigenvalues	8.51	2.27	1.03	0.98	0.87	0.61

[a] The factor analysis was a principal factor method with iteration and oblique rotation to a terminal solution. The pattern matrix is reported.

factor. Factor four is most highly correlated with roads and streets and zoning. The fifth factor captures the qualities of public health dimensions in public sewer and water services. Finally, the underlying dimensions of emergency health and safety services are represented in factor six. In sum, the application of factor analysis to the service assessments yields six meaningful service dimensions each constituting a similar area of local service as perceived by residents.

A quality of service index was constructed using the Illinois survey data to provide a comparative assessment across all services in a county.

The index was derived using the respective factor scores from the first principal factor of the unrotated terminal factor analysis solution to weight the standardized difference between the mean Likert scale for each service and the average scale for all counties. The weighted products were summed across services to obtain a composite measure of perceived service quality (QS) for each county. All services were used in QS to control for the influences of the entire service menu. The higher the value of the QS index, the better the service quality. The index, along with expenditures, employment, and objective measures of individual services are described in the next section.

Data Description

Correlations identifying the bivariate relationships between subjective and objective measures of local public services plus per capita expenditures, as an indicator of input, and local government organization are presented in Table 6.7. In addition to aggregate comparisons, detailed information about parks, libraries, and local schools are presented. A satisfactory aggregate objective measure of local government output could not be found.

A statistically positive correlation between mean Likert scores, subjective measures of output, and objective indicators of service is reported for libraries and schools. The r of .06 for acres of parks per capita and the subjective perception of local park services is not significant at or above the ten percent level of probability. This may occur because, in some instances, park acres per capita includes acres of state and federally owned property and the residents' responses focused on "local" services. The low negative correlation between per capita park expenditures and the objective indicator of park services, while not significant, reinforces the problem with reported park acreage. The correlations, however, provide evidence that citizens are fairly accurate in their perception of service attributes reflected in objective indicators of local government output.

In general, per capita expenditures are not correlated with either subjective or objective output measures. The exception is pupil-teacher ratio which is moderately correlated with school expenditures. On the other hand, full-time equivalent employment adjusted for population is correlated with both subjective and objective measures as well as aggregate per capita expenditures. While the correlation is not high, park employment is inversely associated with acres of parks per capita and perception of park service quality. The first relationship may reflect the trade-off between labor intensive recreational services and park land in local recreation service budgets. However, the inverse relationship between

Table 6.7. Correlations with Descriptions for Public Service Measures

Public Service Measure	Input	Output		Governmental	Mean	SD	Maximum	Minimum
	Expenditures	Objective	Subjective	Structure[a]				
Parks[b]								
Per Capita Expenditures	—	—		.04	$ 11.18	10.16	51.32	0.23
Acres Per Capita	-.15	.06		.40*	.38	.90	5.95	.002
Mean Likert Score	-.01	-.17**	—	.18**	3.30	.22	3.70	2.74
Park Employment[c]	.53*	—	-.20*	-.21*	3.25	3.37	18.90	0
Libraries[b]								
Per Capita Expenditures	—	—		-.02	3.25	3.08	11.56	.07
Books Per Capita	-.05	.50*		-.20	2.03	.83	4.44	0.54
Mean Likert Score	.12	.55*	.45*	-.38*	3.51	.19	3.81	3.00
Library Employment[c]	.58*	—	—	-.60*	2.98	1.06	4.97	0.34
Schools[b]								
Per Capita Expenditures	—	—		-.08	101.78	16.15	173.62	70.18
Pupil Teacher Ratio	-.36*	.20*		-.08	14.22	1.77	19.80	8.22
Mean Likert Score	.09	—	—	.17*	3.01	.21	3.62	2.44
School Employment[c]	.40*	-.91*	-.30*	-.01	101.78	16.15	173.62	70.18
Aggregate[b]								
Per Capita Expenditures	—	—	—	-.10	657.39	157.22	1442.08	390.74
Employment[c]	.40*	—	-.13**	.01	322.66	69.48	636.69	214.17
Quality Index (QS)	-.03	—	—	-.05	100.00	.98	101.83	96.45

* Significant at the five percent level.
** Significant at the ten percent level.
[a] Structure is measured as the number of units per 10,000 population except for aggregate structure measured by the structural index. See Chapter 5 for further discussion.
[b] For aggregate and schools N=101; Parks N=63; and Libraries N=33.
[c] Employment is measured in FTE per 10,000 residents except schools where it is measured in FTE per 1,000 pupils.

park employment and perceived park service quality is not as easily explained. One possibility is that influential factors, uncontrolled in the bivariate analysis, are indirectly causing the statistically significant negative relationship.

The structure of local government was not strongly correlated with the subjective indicators of local government performance. The largest correlation coefficient (r=.40) was for park services. The positive relationship between structure and perceptions of service quality suggests that the activities of fragmented, decentralized governments (more governments per 10,000) are rated better than those of more centralized organizations. Parks and schools are examples. However, the negative correlation coefficient between library services and library structure indicates the opposite. To determine the effect of alternate local governance structures and size on public sector output, measured subjectively and objectively while controlling for expenditures, preferences, and income variation, a series of simple regression analyses were conducted. These regressions are reported in the next sections.

Service Quality and Structure

A quality of service model statistically isolates the effects of political organization and size on the subjective output of local governments. The dependent variable, the quality of service index (QS) derived from the factor analysis, is the comprehensive measure of residents' perceptions of public service quality. Using QS as the dependent variable incorporates a broad range of services into a single quality measure. Including all services, however, does not illustrate the effects of structure on the subjective output or quality of a specific service. To offset this limitation, library services, parks, education, and local roads and streets are each examined separately. The mean score on the Likert scale is the dependent variable in these analyses.[19]

To investigate the effects of local government structure on perceived service quality, the following quality of service model was estimated:

$$QS_i = a + \sum_{j=1}^{n} b_j X_{ji} + b_e E_i + b_g G_i + e$$

where:

QS_i = the quality of service index or the mean Likert score in county i,

X_{ji} = demographic or economic variable j in county i,

E_i = per capita local government expenditures for all services or for a specific service in county i,

G_i = a measure of local government structure or size in county i,

a,b = constant term and vector of coefficients to be estimated, and

e = error term.

The first demographic variable included is percent net migration, 1970–1980. Inmigrants with different preferences and experiences may not be pleased with existing community services.[20] Furthermore, population growth places stress on local services with fixed short run capacities, such as schools or sewers. Higher net inmigration is expected to be related to a lower overall valuation by residents of local public services.

The second demographic variable is percent of nonwhite population. The impact of race on service quality perception is less easily assessed. No a priori relationship is hypothesized.[21] To assess the impact of the rural character of a locality on the relation between government structure and performance, a binary variable is included to distinguish rural counties from metropolitan counties.

Per capita expenditures for local public services are usually higher in communities with relatively higher personal incomes. Higher income communities provide better services as well.[22] If these qualitative differences are recognized by residents, then a positive relationship between QS_i and per capita income will exist.

The impact of citizen participation on the relationship between structure and performance is tested with a subjective evaluation of citizen involvement in local government measured by a mean Likert score.[23] Claims are that small, decentralized political organizations facilitate citizen participation in the collective choice process selecting community service levels. However, because of increased information costs with fragmented structures, three to five overlapping separate local governments may be optimum.[24] Accordingly, a positive relationship between citizen participation and perceived public service quality is expected.

Higher per capita expenditures (E_i) will be positively associated with subjective output measures of services if expenditures denote effort or input.[25] Three measures of local public sector size and two indicators of organizational structure (G_i) are used to test for the effects of size and structure on QS_i. Number of FTE employees, employees per 10,000 residents and employees per administrative unit denote size of government.[26] If perceived quality is influenced by local public sector size, then size and quality will be positively related. Christenson and Sachs found all three size measures positively associated with perceived service quality in North Carolina.[27]

The number of local governments adjusted for population serving a locality and the number of special districts scaled for population are two alternate indicators of political organizational structure. The latter measure is a more direct indicator of the relationship between number of single-purpose districts and perceptions of service quality. In the analysis of selected services, number of the special districts per 10,000 residents was used. If smaller units or those with specialized functions are particularly responsive and provide services more in accordance with tastes and preferences of residents, a fragmented governmental system characterized by special districts should be positively associated with QS_i. The evidence from a California study supports this claim but results from North Carolina do not.[28] In North Carolina there is evidence that services provided by more centralized, less fragmented local governance systems were evaluated as better than services in localities with a more decentralized local government organization.

The regression estimates of the quality of service model using data from Illinois counties are presented in Tables 6.8 and 6.9. The five equations in Table 6.8 use the comprehensive index of service quality (QS_i) as the dependent variable. No relationship was found in these analyses between any of the government size measures, Models (3), (4), and (5), and the level of perceived quality of service. This is not consistent with the evidence from North Carolina. The coefficients of the size variables are not statistically different from zero. In contrast, the analysis indicates that fewer taxing units per 10,000 people are significantly related to higher perceived quality of public services (Models (1) and (2) in Table 6.8).

In general, per capita expenditures are not statistically associated with the service quality index. The per capita expenditure coefficients are negative but not statistically different from zero. Citizen participation and income are both positively associated with perceived local government performance, while net migration is negatively associated with service quality. The metropolitan binary variable did not influence perceptions of composite local government performance. The coefficient of the race variable was negative and significant in all equations. The independent variables in Table 6.8 are associated with approximately fifty percent of the variation in the comprehensive measure of service quality, QS_i. Most coefficients were stable across various model specifications, particularly Models (1) and (2).

Estimates for selected services are presented in Table 6.9. For library services and education, median years of schooling were included as an explanatory variable. Regression models for specific services were estimated in a similar manner to the composite quality of service model. In each model, however, certain independent variables were not significant determinants of perceived quality for selected services. For example, race was not significant in the roads and streets model. The coefficient of net migration was not significant in either the roads and streets

Table 6.8. Quality of Service Index Regressions[a]

Model	Variable	Government Structure and Size Factors Coefficient	County Characteristics Metro/ Nonmetro	Percent Net Migration	Percent Nonwhite	Per Capita Income	Citizen Participation	Expenditures Per Capita	R²	Constant	F-Ratio
1	Taxing units/ 10,000	-.2136* (3.08)	2.6456* (0.96)	-.2466* (2.80)	-.5106* (3.21)	.0061* (3.88)	19.0477* (5.60)	-.0073 (1.17)	.52	-68.11	16.64
2	Special dist./ 10,000	-.2892* (2.05)	.8993 (0.33)	-.2555* (2.80)	-.4480* (2.79)	.0066* (4.04)	18.1380* (5.22)	-.0076 (1.18)	.50	-69.45	15.09
3	Employ- ment/ 10,000	.0024 (0.19)	-1.042 (0.40)	-.2310* (2.49)	-.4136* (2.53)	.0062* (3.56)	17.5974* (4.95)	-.0072 (0.96)	.47	-68.25	13.88
4	Employ- ment/ gov't.	.0641 (1.12)	.7258 (0.24)	-.2271* (2.47)	-.4594* (2.74)	.0059* (3.55)	18.4363* (3.14)	-.0087 (1.27)	.48	-70.09	14.23
5	Employment	.0003 (0.68)	-.1502 (0.05)	-.2337* (2.53)	-.4419* (2.62)	.0057* (3.26)	17.7263* (5.02)	-.0074 (1.10)	.48	-66.59	14.10

[a] n = 101, absolute value of t statistics are in parentheses. The dependent variable is an index of service quality constructed using the factor scores of the first factor from a factor analysis.

* Significant at the five percent level.

Table 6.9. Quality of Service Regressions for Selected Services[a]

	Service			
	Libraries	Parks	Roads/Streets	Education
Metro/Nonmetro	.0387	.0549	.1491**	−.0704
	(0.75)	(0.80)	(1.69)	(1.16)
Percent Net Migration	−.0036*	−.0094*	−.0003	.0024
(1970–1980)	(1.96)	(3.73)	(0.10)	(1.04)
Percent Nonwhite	−.0063*	−.0299*	−.0021	−.0100
	(2.02)	(7.07)	(0.41)	(2.70)*
Per Capita Income	.0001*	.0001	.0001**	−.0001
	(2.95)	(1.03)	(1.67)	(1.25)
Median School Years	.0195	−	−	.0593*
	(1.19)			(2.96)
Citizen Participation	.2970*	−	.5099*	.2670*
	(4.33)		(4.72)	(3.39)
Service Expenditures[b]	.0023	.0035	.0037*	−.00001
Per Capita	(0.87)	(1.43)	(2.24)	(0.02)
Library Districts/10,000	−.1074*	−	−	−
	(2.72)			
Park Districts/10,000	−	.0294**	−	−
		(1.76)		
Street Units/10,000[c]	−	−	−.0160*	−
			(2.51)	
School Districts/1,000 Pupils	−	−	−	.0568*
				(2.26)
Constant	2.0339	3.0731	0.3537	1.8822
R²Adjusted	.49	.47	.34	.43
S.E.E.	.13151	.1877	.2120	.1501
F-Ratio	12.26	14.77	8.00	7.69
n	94	93	95	92

*Significant at the five percent level.
**Significant at the ten percent level.
[a]Absolute value of t statistics are in parentheses. The dependent variables are the mean Likert scores of service quality for the respective services.
[b] Expenditures are for library, parks, roads and streets and schools for the respective models. All except school expenditures are scaled for population. School expenditures are measured per 1,000 pupils adjusted for grade levels.
[c] Street units are the number of jurisdictions of all types (municipal, township, and county) with road and street responsibilities.

or the education model. Per capita income was significant only to perceived quality of library and road and street services. The coefficient of the metropolitan variable was positive and significant (at the ten percent level) in the roads and streets model demonstrating that, on average, residents in nonmetropolitan Illinois counties were more satisfied with these services.

Of major interest is the relationship between expenditures for selected services and perceived quality and the impact of government organization structure on perceived quality. In each case, except roads and streets, the structural measure was number of single function governments providing the service adjusted for county population. For roads and streets the structural measure was the sum of municipalities, townships, and county, all of which are responsible for streets or local roads.

The coefficient of the expenditure variable was not significant in any of the individual service models except roads and streets. Greater spending for roads and streets was associated with a higher perceived quality of service. The more complex the government structure providing library services and roads and streets, the lower the perceived quality of service. This is consistent with the findings for comprehensive index of service quality. However, the positive and significant coefficient (at the ten percent level) for the number of park districts per 10,000 people, and the positive and significant coefficient (at the five percent level) for school districts per 1000 pupils indicate the opposite. A larger number of park districts and school districts are associated with a better rating for park services and education.

The evidence presented suggests that while more fragmented governmental organizations generally result in lower perceived service quality, this relationship does not hold for all types of services. Park services and education are exceptions. Also, except for roads and streets, per capita expenditures were not significantly related to perceived service quality. Government size was not found to be related to quality of services.

Objective Measures and Structure

The objective measures of local government activity for parks, libraries, and education are acres of park land per capita, books per capita and pupil-teacher ratio. The relationships between these objective measures and local government organization were also investigated through a regression analysis. Within each public service a separate equation was estimated regressing sociodemographic independent variables and expenditures, as an indicator of effort, against the objective performance measure. The park and library models were unsuccessful. The measurement problem with park acres per capita could be one explanation for the poor park results. For libraries, the number of books per capita, at least in Illinois communities, may not be a good objective measure of overall services.

Objective Measure of Education. No single objective measure is sufficiently comprehensive to capture both the quality and quantity dimension of educational services. A variety of approaches have been used to quantify these dimensions, though the most common measure of educational output has been some type of student standardized test scores. Other measures, including the proportion of youth completing a given year of school, the dropout rate, the pursuit of advanced, post high school education, student grade point averages, and pupil-teacher ratios or classroom size have also been used. Applying an education production model, the measure of educational output is analyzed and related to variation in input factors, the socioeconomic environment within the community, the state of technology and institutional arrangements.[29]

Pupil-teacher ratios are the surrogate measure of educational service used in this analysis. Table 6.10 reports the determinants of pupil-teacher ratios across Illinois localities.[30] The determinants include measures of community tastes and preferences, institutional arrangements, and inputs as captured by education spending. The same taste and prefer-

Table 6.10. Determinants of Pupil-Teacher Ratios in Illinois Counties[a]

Variable	Model A	Model B	Model C	Model D
Metro/Nonmetro	−0.2775	−0.2043	−0.1485	−0.0890
	(0.68)	(0.50)	(0.36)	(0.22)
Percent Net Migration	0.0849*	0.0842*	0.0750*	0.0750*
	(5.88)	(5.82)	(5.35)	(5.44)
Percent Nonwhite	−0.1048*	−0.1068*	−0.1098*	−0.1112*
	(3.42)	(3.50)	(3.52)	(3.60)
Per Capita Income	0.00007	0.00009	0.0004	0.0004
	(0.23)	(0.33)	(1.53)	(1.45)
Median School Years	0.3042*	0.2656**	−	−
	(2.19)	(1.86)		
School Expenditures	−0.0077*	−0.0075*	−0.0069*	−0.0069*
Per Capita	(5.43)	(5.50)	(4.92)	(5.14)
School Districts Per	0.0090	−	−0.0611	−
10,000 Population	(0.11)		(0.76)	
School Districts Per	−	−0.0908	−	−0.2264
1,000 Pupils		(0.54)		(1.47)
Constant	14.59	14.78	15.71	15.88
R²Adjusted	.49	.49	.46	.47
F-Ratio	11.86	11.94	12.32	12.77
S.E.E.	1.01	1.01	1.04	1.03
N	93	93	93	93

[a]Absolute values of t statistics are in parentheses. The dependent variable is the pupil-teacher ratio.
* Significant at the five percent level.
** Significant at the ten percent level.

ence variables as in the subjective quality of services analyses were included. Significant coefficients are reported for the taste and preference variables: percent net migration, percent nonwhite, and median school years. For example, on average, a one percent increase in net migration was associated with an increase in the pupil-teacher ratio of close to one pupil. Unexpectedly, the median school years variable was positively related to the pupil-teacher ratio. A relatively strong correlation between median school years and per capita income could account for this unexpected relationship. Models C and D in Table 6.10 exclude the education variable. The coefficient of per capita income increases in magnitude with this specification.

Per capita educational expenditures are negatively associated with the objective measure of schooling. On average, for every $100 increase in spending, the ratio declines by about one student. Of major interest is the effect of government (school district) organization on pupil-teacher ratios. In contrast to the subjective measure of education, no significant relationship is found between either of the two structural measures and pupil-teacher ratios. The two structural measures are school districts adjusted for population and pupils, respectively. This finding suggests that the implications drawn about the effects of school district organization on education output are dependent, at least in this case, on the way outputs from schools are measured. Fragmented school organizations with more units per 1000 pupils were perceived as having better services by residents. On the other hand, the objective measure of schooling (pupil-teacher ratio), was not statistically associated with structure.

Employment as a Service Measure. The rationale for using public employment as an objective measure of local government service is that public services are represented by the number of persons employed in the provision of services. This reflects the preferences of communities for local government activities.[31]

The demand for public employees is specified as a function of the cost of a public employee, income and intergovernmental aid, taste and preference variables, and local government organization. This relationship is symbolically represented as:

$$N_i = a + \sum_{j=1}^{n} b_j X_{ji} + b_w W_i + b_g G_i + b_a A_i + e$$

where:

N_i = number of FTE employees scaled to population or pupils in county i,

X_{ji} = taste and preference factor j in county i,

W_i = price of public employee in county i measured by average wages,

G_i = measure of local government structure in county i, and

A_i = intergovernmental revenues per capita in county i,

a,b = constant term and vector of coefficients to be estimated, and

e = error term.

Conceptually N_i is negatively related to W_i and positively related to A_i. As the cost of an employee increases, the number demanded decreases. Alternatively, more intergovernmental revenues in a locality increases the number of public employees demanded. If more fragmented, smaller government systems are relatively more responsive to consumer preferences, then higher employment, as an output measure, may be associated with more governments per population of 10,000. The rationale for this result is not unambiguously distinguishable from a supply-cost explanation for a positive relationship between public employment and government structure. Small, fragmented overlapping systems could be argued to be inefficient and duplicative resulting in higher employment.

The determinants of total local government employment and for park, library, and school services in Illinois counties are presented in Table 6.11. In general, average earnings, the price variable, is negatively related to employment per 10,000 residents while intergovernmental aid is positively related. On average, an increase in average earnings of $100 per FTE is associated with a decrease of slightly more than one person in total employment per 10,000 residents. For every additional $10 in grants-in-aid per capita, employment per 10,000 people increased by about four.

Three measures of local government structure are employed including taxing units per 10,000 residents, special districts per 10,000, and a comprehensive structural index used in Chapters 4 and 5. For the separate service employment analyses, the number of special districts adjusted for population was used to measure structure. The number of school districts was divided by the number of pupils.

No significant relationship is reported between government structure and employment in parks, libraries, and schools. For aggregate employment, however, taxing units per 10,000 and special districts per 10,000 have positive significant coefficients at the ten percent level of probability. This finding suggests that government structure may affect demand for public employment as a measure of local public services. More research is clearly needed.

In general, the proportion of variation in public employment related

Table 6.11. Determinants of Local Government Employment[a]

Variable	Total Employment			Park Employment	Library Employment	School Employment
	Model A	Model B	Model C			
Average Earnings	-0.0121* (4.62)	-0.0122* (4.67)	-0.0120* (4.51)	-0.0001 (0.64)	0.0001 (1.30)	-0.00003 (0.06)
Percent Rural	-0.6600** (1.69)	-0.4643 (1.37)	-0.2530 (0.80)	-0.0386** (1.80)	0.3186 (1.25)	-0.1378* (1.99)
Per Capita Income	0.0163 (1.08)	0.0165 (1.10)	0.0198 (1.30)	0.0021* (2.76)	0.0008* (2.68)	-0.0050** (1.86)
Intergovernmental Revenues[b]	0.4502* (5.06)	0.4498* (5.07)	0.4223* (4.76)	0.0081 (1.13)	-0.0001 (0.19)	0.0038 (0.13)
Population	-0.0001 (0.88)	-0.0001 (1.05)	-0.0001 (1.38)	—	—	—
Median School Years	—	—	—	—	0.3186 (1.25)	-2.2013 (1.59)
Taxing Units Per 10,000 Pop.	1.1989 (1.71)**	—	—	—	—	—
Special Districts Per 10,000 Pop.	—	2.1142** (1.75)	—	—	—	—
Structural Index	—	—	59.5035 (0.40)	—	—	—
Park Districts Per 10,000 Pop.	—	—	—	-0.5724 (0.75)	—	—
Library Districts Per 10,000 Pop.	—	—	—	—	-0.0445 (0.79)	—
School Districts Per 1,000 Pupils	—	—	—	—	—	0.3972 (0.44)
Constant	281.97	285.35	264.96	-4.85	-4.91	153.99
R²Adjusted	.36	.36	.34	.30	.52	.08
F-Ratios	10.28	10.32	9.54	6.57	6.84	2.34
S.E.E.	55.68	55.64	56.49	2.79	0.73	10.84
N	101	101	101	67	33	95

*Significant at the five percent level.
**Significant at the ten percent level.
[a] Except for school employment, the dependent variables are FTE employment per 10,000 residents. For schools employment is measured per 1,000 pupils. The absolute value of the t statistics are in parentheses.
[b] For school employment includes only school aid.

to the variation in the explanatory factors was low.[32] While most coefficients had the expected signs, many were not statistically significant, thus restricting the applicability of the results.

SUMMARY

This chapter extends the empirical analysis on the implications of alternate local organizational structures for performance by considering subjective and objective measures of public services. In this context, public expenditures are viewed as indicators of input or effort. Accordingly, the subjective measures using residents' perceptions of service quality suggest that the value of local government output is not the intrinsic properties of services but perception of these properties by consumers.

In describing public output, perceptual data on service quality from a citizens' survey, selected objective measures of output, and the employment proxy were compared and contrasted. A significant relationship was reported between objective measures and perceived quality measures of libraries and schools.

The significant bivariate relationships between government structure and subjective measure of local government performance generally held when community tastes and preferences and incomes were considered. Attempts to account for variation in acres of parks per capita and books per capita were not successful.

However, the factor analysis of citizens' perceptions of service quality indicated the evaluations of the twenty-five common public services could be reduced to six factors representing common underlying dimensions. In general, neither government size nor expenditures influenced service quality. The exception is roads and streets where higher expenditures were associated with a higher perception of service quality. Higher service expenditures, within the range found in Illinois, may have little effect on the degree of satisfaction derived by citizens.

The evidence on local government structure and citizens' perceptions of service performance is not consistent. While fewer governments per 10,000 residents resulted in a higher perception of service quality in the aggregate, a more centralized structure was negatively associated with perceptions of quality for certain services. The perceived quality of parks and education was positively associated with the degree of fragmentation. This indicates that consolidation efforts may result in a lower level of individual satisfaction with the service in some communities. In such cases, local officials may experience more difficulty satisfying service demands.

The findings also caution against universal application of policies, such as boundary commissions, to generally limit or restrict use of single-purpose special districts. Blanket restrictions on decentralization of public services may not always result in a higher perception of quality in the services provided. Perceptions of service quality may be maximized when certain services are provided through more centralized systems and others through a more fragmented structure. A possible beginning point is to separate those services where marked differences in preferences are expected (like education) from those where preference variation is likely to be minimal (like sanitation services). Such a dichotomy is certainly supported by the evidence presented in this chapter.

Overall, public employment as a measure of local government output was higher in areas served by fragmented systems of local government. The unambiguous interpretation of this result is difficult, however. This finding may reflect either the demand driven political responsiveness of small fragmented local governments, or the supply driven higher service cost, measured by more employment, claimed to be characteristic of decentralized government organizations. In the following chapter, the implications of local government structure for service responsibilities, political responsiveness, revenue systems, expenditure patterns and citizens' subjective evaluation of performance are summarized.

NOTES

1. Elinor Ostrom, "Metropolitan Reform: Propositions Derived from Two Traditions," *Social Science Quarterly*, Vol. 53, No. 3, December 1972, pp. 474–493.
2. See Thomas F. Stinson and Edward F. Krahmer, "Local School Expenditures and Educational Quality: A Correlation Analysis," *American Journal of Agricultural Economics*, Vol. 51, No. 5, December 1969, pp. 1153–1560; Thomas I. Ribich, *Education and Poverty* (Washington, D.C.: The Brookings Institution, 1968); Herbert J. Kiesling, "Measuring a Local Government Service: A Study of School Districts in New York," *Review of Economics and Statistics*, Vol. 49, No. 3, August 1967, pp. 356–367; Henry M. Levin, "The Effect of Different Levels of Expenditure on Educational Output," in Roe L. Johns, et al., eds. *Economic Factors Affecting the Financing of Education* (Gainesville, FL: National Educational Finance Project, 1970), pp. 173–206; Jerry G. West and Donald D. Osburn, "Quality of Schooling in Rural Areas," *Southern Journal of Agricultural Economics*, Vol. 4, No. 1, July 1972, pp. 85–87, and James A. Christenson and Gregory S. Taylor, "Determinants, Expenditures and Performance of Common Public Services," *Rural Sociology*, Vol. 47, No. 1, Spring 1982, pp. 147–163.
3. Roy Bahl and Jesse Burkhead, "Productivity and the Measure of Public Output," in Charles H. Levine, ed. *Managing Human Resources: A Challenge to Urban Governments* (Beverly Hills, CA: Sage Publications, 1977) pp. 253–269.
4. See Donald M. Fisk and Richard E. Winnie, "Output Measures of Urban Government: The Current Status and Likely Prospects," *Social Science Quarterly*, Vol. 54, No. 4, March 1974, pp. 725–740 and D. C. Shin, "The Quality of Municipal Services: Con-

cept, Measure and Results," *Social Indicators Research*, Vol. 4, 1977, pp. 207–229 for additional discussion.

5. Fisk and Winnie, 1974. Also see Urban Institute and International City Management Association, *Measuring the Effectiveness of Basic Municipal Services* (Washington, D.C., no date).

6. Elinor Ostrom, "Why Do We Need Multiple Indicators of Public Service Outputs" in *National Conference on Nonmetropolitan Community Services Research* (Washington, D.C.: Senate Committee on Agriculture, Nutrition and Forestry Print, 1977), pp. 277–286, and Christenson and Taylor, 1982. However, Christenson and Taylor found no relationship between objective and subject performance measures for education, medical services and libraries in their study of North Carolina county areas.

7. See Roy Bahl, Jesse Burkhead and Bernard Jump, Jr., eds. *Public Employment and State and Local Government Finance* (Cambridge, MA: Ballinger Publishing Co., 1980), especially Chapters 3 and 4, for a formal presentation of this approach and empirical applications to police services and local schools.

8. This framework was adapted from Christenson and Taylor, 1982.

9. Christenson and Taylor, 1982.

10. Robert E. McArthur, "Impact of City-County Consolidation of the Rural-Urban Fringe: Nashville-Davidson County, Tenn." AER 206, Economic Research Service, (Washington, D.C.: U.S. Department of Agriculture, 1971).

11. Elinor Ostrom and Gordon P. Whitaker, "Community Control and Governmental Responsiveness: The Case of Police in Black Communities" in David Rogers and Willis Hawley, eds. *Improving the Quality of Urban Management* (Beverly Hills, CA: Sage Publications, 1974); Elinor Ostrom, "Size and Performance in a Federal System," *Publius*, Vol. 6, No. 2, Spring 1976, pp. 33–73.

12. Bruce D. Rogers and C. McCurdy Lipsey, "Metropolitan Reform: Citizen Evaluations of Performances in Nashville-Davidson County, Tennessee," *Publius*, Vol. 4, No. 4, Fall 1974, pp. 19–34.

13. Robert B. Hawkins, Jr. "Special Districts and Urban Services," in Elinor Ostrom, ed. *The Delivery of Urban Services: Outcomes of Change* (Beverly Hills, CA: Sage Publications, 1976) pp. 171–187.

14. Bengt Owe Birgersson. "The Service Paradox: Citizen Assessment of Urban Services in 36 Swedish Communes," in Vincent Ostrom and Frances Pennell Bish, eds. *Comparing Urban Service Delivery Systems* (Beverly Hills, CA: Sage Publications, 1977), pp. 243–267.

15. James A. Christenson and Carolyn E. Sachs, "The Impact of Government Size and Number of Administrative Units on the Quality of Public Services," *Administrative Science Quarterly*, Vol. 25, No. 1, March 1980, pp. 89–101.

16. The cooperation of Professor R. J. Burdge, University of Illinois at Urbana-Champaign, and the *Illinois Today and Tomorrow* project is gratefully acknowledged. In addition to several other questions, respondents were requested to score the degree to which they felt there was a problem with the respective local services. The response categories were (4) no problem, (3) slight problem, (2) medium problem, or (1) severe problem. A Likert procedure was used to score the responses for each county. A complete summary of the survey is available in the tabloid *Illinois: Today and Tomorrow: A Statewide Study* (Urbana, IL: University of Illinois Institute for Environmental Studies, May 1978).

17. See Howard Ladewig and Glenn C. McCann, "Community Satisfaction: Theory and Measurement" *Rural Sociology*, Vol. 45, No. 1, Spring 1980, pp. 110–131 and Jeffrey L. Brudney and Robert E. England, "Analyzing Citizen Evaluations of Municipal Services: A Dimensional Approach," *Urban Affairs Quarterly*, Vol. 17, No. 3, March 1982,

pp. 359–369. A study using Guttman Scales to analyze the unidimensionality of common public services is James A. Christenson, "Quality of Community Services: A Micro-unidimensional Approach with Experiential Data," *Rural Sociology*, Vol. 41, No. 4, Winter 1976, pp. 509–525.

18. Cook County was excluded from the analysis because of its atypical size and characteristics. Including Cook County resulted in little change from the factor analysis reported. Small loadings are commonly < 0.20 in absolute value. Here heavy loadings are those with an absolute value > 0.40. To investigate the commonality across services, the oblique (unrelated) rotation was employed. However, the unrotated matrix was the base for the quality of service index (QS_i) which captured the common structure of all twenty-five services. See Benjamin Fruchter, *Introduction to Factor Analysis* (Princeton, NJ: D. Van Nostrand Co., 1954).

19. The dependent variables are constructed by averaging the discrete responses of the citizens from each county. The result is a continuous limited dependent variable with a maximum of four and a minimum of one. However, there are no observations at the limiting values. Ordinary least squares estimations are, then, not problematical. For a discussion of qualitative response models see Takeshi Amemiya, "Qualitative Response Models: A Survey," *Journal of Economic Literature*, Vol. 59, No. 4, December 1981, pp. 1483–1536 and George G. Judge, William E. Griffiths, R. Carter Hill, and Tsoung-Chao Lee, *The Theory and Practice of Econometrics* (New York, NY: John Wiley and Sons, 1980), Chapter 14.

20. The independent socioeconomic and demographic factors are similar to those reported in Christenson and Sachs, 1980. Evidence of the difference between the public service preferences of inmigrants and existing residences is found in Andrew J. Sofranko and James D. Williams, eds. *Rebirth of Rural America: Rural Migration in the Midwest* (Ames, IA: North Central Regional Center for Rural Development) especially pp. 121–134. Also see Stephen B. Lovejoy, Deborah J. Brown and Janet S. Weitz, "Inmigrants in Nonmetropolitan Communities: More Dissatisfied with Public Services?" *North Central Journal of Agricultural Economics*, Vol. 5, No. 2, July 1983, pp. 39–45 and Deborah J. Brown, Stephen B. Lovejoy, and Janet S. Weitz, "Satisfaction, Length of Residence and Per Capita Multiplier Models," *Land Economics*, Vol. 58, No. 2, May 1982, pp. 204–216.

21. J. D. Aberbach and J. L. Walker, "The Attitudes of Blacks and Whites Toward City Services: Implications for Public Policy," in John P. Crecine, ed. *Financing the Metropolis: Public Policy in Urban Economics* (Beverly Hills, CA: Sage Publications, 1970), pp. 519–537.

22. Brian J. Berry and John D. Kasarda, *Contemporary Urban Ecology* (New York, NY: MacMillan Publishing, 1977).

23. The subjective evaluation of citizen participation in local government decision making was available in the survey data from which the perceptions of service quality were obtained.

24. See Hawkins, 1976 and Gordon Tullock, "Federalism: Problems of Scale," *Public Choice*, Vol. 6, Spring 1969, pp. 19–29.

25. See Ostrom, 1972. However, the limited research on this relationship reports that expenditures are not a significant determinant of either perceptions of overall service quality or quality of selected services. See Christenson and Sachs, 1980 and Christenson and Taylor, 1982.

26. Number of employees is most common measure of organizational size. See John R. Kimberly, "Organizational Size and the Structuralist Perspective: A Review, Critique and Proposal," *Administrative Science Quarterly*, Vol. 21, No. 4, December 1976, pp. 571–597.

27. Christenson and Sachs, 1980.
28. Hawkins, 1976 and Christenson and Sachs, 1980.
29. For example, see Richard Raymond, "Determinants of the Quality of Primary and Secondary Education in West Virginia," *Journal of Human Resources*, Vol. 13, No. 4, Fall 1968, pp. 450–470; James S. Coleman, et al., *Equity of Educational Opportunity*, U.S. Department of Health, Education and Welfare (Washington, D.C.: Government Printing Office, 1966); Eric A. Hanushek, "Teacher Characteristics and Gains in Student Achievement: Estimation Using Micro Data," *American Economic Review*, Vol. 61, No. 2, May 1971, pp. 280–288; West and Osburn, 1972; and Lewis J. Perl, "Family Background, Secondary School Expenditure and Student Ability," *Journal of Human Resources*, Vol. 8, No. 2, Spring 1973, pp. 156–180. These and other studies of education are reviewed in Brady J. Deaton and Kevin T. McNamara, *Education in a Changing Environment: Impact of Population and Economic Change on the Demand and Cost of Public Education in Rural America*, SRDC Series No. 17 (Mississippi State, MS: Southern Rural Development Center, 1984).
30. No standardized test scores were available for Illinois counties. Pupil-teacher ratios were used as the measure of output. For a review and study of pupil-teacher ratios see Gene V. Glass, Leonard S. Cahen, Mary Lee Smith and Nikola N. Filby, *School Class Size: Research and Policy* (Beverly Hills, CA: Sage Publications, 1982).
31. Literature is limited on the employment approach to analyzing local government performance. See Roy Bahl, Richard Gustely, and Michael Wasylenko, "The Determinants of Local Government Police Expenditures: A Public Employment Approach," *National Tax Journal*, Vol. 31, No. 1, March 1978, pp. 67–79; Marvin Johnson, "Fiscal Behavior of Wisconsin School Districts: An Application of the Public Employment Model," Staff Paper 161, Department of Agricultural Economics (Madison, WI: University of Wisconsin, 1980); Bahl, Burkhead and Jump, 1980, Chapter 4, and Teri L. Perkins, "A Rural Test of a Public Employment Model of School District Expenditure Determinants," Paper presented at American Agricultural Economics Association Meetings, Logan, UT: August 3, 1982.
32. These results, however, are as strong as other employment determinant analyses. For example see Bahl, Burkhead and Jump, 1980, Chapter 4.

Chapter 7

Summary and Conclusions

With technological advances have come problems that the private sector can not easily solve. Pollution, for example affects more than one unit of local government. Residents' preferences for open space and freedom from heavy tax burdens in declining central cities, as well as for specific special services such as libraries or parks, lead to the creation of special districts. In some instances, particularly in rural areas, there is no suitable alternative for providing services other than through special districts.

Numerous independent governments also have detractions. The tax base is fragmented and services frequently are not coordinated. Furthermore, when special districts are used to bypass state tax rate or debt limits, citizens in the same locality receive similar services but pay different property tax bills. This phenomenon occurs because special districts have incongruent boundaries and split general-purpose governments. These complex arrangements spur residents' resentment toward property taxes as a revenue source. They perceive the tax as inequitably administered perhaps partly because of the spatial configurations of the governments collecting it.

Many criticize the fractured governmental structure in states such as Illinois and call for reform, reorganization, and elimination of duplication. The system of overlapping governments, however, persists, and there is no immediate indication of major change. In fact, some have recently defended the fragmented structure and have claimed that the competition among governments pressures local officials to more effectively meet the needs of residents and provide services more efficiently than a centralized general-purpose government. The latter supposedly exercises monopoly power resulting in higher expenditures and lower output.

While ad hoc arguments can be advanced for either side of the issue, information about the precise outcomes of governmental proliferation is limited. Research methods differ, samples are not similar, and difficulties in measuring budgetary outcomes make consistent findings rare. Compounding the research difficulties is the fact that when offered an opportunity for consolidating governmental units, taxpayers show little enthusiasm.

The findings of this study contribute to the literature by offering a consistent approach to the governmental fragmentation issue through an examination of the effects of governmental structure on various facets of local public finance. The study offers two main advantages. First, a single state in which local governments have similar responsibilities was studied. Illinois has a rich collection of local governments providing services through virtually every conceivable arrangement. The governments offer a rich variety of socioeconomic characteristics, permitting an examination of the importance of traditional local public finance variables.

A second advantage is the fact that the effects of fragmentation on local finance were examined regarding methods of financing, expenditures for services, and public perceptions of the services delivered. Attention was also paid to institutional factors associated with more or less governmental fragmentation to test some of the commonly held perceptions about the reasons for differences in governmental structure. In particular, attention was paid to the importance of state tax rate limits and the possibility of circumventing them through local government creation.

RESEARCH FINDINGS

Constraints on local governments by state legislatures create incentives for local officials to seek methods of circumventing regulations for financing what they perceive to be necessary services. Certainly this is true of tax rate and debt limits. For many years the claim has been that imposing more restrictive tax rate limits on local governments leads to the formation of additional governments with additional taxing and debt limits. The result is to increase the liability of the public for property taxes or debt.

Illinois municipalities larger than 25,000 and those passing a referendum have home rule authority granting wide-ranging powers, including elimination of tax rate and debt limits. As a result, counties in which a greater portion of the population resides in home rule units should have fewer special districts or less governmental fragmentation. Presumably, in these areas the need and/or incentive for creating additional governments when taxing limits have been reached is reduced. The Illinois data provide a limited test of this proposition. The results demonstrate that counties with a larger proportion of the population residing in home rule units have fewer governments per 10,000 residents. While this finding is not conclusive, it suggests that additional research along these lines may be fruitful. Recent calls for stricter statewide tax rate limits may increase the number of governments and may ultimately increase the use of the property taxes.

Some potentially interesting research extensions might include a more detailed examination of the revenue bases in the localities involved. One might expect to find greater pressure to create additional governments in communities more dependent on property taxes. Also, a more detailed comparison of the types of governments created during periods of population growth would be useful. When governments reach overall tax limits, what types of districts are proposed first? Data to make this comparison unfortunately are not readily available. Studies of governmental structure have to be conducted at the county level. However, governments within a county may exhibit wide differences in tax rates, proximity to rate limits, and population change.

Property Taxes

While there is evidence to support the notion that tax rate limits are associated with a greater number of governments per 10,000 residents, the important question surrounds the effect of governmental structure on local public finance. In particular, do areas with fragmented governments, more governments per 10,000 residents, differ with regard to revenues used in financing services? Based on the analysis of local governments in Illinois, the answer is yes.

Using the traditional median voter model, property taxes as a percentage of total revenues available to local governments were found to be significantly and positively associated with governmental fragmentation. Counties with more units of government per 10,000 residents relied more heavily on property taxes to finance services. This finding occurred when three measures of governmental structure were employed: number of taxing units per 10,000 residents, number of special districts per 10,000 residents, and an index of concentration adapted from the industrial organization literature.

There are several reasons for these findings. One of the most plausible is that fragmented governmental structures mask the responsibility of local officials for property taxes. Each local government represents a small portion of the property tax, and taxpayers encounter difficulty determining the governments responsible for the taxes. Another explanation is that some of the special districts have limited access to revenue sources other than property taxes. Creating new governments, therefore, increases the use of property taxes.

Several other findings are particularly interesting. Intergovernmental aid from federal and state governments was negatively associated with reliance on property taxes. At least a portion of the intergovernmental assistance is used either for property tax relief or to prevent increases in property taxes. The importance of this finding is that state and federal aid is under close review. General revenue sharing, for example, is scheduled for elimination in 1985. This program expanded the spending authority of townships in states such as Illinois where there could be valid debate about the status of townships as general purpose governments. The general revenue sharing program fostered state legislation to broaden township government authority. The new authorizations extended not only to general revenue sharing funds but to local revenues as well. The outcome was a strengthening of townships, with no consideration for their need in urbanized areas.

Public Spending

The professional and academic literature has shown interest in the effects of governmental structure on local public spending. Previous research generally found an inverse relationship between number of governments and per capita local spending. This finding may be surprising. If the centralist position, that numerous local governments are duplicative and possibly wasteful, is true, then one might expect government fragmentation to be associated with higher expenditures. A significant difficulty with expenditure analyses is that quality and quantity of services differ among governments. Any examination of total spending on local public services masks service variations among the governments involved. A more meaningful approach is to compare spending on specific services.

A comparison of aggregate county spending by local Illinois governments was conducted both for total expenditures and for administration, parks and recreation, libraries, roads and streets and education spending. Duplication of effort and resulting higher expenditures were expected to be evident in overall administrative expenditures. Pressures for additional services by special interest groups using single-function districts should surface in the parks and recreation and library expenditures, for example.

The findings for Illinois are mixed. For aggregate local government expenditures, the relationship between local government structure, measured by the number of taxing units per 10,000 residents and the number of special districts per 10,000 residents and aggregate per capita expenditures was not significantly different from zero at the five or ten percent level. However, a more inclusive measure of governmental fragmentation, namely a structural index adapted from studies of industrial organization was negative and significant at the ten percent level. This suggests areas with a more fragmented political structure are associated with higher per capita expenditures.

Although only a tentative positive association between governmental fragmentation and aggregate spending on local services was found, a more detailed comparison by service reinforced the general finding. In separate analyses of expenditures for financial administration, libraries, roads and streets, and education, a strong positive relationship was found between number of governments and per capita expenditures. Greater governmental fragmentation leads to higher spending for these services. In interpreting these findings, one cannot necessarily impute evidence of inefficiency. Regression analyses involving local spending frequently are not sophisticated enough to completely adjust for quantity and quality of service differences. Attempts are usually made to measure these variables indirectly but under close scrutiny they are often found to be lacking.

Reasonably clear findings of the importance of governmental structure for aggregate financial administration expenditures were found. There were strong positive relationships in regressions involving taxing units per 10,000 residents and number of special districts per 10,000 residents. These relationships exist even when number of employees was included. One explanation for this finding is that a larger number of governments nearly always will require additional administration expenditures. There may be need for headquarters and clerical functions which might otherwise be absorbed in a department of a general-purpose government. The Illinois findings indicate that, on the average, one additional governmental unit per 1000 residents adds $1.21 per capita for financial control spending and one additional special district per 1000 residents increases these expenditures by as much as $2.03 per resident. These are rough estimates but they are consistent with the complementarity of many public services and with the commonly held view of duplication of effort. Greater cooperation in provision of services could reduce expenditures.

Perceptions of Public Services

A strong justification for numerous independent governments providing services is the greater responsiveness of the small governments to needs and desires of residents. Allegedly, large centralized governments are better insulated from citizens' complaints and demands for change. In fact, one claim is that additional governments are created to avoid the established bureaucratic budgetary procedures and competition with traditional services for a share of the annual budget.

If this is true, citizens in fragmented areas would rate services higher. Detailed information on citizen ratings of services, by county, is available for Illinois from a statewide survey undertaken in 1977. An index of service quality perceptions was constructed for all services and a series of citizens' ratings for four specific services including libraries, parks-recreation, roads and streets, and education were used to examine the importance of governmental structure on citizens' perceptions.

Three findings are of particular importance. First is the lack of significance between size of government, as measured by employment levels, and perceptions of public services. This is contrary to findings reported in earlier studies.

Second is the fact that governmental fragmentation, as measured by number of governments per 10,000 residents, and number of special districts per 10,000 residents was significantly negatively associated with citizens' perceptions. Governmental fragmentation was associated with lower perceptions of services. This was true when either number of taxing units or number of special districts is used. These results are not supportive of the notion that smaller governments are more receptive to citizens' desires. The survey information is not adequately refined to evaluate only those services provided by special districts or to compare the findings in areas served by only centralized governments. In each county, examples of each arrangement exist and the evaluations are aggregated to the county level to be compatible with the remainder of the information.

A third important general finding is that per capita expenditures for local services are not significantly related to citizens' perceptions. This result was unexpected since additional inputs are expected to raise the visibility of the services, causing residents to rate them more favorably. However, this was not the case in either the aggregate or individual service model. The single exception was for roads and in this case more spending increased the perceptions of service quality. A possible explanation is that higher expenditures mean more inputs which are very visible to residents. Newly upgraded road surfaces can be immediately seen by most residents whereas additional library acquisitions, playground equipment, or teachers are less visible.

The models for specific services were not as clear-cut in the importance of governmental structure as the overall service equations. For library services and roads-streets, a negative relationship between governmental fragmentation and citizens' perceptions was found indicating that more governments are associated with lower perceptions of service. A plausible explanation is that economies of scale exist for libraries and roads, so that small districts are not able to offer the same level of services. In libraries, for instance, patrons have access to a larger collection of books with easier and faster retrieval than a series of small libraries using interlibrary loan facilities. In the provision of roads, use of large equipment and discounts on purchases may provide cost savings in large operations. However, in both cases, available information permits little more than conjecture as to an explanation for the findings.

In education and park services, a positive relationship was found between governmental fragmentation and public perceptions of services. The rationalization for these findings may lie in the desire of residents to have closer access to both schools and parks. More school districts or more park districts could possibly mean that programs are more clearly geared to preferences of the communities. Summer programs for youngsters conducted by park districts are popular with residents. More school districts and governing boards mean a larger number of officials to which residents can express complaints and desires. The outcome of these better opportunities for citizen input may mean higher ratings for public services.

Perhaps the most useful finding from this analysis is the fact that citizens' perceptions of services depend on many factors including the governmental structure through which services are provided. Since perceptions of service quality are important considerations in determining voting patterns on bond issues and tax rate limits, it is critical that policymakers recognize the differences among services when designing delivery systems. Creating additional library districts in response to citizens' requests for new services, for example, may lead to a lower perception of the services provided by residents. An outcome of this lower perception in later years could mean reduced taxing powers. The opposite may hold for schools and parks. Thus, local policymakers need to evaluate service delivery systems on a service by service basis, if citizens' perceptions of quality are important.

POTENTIAL POLICY IMPLICATIONS

The findings of this analysis naturally lead to several policy questions and implications. First is that areas relatively free of tax rate limits were associated with fewer governmental units. While there is certainly more than one interpretation of this finding, it does suggest that state policymakers acting on requests for statewide tax rate limits need to consider the possibility that tighter limits may stimulate additional governments in some areas ultimately leading to even higher aggregate property taxes.

It seems then that policymakers, when reviewing statewide tax rate limitations, must carefully examine where the rate increases are occurring and the governmental arrangements for providing services. There may be several methods for reducing dependency on property taxes while providing comparable services. Access to a broader range of revenues is one alternative. Local governments in areas where property taxes are the dominant local revenue source will be more adversely affected by property tax rate limits than areas in which sales taxes, for instance, are a dominant revenue source. In this study, the inverse relationship between intergovernmental assistance and property taxes is strong.

A second policy implication is that state governments should review opportunities for local governmental cooperative projects to lessen the incentive for creating additional governments to bypass legislative barriers. There are many reasons why single-function districts provide services. When threshold sizes are needed to finance large capital projects the special district approach may be the most economical. However, there is little reason to provide an incentive to form new governments in order to carry out a socially beneficial cooperative project when outdated statutes or constitutional restrictions are the cause. There may be considerable room for improvement in this area.

A third area worth examining is the need to revise local property tax collection systems so that citizens can more clearly identify governments responsible for taxes. States such as Illinois have already undertaken programs in this area whereby tax bills facilitate efforts by taxpayers to determine where the tax payments are being distributed. These improved systems can increase the responsiblity of local leaders for decisions regarding taxing levels.

A fourth policy implication is the need to recognize citizen attitudes in making policy recommendations. This study has focused on number of governments and the extent to which they affect taxing and spending levels. However, we also found that citizens differ in the way they perceive services. A positive relationship was found between perceived quality of services and number of school districts. In the case of overall services, on the other hand, there was a significant negative finding. Thus, as a general rule, one might conclude that fewer governments are associated with better perceptions of service quality. However, in the case of schools this may not be true. One might argue, for instance, that a movement to cut back the number of school districts could lead to increased citizen dissatisfaction with the services provided and perhaps less future support for local school taxes.

The point is not that the number of school districts should be increased or decreased. Rather it is that serious consideration of public perceptions of service quality is needed before far-reaching policy decisions are made, especially at the state government level. Conditions and preferences differ throughout a state and one statewide policy may not be effective. Local differences must be considered.

Perhaps the most important implication of this study is the need for a more detailed examination of the need for better coordination of local public services. Population has shifted and tax bases have changed markedly since the current structure of local governments was created. The overriding tendency has been to add more governments with little consideration of the overall effects on provision of local services.

It is not uncommon to find residents in a city being served by a city park department and a park district. Alternatively, situations exist in Illinois in which a municipal fire protection department serves a portion of the city, while one or two fire protection districts serve other sections. Through mutual aid pacts it is possible that subsidies from some residents are used to provide services to other residents paying lower tax rates in the same city. A fire protection district charges for volunteer service but generally provides for relatively low levels of fire protection. However, if a major fire were to occur, the fully operated municipal fire protection crew would be expected to provide assistance. The number of these instances is not known and an estimate of the difficulties created is not available. However, instances such as these aggravate citizens' already negative attitudes toward property taxes.

The presence of special districts covering only a portion of the central city creates another problem, namely increasing resistance by suburban residents for annexation to the city. As residents in central cities move to the suburbs with higher quality housing and lower population densities, the central city experiences the well-documented tax base decline. By creating certain special districts, residents in unincorporated areas are able to receive only select services in which they are interested but are still able to take advantage of the traditional city services while employed in the central city. Given state fiscal restraints on revenue sources available to the central cities, it is difficult to tax the commuters. By allowing special districts to be created easily, without consideration for the overall effect on the tax base in the area, a significant reason for annexation is removed. The free-rider problem is made more serious and central cities are left to face even greater tax base declines.

Special districts, however, may be the most efficient and effective way to provide services whose benefits are not confined to a single community. By creating a special district, fiscal equivalence is achieved with the cost of the service borne by those benefiting. For many low density rural areas, the judicious use of special districts when combined with county special service areas may provide the only alternatives for providing demanded services.

SUGGESTIONS FOR ADDITIONAL RESEARCH

While readers may disagree with some of the interpretations of the findings in this analysis, it is difficult to argue with the concept that governmental structure and institutions are important both in the financing of local public services and in citizens' perceptions. As important as governmental structure appears to be, it is still in its infancy in empirical analyses. Several avenues of research are warranted.

First is the development of a more comprehensive theory of local government formation and development. Many questions remain unanswered. The present study supports the concept that additional governments may be a response to tax rate limits restricting the provision of demanded services. The results presented in this book, however, can be considered preliminary at best. More thought needs to be given to the reasons why special districts are formed and hypotheses need to be tested with more complete data.

Second is a critical need for more sophisticated information on the types of services provided and the unit cost of producing them under alternate arrangements. Given the current status of public sector accounting systems, this will be difficult since data are not regularly coded by subfunction or department in many of the smaller governmental units. Particular attention should be paid to the possibilities for more effective services provided through alternate governmental structures.

Third is a need for aggregation across governmental units in expenditure, revenue, and debt comparisons in order to obtain an overall perspective of the total cost or liability to the public. Many of the current studies do not recognize that other governmental units also have claim on the property tax base and that there is an effective limit as to what taxpayers will pay to all governments providing services. Likewise, there is an effective limit to the debt that can be serviced with the existing property tax base.

In the latter half of the 1970s taxpayers sent a message to state and local officials in many states that they were frustrated with many aspects of local public finance. An era of property tax relief began. While the fiscal restraint era may have subsided, there is no guarantee that it will not resurface. The confusion surrounding numerous local governments responsible for a vast array of services likely adds to that frustration.

While it is difficult to assess the importance of governmental structure, the findings of this analysis are quite clear that structure is an element to be considered. More complex governments may not increase overall local public spending but they seem to increase property tax reliance and may be associated with lower perceptions by residents of the quality of the services provided.

Index

About the Authors

David L. Chicoine is associate professor of agricultural economics at the University of Illinois at Urbana-Champaign. He also holds appointments with the Cooperative Extension Service and the Institute of Government and Public Affairs, University of Illinois. He received a Ph.D. from the University of Illinois at Urbana-Champaign in 1979. His scholarly research is on state and local public finance issues with some focus on taxation and agriculture, and land and water economics. His articles have appeared in *Land Economics, National Tax Journal, American Journal of Agricultural Economics,* and *Property Tax Journal,* among others. He is co-editor, with Norman Walzer, of *Financing State and Local Governments in the 1980s.* Chicoine has served as a consultant on taxes, farmland property tax assessments, and local government education programs and as an advisor to the Illinois General Assembly. He also serves on the Illinois Farmland Assessment Technical Advisory Board.

Norman Walzer earned a B.S. in business administration from Illinois State University and a Ph.D. in economics from the University of Illinois at Urbana. He is actively engaged in state-local public finance studies and research on urban-regional economic development. Professor Walzer serves as consultant to state and local government agencies and as research director for a state commission studying problems facing cities. Currently Professor and Chairman of the Economics Department at Western Illinois University, he has published articles in *Review of Economics and Statistics, Industrial and Labor Relations Review, Land Economics, and National Tax Journal.* He also has co-authored *Cities, Suburbs, and Property Taxes* with Glenn W. Fisher and co-edited *Financing State and Local Governments in the 1980s* with David L. Chicoine.